The Tea Party
and the Remaking
of Republican Conservatism

The Tea Party

and the Remaking

of Republican Conservatism

THEDA SKOCPOL AND
VANESSA WILLIAMSON

OXFORD
UNIVERSITY PRESS

OXFORD
UNIVERSITY PRESS

Oxford University Press is a department of the University of Oxford.
It furthers the University's objective of excellence in research,
scholarship, and education by publishing worldwide.
Oxford is a registered trade mark of Oxford University Press
in the UK and certain other countries.

Published in the United States of America by
Oxford University Press
198 Madison Avenue, New York, NY 10016

Library of Congress Cataloging-in-Publication Data
Skocpol, Theda.
The Tea Party and the remaking of Republican conservatism/ Theda Skocpol
and Vanessa Williamson.
     p.   cm.
Includes bibliographical references and index.
ISBN 978-0-19-983263-7 (hardback); 978-0-19-997554-9 (pbk.); 978-0-19-063366-0 (update)
1. Tea Party movement. 2. Conservatism—United States.
I. Williamson, Vanessa. II. Title
JK2391.T43S56   2012
320.520973—dc23   2011038685

Contents

List of Figures

Preface and Acknowledgments

Surprise and curiosity prompted us to do research on the Tea Party.

Most scholarship on U.S. politics addresses established academic questions, pulls concepts and hypotheses off the library shelf, and chews over computerized datasets. But when the Tea Party burst on the scene starting in 2009, it challenged assumptions about how U.S. politics would play out following the big Democratic victories in the 2008 elections. No canned datasets would be of much use to track an emergent set of protests; and the Tea Party as a whole could not be plopped into available conceptualizations about third parties, social movements, or popular protests during sharp economic downturns. Perfect! Many in academia turn away if something doesn't fit. But we were fascinated and intensely curious about this puzzling outburst. We wanted to get off our duffs, figure it out—and tell others what we found.

In 2009 and early 2010, Theda was doing research on the Obama presidency and the politics of health reform when the surprise victory of Republican Scott Brown in the Massachusetts special election put a spotlight on Tea Party activists and funders. In fact, the Tea Partiers were out there on the Massachusetts roadways, dressed in costumes and waving their signs. Clearly, the Tea Party was becoming a force in electoral politics, countering if not upending the policy agendas of the Obama administration. But who was involved in the Tea Party? How did it work, this combination of grassroots activism with sudden infusions of hundreds of thousands of dollars into campaigns such as Scott Brown's for the U.S. Senate? Would the Tea Party impact on electoral politics and public policy-making prove minimal and ephemeral—or was something bigger afoot? The answers were not obvious at all—so the questions kept nagging.

Around the same time, Vanessa was interested in grassroots activism about health reform, and decided to launch a research project for one of her graduate seminars comparing citizen mobilization around health reform on the left and right. She intended to look at both the Tea Party and Organizing for America (OFA), the organization founded to follow up on activism in the Obama presidential campaign of 2008. But very quickly she discovered that OFA was essentially dormant at the grass roots, with phone banking and email alerts proceeding in ways typical for routine party politics. Tea Party activists, by contrast, were holding meetings and plotting dramatic protests to oppose health reform legislation pending in Washington DC. Vanessa had originally presumed the Tea Party to be little more than a media phenomenon, pushed by conservative big-money funders. Her assumptions upended, she decided to look more closely at the Tea Party activists. Working with a fellow graduate student, John Coggin, she contacted Massachusetts Tea Partiers and arranged observations and interviews during the spring of 2010.

In the summer of 2010, Vanessa and John teamed up with Theda to write an article, "The Tea Party and the Remaking of Republican Conservatism," that was accepted by *Perspectives on Politics* to appear in March 2011. Research for that article raised additional questions and suggested further lines of investigation. With encouragement from David McBride at Oxford University Press, Theda and Vanessa hatched the plan for this book.

We set out to learn more about the Tea Party's impact on the Republican Party, its role in the 2010 elections, and its impact on national political debates. We recruited two undergraduates to help us assemble a nationwide database on local Tea Parties, and we reached out to Tea Party activists in states beyond Massachusetts to arrange to observe meetings and talk with people at the grassroots in other states. A huge amount of new research needed to get done in a few short months so that this book could appear by the end of 2011.

Many people have helped us develop arguments, complete the research, and produce the book. Of course, people at Oxford University Press have been central, and we thank David McBride, Alexandra Dauler, Amy Whitmer, and others at the Press for their wise advice and efficient professional efforts.

We are grateful to John Coggin for his contributions to the field research in Massachusetts. His incisive observations and tireless good cheer made this book's earliest field research a great deal of fun. We benefited from discussions with Emily Ekins, who is working on a UCLA PhD dissertation about the Tea Party. Adam Bonica, visiting at Princeton's Center for American Politics during 2010-11 and now on the faculty at Stanford University, contributed the data and developed the measures for Figure 5.1 on ideological polarization in the House of Representatives. His willingness to help us document a key political transition is much appreciated. We also thank Harvard graduate student Rich Nielsen for introducing us to the Jon McNaughton painting, "One Nation Under God." For their work on the nationwide database of local Tea Parties, we are deeply grateful to Andrew Crutchfield and Will Eger, two Harvard undergraduates who did hundreds of hours of skillful sleuthing on the Internet during the spring semester of 2011. They not only coded data; they also alerted us to fascinating features of specific groups around the country.

Although this book was developed in a compressed time, we nevertheless took opportunities to make presentations to fellow scholars along the way, and picked the brains of colleagues willing to read papers and drafts. We are grateful for comments and insights offered by Dan Carpenter, Gregorz Ekiert, Claudine Gay, Peter Hall, Jennifer Hochschild, and Robert Putnam—all colleagues in the Harvard Department of Government. We also benefited greatly from lively discussions of our research at the seminar for the March 23, 2011 Alexis de Tocqueville Lecture sponsored by the Center for American Political Studies at Harvard, and at the April 28, 2011 meeting of the Boston Area Research Workshop on History, Institutions, and Politics, where Mark Helbling and Alex Hertel-Fernandez provided very helpful comments. At the Tocqueville event, the official discussants Suzanne Mettler of Cornell, Larry Bartels of Princeton, and Mickey Edwards of the Aspen Institute each offered sharp observations; and Jane Mansbridge of the Harvard Kennedy School asked a thought-provoking question about democratic participation. And in both group discussions, colleagues posed telling questions about data and interpretations. We have not answered all of their points, but their arguments made an impression and allowed us to improve our manuscript up until the last minute.

Perhaps our greatest debt is to the Tea Party participants in Massachusetts, Virginia, and Arizona who hosted our visits and were willing to meet with us for personal interviews and allow us to attend and observe local meetings. Conservatives all, with political views very different from our views in our personal lives as citizens, they nevertheless treated us with courtesy and kindness. The people we met answered our questions with obvious sincerity and willingness to let us better understand their points of view, their values, and their activities. No other source of information we tapped for this project was anywhere nearly as important—and it was a great pleasure to get out of Cambridge, Massachusetts, and visit actual Tea Party meetings and events in other very different parts of our marvelous country. It has been fascinating for us, and very important, to hear directly from Tea Party people about why they got involved, how, and to what ends. We got beyond stereotypes and preconceptions, to learn in person about people's hopes and fears for American democracy.

Christen Varley of the Greater Boston Tea Party was graciously accommodating in the early stages of this research, encouraging our attendance at meetings and sending out our email questionnaire to Massachusetts activists. We are equally grateful to Peter Courtenay Stephens of Gloucester, Virginia, and to others in his local group, the Peninsula Patriots, for sharing so much with us. We thank Carole Thorpe of Charlottesville, Virginia, for inviting Theda to one of her group's meetings and following up by phone and email to answer further questions about their approach to citizen organizing. In Arizona, Jim and Julie Wise and Sandi Bartlett are tireless organizers who found time to welcome Vanessa to their meetings.

We realize that our Tea Party hosts and contacts will not agree with everything we argue in this book. Still, we hope they will feel that we have treated them and others at the grass roots with the respect they deserve as active and committed fellow American citizens. We found each person we met admirable and likeable in many ways, and the warm hospitality they extended to us was encouraging beyond our expectations. The picture of the Tea Party we develop in this book is richer, more accurate, and more insightful because of the time they gave to us.

Finally, we thank our husbands, Bill Skocpol and Brad Johnson, and Vanessa's parents, Liz and Arthur Williamson. They all put up with our preoccupation with this project over many crucial months, and Vanessa's parents did some sharp-eyed editing, too.

Theda Skocpol and Vanessa Williamson

Cambridge, Massachusetts, August 2011

The Tea Party
and the Remaking
of Republican Conservatism

Introduction

"I Want My Country Back!"

On the evening of March 23, 2010, more than forty Tea Partiers filled to overflowing the back room of the Cape Cod Café, a diner on Main Street in the gritty town of Brockton, Massachusetts. Their regularly scheduled monthly meeting fell only hours after President Barack Obama had signed into law the Affordable Care and Patient Protection Act. The passage of "ObamaCare," as Tea Partiers derisively call it, was an especially bitter pill in Massachusetts. Just two months earlier, conservatives had mobilized for a surprise GOP victory in the special election to replace the late Senator Ted Kennedy. Republican victor Scott Brown had promised to provide the forty-first vote needed to block health reform in the U.S. Senate.

By all rights, Bay State Tea Partiers should have been demoralized that rainy evening. But their enthusiasm seemed undampened. A trickle of early arrivals quickly became a flood, and waitresses struggled to navigate the standing-room crowd.[1] ObamaCare needed to be repealed, everyone agreed; yet the group also maintained a determined focus on local endeavors. Amidst talk of an upcoming Tax Day rally planned for the Boston Common, Tea Partiers displayed sophisticated political awareness, sharing tips on how to build a contact list for registered Republicans in each district and brainstorming about how to persuade Tea Party members to run for the legislature. President Obama may have scored a victory, but the faithful still felt energized and on the offensive for the rest of 2010.

As it turned out, Massachusetts Tea Partiers had few additional electoral successes. But it was a different story across much of the rest of the country. In the November 2010 midterm elections, the dreams of many Tea Party activists were realized, as Republicans gained sixty-three seats in the U.S. House of Representatives—sending former Speaker Nancy Pelosi back to the minority leader's office and putting Republicans in charge. Republicans also gained six seats in the Senate and claimed six new governorships and about 700 more seats in state legislatures. Brash Tea Party-aligned governors took charge in places such as Florida, Ohio, and Wisconsin. Indeed, a great many of the victorious GOP candidates of 2010 openly identified with the Tea Party and enjoyed the support of activists and plutocratic funders associated with the cause.

Tea Partiers did not bask for long in the 2010 afterglow. It was no time to relax and let Republicans in office fall into go-along-to-get-along routines of meeting Democrats halfway. Tea Partiers set their sights on still-greater gains at the polls in 2011 and 2012, but would not stand down until then. They would not hear of compromises, and pushed GOP officials to act quickly and unremittingly: to reduce taxes, slash public spending, curb public sector unions, and clear away regulations on business. Policing immigrants, safeguarding Second Amendment gun rights, and promoting pro-life and traditional family values were also important goals for many at the grass roots.

Across America, grassroots Tea Partiers geared up in early 2011 to monitor and push local, state, and national officials. Characteristic of their determination was the discussion among about fifty members of the Jefferson Area Tea Party Patriots who, supper trays in hand, crowded into the back room of the Wood Grill Buffet on the north side of Charlottesville, Virginia, on February 24, 2011, to discuss future priorities.[2] A lively give and take was skillfully orchestrated by Carole Thorpe, the energetic woman in her late forties elected to head the group. Did people want to endorse candidates for office? Most were wary. Endorsements might divide their ranks and encourage candidates to sweet-talk Tea Partiers. Perhaps we can endorse when "a great candidate comes along," one man suggested, but we should be "90% watchdogs." His position got general assent, and Jefferson Area Patriots hatched plans to attend meetings of local government boards, track dozens of specific bills in the Virginia legislature and Congress, take over local GOP committees—and, last but not least, keep a close watch on Robert Hurt, the Virginia fifth district Republican recently elected to the House of Representatives. Even GOPers supported by Tea Partiers could "disappoint," explained Carole, who cited Scott Brown of Massachusetts as a "textbook case." To avoid such betrayals, Tea Partiers must "organize for the long-term to carry the movement into the halls of government."

A similar effort was under way a few weeks later in a group near Phoenix, Arizona. On the evening of Wednesday, March 16, 2011, the Pink Slip Patriots of Tempe gathered in a meeting room at a local hotel.[3] Pink Slip members are mostly women, though many have husbands in tow. Most are dressed in pink or sport pink accessories—and, in a clever double entendre, they proclaim themselves ever-ready to "deliver pink slips" to politicians. That night, featured speakers came from the Second Amendment Sisters, a pro-gun group, and from the Arizona branch of Americans for Prosperity (AFP), a national free-market advocacy organization originally funded by the petrochemical billionaire Koch brothers.[4] AFP speaker Tom Jenney told the assembled Tea Partiers about a new "scorecard" for state legislators and gave folks a rundown on what each Phoenix-area legislator had been doing. Pink Slip members took copious notes, and readied themselves to continue the conservative fight at every level of government.

TEA PARTIERS ERUPT AND GET THEIR ACT TOGETHER

The Tea Party's rise to prominence has been stunning. Celebrated by Fox News and urged on by national free-market advocacy groups, Tea Partiers like the ones we have just glimpsed in Massachusetts, Virginia, and Arizona burst onto the national scene, starting in early 2009, just weeks into the Obama presidency. They mounted colorful protests, established local groups and regional networks, and delivered powerful electoral punches in the GOP primaries and the November 2010 general election. Subsequently, Tea Partiers have mobilized to keep Republican officeholders on the conservative straight and narrow.

The turnaround for U.S. conservatives has been remarkable because not so long ago the national tide seemed to be running against them. The elections of 2008 were widely said to portend doom for forces on the right. Not only did the November 2008 election mark the triumph of an African-American Democratic presidential candidate proposing an ambitious reform agenda; voters also sent formidable Democratic majorities to the House and Senate, and handed many statehouses to Democratic governors

and legislators. Outgoing Republican President George W. Bush was extremely unpopular, and the failed presidential campaign of John McCain
left the GOP without a clear leader.[5] Before long, feuds broke out between
the former campaign advisors to McCain and his rambunctious running
mate, Alaska Governor Sarah Palin.

Scrambling to regroup in late 2008 and early 2009, high-ranking
Republicans were far from united behind their new party chair, Michael
Steele.[6] His tenure at the Republican National Committee would leave official party organs mired in controversy and debt. Masterminds like Karl
Rove stepped to the fore to raise funds outside of the Republican National
Committee. Yet who could be the public face of the GOP after Bush? Congressional minority leaders Mitch McConnell and John Boehner appeared
regularly on television, of course, but no one would call either of them charismatic. Flamboyant media provocateurs like Rush Limbaugh seemed to be
pointing the way for ultra-conservatives, but many moderate Republicans
and independents recoiled from the vitriol of Limbaugh and his ilk. No
wonder that in the months after the 2008 elections, pundits debated whether
the Republican Party might be doomed to long-term decline. With rising
cohorts of younger and minority voters energized on behalf of Barack
Obama and the Democrats, the crestfallen GOP looked like a relic of the
past, fast fading into irrelevance.[7]

For the opening months of his term, President Obama enjoyed wide
public approval.[8] Not everyone was on board, of course. Rank-and-file
Republicans remained sullen and strongly opposed to Democratic initiatives; conservatives at the rightward edge of the Republican Party were an-
grier than ever, not just about Democrats in office, but also about what they
took to be Bush-era betrayals of small-government principles. With Washington now dominated by Democrats, right-wingers despaired that things
would just get worse. Not only had Obama promised to pursue long-standing
liberal priorities such as health care reform; he came to office as the United
States was careening into a deepening recession in the aftermath of the
2008 Wall Street meltdown. Many Americans resented the costly bailouts of
banks and auto companies initiated by outgoing President Bush and carried
forward by the incoming Obama Administration. And then came the
hugely expensive economic stimulus package, the American Recovery and
Reinvestment Act passed by President Obama and Congressional Democrats in their bid to revive the fast-contracting U.S. economy. Republican
hostility hardened, and in some circles "Porkulus" became the mocking

shorthand for Obama's recovery efforts.[9] But Porkulus was hardly a catchy rallying cry. And how could any effective resistance crystallize with the Republican brand so besmirched and party organs in such disarray?

On February 19, 2009, an opportunity presented itself. From the floor of the Chicago Mercantile Exchange, CNBC television reporter Rick Santelli burst into a tirade against the Obama Administration's nascent foreclosure relief plan: "The government is rewarding bad behavior!" Santelli shouted. He invited America's "capitalists" to a "Chicago Tea Party" to protest measures to "subsidize the losers' mortgages."[10] Video of the Santelli rant quickly scaled the media pyramid. The rant headlined the *Drudge Report* and was widely re-televised. Within twenty-four hours, it even provoked a public rebuke from White House Press Secretary Robert Gibbs, whose pushback only fueled the media fire. Anyone who hadn't caught Santelli's original outburst could hardly miss the constant replays and escalating responses.

Across the country, disgruntled conservatives perked up. The "Tea Party" symbolism was a perfect rallying point since it brings to mind the original American colonial rebels opposing tyranny by tossing chests of tea into Boston Harbor.[11] It signifies authentic patriotism, and has visceral meaning to people who feel that the United States as they have known it is slipping away. "I want my country back!" one Massachusetts man told us in 2010. "We need to take our country back," echoed a Virginia woman the following year. This plaintive call is perhaps the most characteristic and persistent theme in grassroots Tea Party activism. As Mark Lloyd of the Virginia Tea Party Patriots explains, people gravitate to the Tea Party when they anguish about "losing the nation they love, the country they planned to leave to their children and grandchildren."[12] As a new president of diverse heritage promised to "transform America," perceived threats to the very nature of "our country" spurred many people, and particularly older people, to get involved with the Tea Party.[13]

When Santelli issued the call for "Tea Party" protests, web-savvy activists recognized this rhetorical gold. Operating at first through the online social-networking site Twitter, conservative bloggers and Republican campaign veterans took the opportunity offered by the Santelli rant to plan protests under the newly minted "Tea Party" name.[14] Right-wing radio jocks and bloggers started circulating information on how would-be Tea Partiers could hook up with local and regional organizers to "take back" the country.

Initial Tea Party protests on February 27th drew small crowds in dozens of cities across the country. But after cable giant Fox News took up the rallying cry in March and early April, hundreds of thousands rallied on Tax Day 2009 to reiterate the anti-government message.[15] This was the moment when many people we interviewed got involved for the first time. In the months that followed, rallies and demonstrations continued, featuring mostly ordinary-looking older people waving incendiary signs and dressed up like Revolutionary-era patriots. Conservative news outlets amplified the public attention grassroots Tea Partiers were receiving, and mainstream media outlets became transfixed by the spectacle.

Soon Tea Partiers across the country moved into local organizing. From spring to fall of 2009 and on into 2010, local activists operating without central direction created legions of local Tea Parties meeting regularly, usually once a month, but in some cases weekly. In this book, we pay careful attention to the creation and spread of what grew to be approximately 1000 local Tea Party groups. Their emergence was important, taking grassroots activism from the realm of occasional outbursts connected by Internet communications into sustained, face-to-face community organizing. Typical was the genesis of the local Tea Party in Gloucester and Mathews counties in Virginia. On May 10, 2009, the local newspaper published a letter from Jean Casanave, who lamented that Americans are "losing our way" and declared that we must "fight" for "our Constitution," for "small government, low taxes, [and] religious freedom . . . "[16] Tom Robinson, an area man with considerable organizing experience, tracked Jean down to express interest in joint action. Within weeks, Tom and Jean plus a couple of dozen others launched the Peninsula Patriots, whose members meet monthly to hear lectures and plan lobbying and protest activities.[17]

As local Tea Party clusters formed during 2009 and early 2010, national conservative advocacy organizations and right-wing media stars stepped in to mobilize Tea Party people for contentious August town hall events with their local Congressional representatives, and also planned a national rally in the fall. On September 12, 2009, between 60,000 and 70,000 Tea Party protesters marched on Washington DC.[18] Periodic rallies continued through 2010, and during that pivotal year both grassroots citizens and national advocacy organizations claiming the Tea Party banner exercised significant clout in dozens of electoral races—first in Republican primaries, and then in the dramatic general election contests of November 2010.

After the GOP scored major victories in the 2010 midterms, the Tea Party's national momentum shifted even further to the elites at the top. Several of the well-heeled free-market advocacy groups that had pushed the 2009 Tea Party rallies convened newly elected Republicans in January 2011 to tutor them on how to hold firm, without compromise, for lower taxes, huge spending cuts, and evisceration of government regulations. Dozens of GOP Representatives and Senators joined Tea Party caucuses to exert leverage in the 112th Congress, in which the ideological center of gravity jumped sharply rightward. National media outlets accelerated their recruitment of self-appointed Tea Party spokespersons because producers and columnists were more desperate than ever to have honchos on speed-dial, easy to reach on short notice. And of course the unelected leaders of ultra-free-market advocacy groups based in Washington DC were all too happy to speak in the name of grassroots Tea Partiers, even though most of the DC talking heads rarely attend local meetings or interact with actual grassroots participants.

Indeed, one of the most important consequences of the widespread Tea Party agitations unleashed from the start of Obama's presidency was the populist boost given to professionally run and opulently funded right-wing advocacy organizations devoted to pushing ultra-free-market policies. Along with Republican Party operatives, who had long relied for popular outreach on independent-minded and separately organized Christian conservatives, national free-market advocacy operations would, via the Tea Party, enjoy new ties to grassroots activists willing to prioritize fiscal anti-government themes. One political action committee poured the old wine of GOP consultants and big-money funders into a new bottle labeled Tea Party Express (TPE), which allowed them to seem closely aligned with grassroots citizens.[19] Other existing national organizations, such as FreedomWorks and Americans for Prosperity, suddenly saw fresh opportunities to push long-standing ideas about reducing taxes on business and the rich, gutting government regulations, and privatizing Social Security and Medicare.[20]

There is a certain irony in these newly formed ties. FreedomWorks, for example, is not any sort of insurgent force. As a multimillion-dollar ideological organization advocating "Lower Taxes, Less Government, More Freedom," FreedomWorks operates out of Washington DC and traces its roots back to Citizens for a Sound Economy (an organization founded in 1984 with major funding from arch-conservative petrochemical billionaires, the

Koch brothers). FreedomWorks is currently led by Dick Armey, now in his seventies, who was the Republican Majority Leader from Texas in the 1990s, and has also worked as a lobbyist for many big-business interests. Hard to find more establishment Republican credentials than these. Yet suddenly, in 2009 and 2010, FreedomWorks helped to launch the Tea Party Patriots, an umbrella group that endeavors to orchestrate local and regional grassroots Tea Partiers into a bigger-than-life force in the media and electoral contests. And the unelected Dick Armey, along with his billionaire-backed organization, emerged as a national Tea Party spokesperson and advisor to GOP officials—operating in the name of a grassroots populist movement. In a twinkling, long-standing and top-down became, supposedly, new and bottom-up.

MAKING SENSE OF THE TEA PARTY

From a televised diatribe, to periodic protests, sustained local efforts, and the revitalization of national free-market advocacy—the modern-day Tea Party came together in record time, with remarkable élan and force. The pages to come feature fascinating people, dramatic local activities, and pivotal national maneuvers. But our job is not just to tell stories or describe the many parts of the Tea Party. The goal is to make sense of it all, and answer some pressing questions. What is the Tea Party, taken as a whole? How did it revitalize and remake right-wing conservatism leading into the 2010 elections? And what are the consequences for the Republican Party, for American democracy, and for the chances that governments at all levels will be able to tackle the pressing challenges of the twenty-first century? So far, pundits and analysts alike have offered insufficient understandings of the Tea Party in its totality, and most seem puzzled about how Tea Party efforts have achieved such outsized effects on national debates and Republican politicians. We will tackle these issues head on—and try to do so in ways that avoid oversimplifications and crude stereotypes.

Stereotypes are certainly out there. As one woman involved in the Tea Party told us: where "you come from"—that is, Cambridge, Massachusetts and Harvard University—people believe Tea Partiers are "a bunch of uneducated, racist, rednecks." This is itself an overgeneralization, yet such stereotypes do exist. And they can be misleading. Tea Party participants come from all over the country and range from people with high school diplomas or less, to college graduates and people with advanced degrees. Compared to other Americans, including other conservatives, Tea Party participants more readily subscribe to harsh generalizations about immigrants and blacks. And these views are a crucial part of the generalized societal worries so many Tea Partiers expressed to us. But there is little evidence that most individual Tea Partiers reject normal interactions with people of other races. Organizational leaders jump at chances to invite black speakers, and eagerly welcome—indeed feature—any person of color who wants to associate with the Tea Party. Most responsible Tea Parties strive to marginalize overtly racist and other extreme voices in their rallies or meetings. Organizers have told us about their efforts in this regard, and we have personally witnessed deft efforts to neutralize outbursts in meetings.

Additional exaggerations and distortions come from commentators at both ends of the partisan spectrum. Celebrants proclaim the Tea Party to be "revolutionary," but how new are many of the goals and ideas, really? When we explore the passions of Tea Partiers in detail, we will see that they are new variants of long-standing conservative claims about government, social programs, and hot-button social issues. We will need to listen carefully and probe deeply to figure out exactly what it is about Tea Partiers' beliefs and passions that is specific to our time in the presidential era of Barack Obama.

Many supporters also proclaim the Tea Party to be purely a grassroots rebellion, a "mass movement of . . . 'regular' Americans with real concerns about losing the right to live their lives as they choose."[21] This view captures only a small part of the truth, ignoring the fact that Tea Party participants are in many respects even more ideologically extreme than other very conservative Republicans. Similarly, the "mass movement" portrayal overlooks the fact that the Tea Party, understood in its entirety, includes media hosts and wealthy political action committees, plus national advocacy groups and self-proclaimed spokespersons—elites that wield many millions of dollars in political contributions and appear all over the media claiming to speak for grassroots activists who certainly have not elected them, and to whom they are not accountable. What kind of mass rebellion is funded by corporate billionaires, like the Koch brothers, led by over-the-hill former GOP kingpins like Dick Armey, and ceaselessly promoted by millionaire media celebrities like Glenn Beck and Sean Hannity?

The opposite illusion is also there among those who proclaim the Tea Party to be nothing more than an "astroturf" phenomenon, an illusion pushed by Fox News, or a "billionaire's tea party" in which "corporate America is faking a grassroots revolution."[22] This take on the Tea Party as a kabuki dance entirely manipulated from above simply cannot do justice to the volunteer engagement of many thousands of men and women who travel to rallies with their homemade signs and, even more remarkably, have formed ongoing, regularly meeting local Tea Party groups. The citizens we have met, who spend hours meeting with one another, arguing with officials, and learning about the workings of local, state, and national government—these people do not fit the caricatures espoused by some on the left. They are unglamorous, mostly older middle-class Americans. Billionaire-funded political action committees and longtime free-market advocacy organizations are certainly doing all they can to leverage and benefit from Tea Party activism. But they did not create all that activism in the first place, nor do they entirely control the popular effervescence.

At times, to be sure, national right-wing advocates and media stars are handing out a load of bull to grassroots Tea Party people, who accept outlandish claims a bit too readily. In meetings and interviews, we found that misinformation was prevalent among Tea Party supporters, particularly given their relatively high levels of education. But gaps and manipulative ties between professionally run national advocacy operations and local citizen undertakings are hardly unique to the Tea Party, or confined to conservative politics in the contemporary United States.[23] It is rarely helpful for analysts simply to denigrate the intelligence or autonomy of citizens who believe one false thing or another. What is more valuable is to understand the symbiosis of the various parts of Tea Party activism, and how those interactions strengthen Tea Party ideology and activism.

Considered in its entirety, the Tea Party is neither a top-down creation nor a bottom-up explosion. This remarkable political outpouring is best understood as a combination of three intertwined forces. Each force is important in its own right, and their interaction is what gives the Tea Party its dynamism, drama, and wallop. Grassroots activism is certainly a key force, energized by angry, conservative-minded citizens who have formed vital local and regional groups. Another force is the panoply of national funders and ultra-free-market advocacy groups that seek to highlight and leverage grassroots efforts to further their long-term goal of remaking the Republican Party, pushing it towards the hard right on matters of taxation, public spending, and government regulation. Finally, the Tea Party cannot be understood without recognizing the mobilization provided by conservative media hosts who openly espouse and encourage the cause. From Fox News to right-wing radio jocks and bloggers, media impresarios have done a lot to create a sense of shared identity that lets otherwise scattered Tea Parties get together and feel part of something big and powerful. Media hosts also put out a steady diet of information and misinformation—including highly emotional claims—that keep Tea Party people in a constant state of anger and fear about the direction of the country and the doings of government officials.

Grassroots activists, roving billionaire advocates, and right-wing media purveyors—these three forces, together, create the Tea Party and give it the ongoing clout to buffet and redirect the Republican Party and influence broader debates in American democracy. Our book explores each force and shows how they work together.

HOW WE KNOW: THE BIG PICTURE AND THE HUMAN DETAILS

Using vivid English and avoiding dry academic jargon are things we strive to do. Still, make no mistake, we are social scientists; our research is carefully grounded in the best evidence we can find. The footnotes are there for anyone who wants to look closely. Sometimes scholars and journalists rely on just one kind of evidence—a few interviews, maybe, or percentages from national surveys. We are much more eclectic, because we are trying both to get a sense of the big picture—how the Tea Party fits into American politics; who Tea Partiers tend to be in terms of broad categories like age, ethnicity, and income and education—and at the same time probe much more deeply by observing real groups in action and meeting and talking to fellow citizens who are active in Tea Party efforts.

For the big picture, much of our evidence comes from public records and news reports that help us trace the goals and activities of national advocacy groups and political action committees, and we also look at the elected officials and media figures who speak in the name of the Tea Party. We also track what has happened to the Republican Party in Washington DC and many key states as GOP candidates and officials attempt to harness Tea Party enthusiasm, yet avoid alienating other less conservative citizens.

National social surveys are also helpful. By now, literally hundreds of poll questions have been asked in an attempt to get at the attitudes and social backgrounds of "Tea Party sympathizers" compared to other sorts of

Americans—including self-described Republicans and conservatives who are not part of the Tea Party, as well as independents and Democrats who claim a range of neutral or oppositional stances toward the Tea Party. Not all surveys are equally well done. But there are enough of them by now, spread out over 2009, 2010, and 2011, to let us glean important information—not only from the best national surveys but also from some excellent studies of Tea Partiers in particular states. Because national pollsters ask similar questions again and again, we are also able to track key findings over time. This helps us get a sense of how American attitudes have changed as the Tea Party has become increasingly visible, and to learn how the beliefs of Tea Partiers themselves have shifted compared to the beliefs of other Americans.

But surveys, news accounts, and public information are not enough. To make sense of grassroots activism, we knew we needed to get out there and hear from Tea Party participants face to face. In the early stages of this research, we visited the nearby Greater Boston Tea Party, attended meetings, talked with people, and got to know the whirlwind 39-year-old leader, Christen Varley. She, in turn, sent out an electronic questionnaire from us to Massachusetts activists on her master list. The survey asked about how people got involved, their prior political experience, their age and social background, and the issues they considered most important. We then followed up with open-ended interviews.

Massachusetts is just one state, hardly politically typical, and we wanted to get in touch with Tea Partiers in different parts of America, farther from home. We were not going to run into many Tea Partiers walking across Harvard Yard, nor could we get a real-life perspective with our noses glued to computer screens. Without hearing directly from Tea Partiers in different parts of the country, we could easily fall into misleading generalizations or stereotypes. We also wanted to probe more deeply how local people contacted one another and got endeavors going. We knew how valuable it would be to attend additional local meetings, to witness everything from their ceremonial beginnings, to the lectures or discussions they featured, to the tenor of Tea Party meetings compared to other kinds of civic meetings we have observed over the years.

When opportunities arose to visit groups in Virginia and Arizona, we seized the chance to meet with grassroots Tea Party leaders and members who, almost without exception, were very welcoming and gracious to us. We came from afar, and they all knew or suspected that our political views are different from theirs. But they were still willing to let us get to know them individually—not just in brief phone interviews or hurried snippets at big protest events, but at much greater length at their regular meetings and social events, in visits to their homes, and in hour-long personal interviews.

Just to observe, we also attended a mid-April 2011 meeting of the York County Constitutionalists in North Berwick, Maine, to hear a lecture by a leader of the large Tea Party–affiliated group in Rochester, New Hampshire. At this interesting event, Jerry DeLemus, co-founder of the Rochester 9/12 Project and Chairman of the Granite State Liberty PAC, explained how New Hampshire Tea Party groups organized to take over much of the apparatus of their state's Republican Party, while also electing many Tea Party–influenced candidates in 2010 and pressing them afterwards to remain true to right-wing priorities. This was a chance to hear how Tea Partiers think about the political process at the ground level, as a dynamic organizer from the most mobilized New England state discussed Tea Party tactics with fellow Patriots across the Maine border. National politics also came into view as the speaker highlighted his ongoing interactions with a number of the GOP presidential aspirants gearing up for the critical New Hampshire primary in early 2012.

Through all of our travels, we not only observed real-world groups in operation. We also met some special people. We got to know a blogger and former stay-at-home mom living in small-town Massachusetts who, having been active in politics during college, returned to formal politics through her local Tea Party and now works full time at a local social conservative organization. We spoke with a refugee of World War II now living in Virginia, a woman who came to America knowing two words of English and who was taken in by a family she describes as "hippie sheep farmers." One of us (Vanessa) visited the home of a married couple in Arizona, sunbird migrants to the area, who shared not only their political views, but pictures of their grandchildren and stories of their RV travels across the country. And the other one of us (Theda) corresponded over many months by email with a gentleman in Virginia, who later helped arrange our visit to the Peninsula Patriots. When we traveled south, we were invited to his home for lunch and had the chance to meet the adorable little grandson that he and his wife, both in their seventies, have adopted and are rearing.

We found each person we spoke with admirable and likeable in his or her own way. Though their politics puts them toward the far right of the U.S. political spectrum, the Tea Partiers we have met are at once as typical and as eccentric as any other group of Americans you might run into. Indeed, should the focus not be on politics, the Tea Party meetings we attended could easily bring to mind a run-of-the-mill meeting of a home-owners' association, or a Bible study group, or a get-together at the VFW hall or the Elks' club. We hope that as we try to put the Tea Party into historical and national context, we also convey a human story—and we are very grateful to all who spoke with us for taking the time to participate in our research.

Back in Cambridge, Massachusetts, we have also worked with two lively undergraduates to assemble a comprehensive dataset of Tea Party groups.[24] Our approach to doing this has been different from the approach used by *Washington Post* reporters in the fall of 2010.[25] They started with lists of local groups offered by national organizations such as the Tea Party Patriots, and tried to reach local organizers. Reporters called up to six times, and counted as active those groups whose leaders answered and provided information on the goals, size, funding, and political activities of their local Tea Party. A lot of fascinating data came from the *Washington Post* effort, and we will refer to relevant findings from time to time. But we have also come to believe that the *Post* approach missed a number of active local groups. When we have tried emailing leaders out of the blue, for example, sometimes they answer and sometimes they don't—and we expect it might be the same on the phone. In some cases, local Tea Party leaders distrust national reporters and university researchers and just do not answer. Or people may be very busy and understandably feel they have better things to do. In the state of Virginia alone, we know from our fieldwork of multiple long-standing local Tea Parties not on the *Post* list. So we have gone about our effort to track down local groups using a method that does not require the leaders to respond.

Our team has looked at all fifty states and tracked down every Tea Party throughout the country that has any sort of presence on the Web. By now, most local, regional, and state-level Tea Party groups have some kind of web presence, and many have links to other websites that they consider part of their movement. Tea Party Patriots has done a lot to improve the online capacity of many local groups, and there are strong incentives and resources to help local groups link up. Tea Party websites feature blogs, meeting announcements, and discussion boards that provide a unique window on the people involved in Tea Party activism. We can see, for instance, where groups are located and which states and regions have more or fewer of them in relation to the size of their populations. We can also see which Tea Parties are engaging in local political races, and what news and information sources they consider reliable. We can read their discussions about leading political figures and about the policy issues of the day. The websites also let us track how the small, local Tea Party groups are linking together and organizing at the state and national level. In a few instances, we have even seen how these local groups are responding to our research, as they post messages about our visits and questions! All in all, a tremendous wealth of information can be drawn from the online indications of the Tea Party political phenomenon, and we will use the data where relevant in the chapters to come.

Of course, we could not interview every Tea Partier, visit more than a small number of group meetings, or regularly track many blogs. To ensure that our local results are properly situated in the national Tea Party phenomenon, we regularly check our findings from interviews, meetings, and the Web against broader surveys. In short, we make the different kinds of evidence marshaled for this study speak to each other, noting when information from interviews and observations either fits, or departs from, the broader picture in state or national compilations. Cross-checked in this way, our observations and personal encounters help us to paint an unusually vivid picture of Tea Party activists and groups.

Throughout the book, we introduce readers to Tea Party men and women we have met in person, and we describe what we saw and heard in real-life meetings. We use quotation marks when the precise words of participants appear in our notes; otherwise we provide a faithful synopsis or paraphrase of what people said. We also follow careful rules about using names. In instances where we visited a publicly advertised meeting, or read about one in the newspaper or on a blog, we cite the actual group name and give the date and location of the gathering. The same is true when we talk about state and national Tea Party and advocacy leaders who publicly speak in the name of their organizations. The identities of these people are readily available on the public record, so we use their real names. But in other cases, we use made-up names to protect the privacy of people who sat down for confidential interviews, or who exchanged emails or otherwise interacted with us in ways that presume privacy. In each chapter, we italicize a *pseudonym* the first time we mention a person to whom we promised confidentiality; and we sometimes slightly change incidental details that could make a person identifiable.

The chapters to come deploy the evidence and develop the themes just introduced. We say much more about the characteristics of ordinary Tea Partiers, how they got involved, and what they think. We lay out the complex relationships among the grassroots activists, national advocacy elites, and media purveyors who, together, make up the Tea Party as a whole. Then we probe how and why the Tea Party has had such a major impact on the Republican Party, driving it to the right, and more broadly shifting the focus and center of gravity of U.S. political debates. In conclusion, we will consider what the concurrence of Tea Party outbursts with Barack Obama's presidency means for democracy and governance in the United States.

1

Behind the Costumes and Signs

Who Are the Tea Partiers?

Stanley Ames is 70 years old, a retired Air Force pilot and lifelong conservative Republican.[1] He and his 65-year-old wife, *Gloria*, are active Tea Party participants in a small community on the dusty outskirts of Phoenix. Arriving at the Ames home requires careful navigation through winding suburban streets with names like Dancing Deer Lane, past rows of ranch houses arrayed around a pristine golf course.

Gloria and Stanley are friendly and welcoming, the kind of active older couple whose visits are eagerly awaited by their grandchildren. A tour of their house highlights family photos, artistic snapshots from the national parks they have visited on their many RV trips, and a sizeable collection of books from authors like Sean Hannity, Glenn Beck, and Sarah Palin. In the garage, next to the golf cart, is a gun safe the size of a refrigerator. But the couple owns only three guns, not much of a collection by Arizona standards. Mostly, they have stockpiled ammunition, along with food supplies to last eighteen months. Stan and Gloria want to be ready in case the U.S. economy and social order collapse—a possibility regularly discussed on Fox News, which the couple reports watching for about six hours every day. The home tour ends near a big screen TV, where Stanley jokingly notes that he has revealed what he calls "my secret." In the corner of the room, on a wheeled sawhorse, is a beautifully crafted western-style saddle. Gloria steps in to explain: Stanley, she says, sits on the saddle when he watches "his John Wayne movies."

People in the Tea Party are constantly scrutinized in the media, as well as by pollsters who repeatedly ask Americans what they think of the Tea Party and whether they take an active part in it. Meanwhile, images flit across our television and computer screens, showing costumed people carrying outrageous, homemade signs denouncing the "tyranny" of the federal government.

In all of this, the individuality and humanity of Tea Party participants can get lost. How, for example, did Stanley and Gloria, lifelong conservatives whose previous activism had not gone beyond voting, get drawn into this political mobilization? Are they typical Tea Party participants, these comfortably middle-class folks who come across in person as charmingly everyday?

Spending time with Tea Partiers at protests and in their local meetings, we noticed an interesting phenomenon. The loudest voices at the protests are rarely those of the folks who organize the meetings. The people like Stan and Gloria who are most engaged in Tea Party undertakings at the local level—arranging a meeting or a carpool, running for the precinct committee, quizzing officeholders, attending school board meetings—are not the types of people who shout. Although the views Tea Partiers espouse at rallies are certainly a distilled version of their genuine beliefs—including some very strong fears and furies—the discussions Tea Party people have at their meetings are much more complex and revealing, as are the accounts they give in unrushed personal interviews. As with any political phenomenon, there's only so much you can learn from dropping in on the most visible public dramas staged to capture media attention.

In this chapter and the next, we look beyond the public brouhaha to the people who have found the Tea Party idea compelling. This chapter locates Tea Party people in the overall landscape of U.S. society, showing that they are overwhelmingly older white citizens, relatively well educated and economically comfortable compared to Americans in general. Almost all are Republicans or conservatives to the right of the GOP. To give a broad and representative overview of Tea Party sympathizers and active supporters, we draw on the best available national social surveys. These studies help us pinpoint the social and political backgrounds of Tea Partiers. But we also delve more deeply, using things we have observed and heard from regular Tea Party participants to bring to life key points about their life circumstances and outlooks.

THE PEOPLE AT THE GRASS ROOTS

Stan and Gloria Ames are an older, white, conservative couple who can afford a comfortable though certainly not opulent life-style. They "fit the demographic," as social scientists put it—that is, Stan and Gloria are typical Tea Party participants to the extent that national surveys have been able to pin down what Tea Partiers are like compared to U.S. adults in general. With very few exceptions, the grassroots Tea Partiers we have met fit the same broad social profile—although each man or woman is, of course, more vivid and distinctive in person than the bland categorizations would imply.

Identifying a Distinct Minority

It took pollsters and scholars a while to zero in on the characteristics and outlooks of Americans who support the Tea Party.[2] National surveys during the first year of the Tea Party's evolution consistently found that large chunks of Americans knew little or nothing about this upsurge. Accordingly, small changes in the wording of survey questions resulted in wild swings in the levels of reported sympathy or support for the Tea Party. In due course, however, perceptions and experience spread in the citizenry, and studies became sophisticated enough to get at various levels of support and active involvement.

From late 2009 on, about 30% of American adults reported having a generally favorable impression of the Tea Party. Reported support bounced around that same level into 2011.[3] Included in this 30% are a lot of Americans who tell pollsters that they generally agree with Tea Party positions. But many of these sympathizers may not be all that passionate in their views. Vague questions about support or sympathy do not get at the firm core of Tea Party believers, let alone at those who actively participate.

"Strong" Tea Party supporters, nailed down in various ways, amount to about one-fifth of voting-age adults, or roughly 46 million Americans.[4] That is a lot of people, no question, an important minority of the U.S. electorate who probably account for most of the roughly two-fifths of all voters in the 2010 midterm elections who told exit pollsters that they support the Tea Party.[5] But we still have not pinpointed those who deem themselves truly *active* Tea Partiers because only a fraction of strong supporters with heartfelt views claim to have ever taken actions such as attending a rally or giving money to a candidate or organization.[6] An even smaller subset constitute the genuinely loyal Tea Partiers who regularly attend local meetings, the people who do the ongoing work of organizing events and following through on group goals.

Our nationwide survey of local Tea Parties turned up about 1000 groups spread across all fifty states, including about 800 groups that appeared to be active in the spring and early summer of 2011.[7] Some local Tea Parties are very large, with online membership lists of 1000 people or more. But most local Tea Parties have much smaller contact lists, and the typical local meeting has a few dozen people in attendance.[8] Overall, a generous assumption is that approximately 800 active local Tea Parties have, on average, 200 members apiece—that is, people who sign up to be regularly notified and attend gatherings at least occasionally.[9] That multiplies out to 160,000 very active grassroots participants in Tea Parties across the United States. If we decide to err on the upside to take account of the possibility that some local Tea Parties may have been overlooked and some participants may have been missed, we arrive at about 200,000 U.S. adults who are on the rolls of active local Tea Parties.

Stan and Gloria Ames are, in short, part of a very special minority of very engaged Tea Party citizens. They are not alone; there are many other activists like them. But the totality of active grassroots Tea Partiers who regularly attend meetings or take overt actions in support of the cause add up to just a tiny fraction of the U.S. electorate. To make this observation is not in any way to denigrate grassroots Tea Party energy. In any political formation, true activists are just a tiny fraction of wider circles of sympathizers. The core activists are surrounded by an intermediate circle of attentive supporters—people on email lists, perhaps, who occasionally send a check or drop in on a well-publicized event. Both activists and attentive supporters are, in turn, surrounded by a ring of mostly passive sympathizers, the "couch potatoes" of the movement.

The Social Backgrounds of Tea Party People

From all available evidence, active participants and the broader circles of Tea Party supporters come from similar social backgrounds.[10] The first really detailed and accurate national survey was completed by the *New York Times* and CBS News in April 2010—about a year after the Tea Party idea first spread. According to that survey, whose findings have been echoed in subsequent studies, "the 18 percent of Americans who identify themselves as Tea Party supporters tend to be Republican, white, male, married and older than 45."[11] A number of studies have found that the vast majority of Tea Party supporters are middle-aged or older.[12] Not surprisingly, given their age, Tea Party supporters and activists are better-off economically and better-educated than most Americans. Many are regular church-goers.[13] And compared to all other Americans, Tea Partiers are more likely to be evangelical Protestants than mainline Protestants, Catholics, Jews, or nonbelievers.[14]

Given the disproportionate number of older whites, it is not surprising that Tea Party activists and supporters are found to have somewhat higher incomes than typical Americans.[15] Most are not truly wealthy, however. Comfortably middle-class might be the best way to describe grassroots Tea Partiers—in contrast to many of the professional advocates and media stars who promote and profit from the Tea Party label on the national stage. The homes of Tea Partiers we visited are modest in size and peppered with family pictures and mementos. These domiciles were not the professionally decorated, oversized pseudo-mansions so prevalent among America's well-to-do business chieftains and elite professionals. One of the Tea Party families we visited had a well-manicured, medium-sized home on a compact tract in the corner of a neighborhood of modest, closely spaced homes. This family is not suffering economically, but it is not rolling in wealth, either.

Nearly all the Tea Party people we met had at least some college education, including the women who had primarily stayed at home and reared children. Our contacts included participants currently or formerly in professional occupations such as medicine and engineering. Yet the plurality seemed to be small business owners, often in fields like construction, remodeling, or repair. Virginia Tea Partier *James Morrow*, for instance, is retired from his job as a contractor. A fair number of others worked in technology, insurance, or real estate. Although we met a retired police officer, a social worker, and a few teachers, only a relatively small portion of Tea Party participants were employed in the public sector—with the exception of the military. Quite a few of the men we met were veterans of the Vietnam War, and a number of Tea Party men and women had military careers behind them. Military people make up an especially prominent part of the Tea Party population in Virginia, a state with a proud military tradition.

Do Tea Partiers hail from particular parts of the United States? We will see in Chapter 3 that southern states tend to have larger Tea Party groups. But the geographical location of local groups is not necessarily indicative of the home regions of individual Tea Partiers. Americans move around a lot, and many Tea Partiers we spoke to are not long-standing residents of, or native to, the areas where they currently reside and attend Tea Party meetings. A lot of them arrived at their current homes after retirement, and some told us that attending Tea Party meetings was a way to connect with like-minded fellow residents in their new regions.

We should not be surprised at this, because so many Tea Party participants are comfortably well-off senior citizens. Like many of their peers not in the Tea Party, they decided after leaving the workforce to escape the cold northern winters and enjoy their retirement years in sunnier southern and western climes. At one meeting outside of Phoenix, it did not seem that any of the two dozen or so attendees were actually born or raised in Arizona. The Tea Party emerged only in 2009, so we cannot say the people at that meeting were Tea Partiers as such in their pre-retirement days. Yet their current involvement arises from long-standing attitudes and worldviews, which they brought to Arizona as they arrived from all over the United States.

Proud to Be Older

Although not every active Tea Partier is a senior citizen, most are middle-aged and beyond—a key social characteristic. In addition to participating in the group in their retirement community, Stan and Gloria have attended Tea Party meetings in Flagstaff, where they tell us there are quite a few nonelderly participants, people still employed at full-time jobs. At meetings in Boston proper, we saw younger Tea Partiers, too—a sprinkling of twenty-somethings plus others in their prime working years. A political science colleague who studies Tea Partiers in Ohio told us that he saw a relatively wide spread of ages at a Tea Party meeting in Akron.[16] Probably the age profile of the Tea Party nudges younger in urban areas, especially in locales where libertarian college students may turn up. But at the Tea Party meetings we attended in rural and suburban venues, graying hair topped almost every head. Although quite a few of the group leaders we met were women in their forties, the bulk of those in attendance were unmistakably in their fifties, sixties, seventies, and even older. Older husbands and wives often attended together, leaving big cars in the parking lot festooned with Tea Party stickers that symbolized their new joint passion. At a supper meeting in Virginia, a few members arrived with children or grandchildren, all pre-teens and youngsters who fidgeted as they sat through the adult talk-fest. Adults age 25 to 45 were not much in evidence.

Some Tea Party members aspire to recruit younger adults to the cause. "You brought a young person!" exclaimed one Arizona member with delight, when one of the authors (29-year-old Vanessa) arrived at a meeting along with Gloria and Stanley Ames. A link on the website of the Greater Phoenix Tea Party Patriots featured a notice about "Weekend Camps" run by American Leadership Teen Camps—though we have no idea how many teens actually attend with support from their parents or grandparents.[17] In Charlottesville, Virginia, the local Tea Party leader told us about efforts to do organized outreach to local schools, and mentioned one session for high school students already scheduled for the spring of 2011, sponsored by an association of home-schoolers in the area. In a truly creative flourish, one Tea Party participant in Virginia suggested outreach to hunting clubs that might have younger and more diverse memberships interested in Second Amendment issues.

Despite occasional efforts at intergenerational outreach, Tea Partiers do not seem anguished about their upward-tilted age profile. The paucity of younger participants is usually taken in stride. Tea Partiers are "older and wiser," one member in Arizona told us. Similarly, Virginian *John Patterson* explained that older Americans are more attuned to Tea Party priorities. "Twenty-eight-year-olds are not paying the bills" and so they are not as attracted to the Tea Party as people over fifty, who worry about fiscal matters. In everyday human terms, the Tea Party perspective resembles how grandparents routinely look at those following them through life: there is hope for the grandkids, who may respond to education, but younger adults are unseasoned and often irresponsible.

The generational perspective of most Tea Partiers is unmistakable. The vast majority are looking at society and politics with the expectations, hopes, and fears of long-standing staunch conservatives.[18] Tea Partiers seem less concerned about flocking to meetings with other oldsters than do the Sixties-generation liberals whose meetings we have also attended. Older liberals often obsess and strategize about how to rope in future generations and hand over some leadership roles to them, whether or not they are very effective at actually doing this. Elderly conservative and liberal activists in early twenty-first century America share an important commonality: both kinds of activists are equally confident that their perspectives *should* have cross-generational legs. The truth, after all, should appeal to young and old alike. But older liberals think they have to recruit and empower younger activists, whereas Tea Partiers tend to take satisfaction in their own special wisdom.

TEA PARTIERS ARE *VERY* CONSERVATIVE

Political dispositions matter more than social characteristics in pinpointing exactly who has gotten on board the Tea Party train. Although the race, age, and general social status of Tea Partiers certainly have relevance, these broad background characteristics do not distinguish supporters or activists from millions of other Americans. Indeed, the social profile of Tea Partiers— older, white, middle class, and often religious—fits most Republicans and most conservatives. What distinguishes Tea Party supporters more precisely are their very right-wing political views, even compared to other conservatives. Long-standing right-wing views prompted prospective Tea Partiers to look for a new political home amidst the detritus of the GOP in late 2008. And their more pessimistic version of conservatism caused them to be acutely worried about the economic crisis and what Obama might do to address it.

Conservative Republicans—and Beyond

Tea Partiers are very conservative Republicans, but in saying this we need to be careful to specify exactly what we do and do not mean. When talking about the relationship of Americans to the two major political parties, it helps to keep in mind that U.S. parties are not mass membership organizations. Ordinary citizens express levels of identification with a party by saying they accept the label, or by regularly voting for the party's candidates. Analysts use such measures when they speak of regular citizens as "Republicans." But U.S. party organizations as such consist of relatively small numbers of national, state, and local officials and committees. Citizens can be Republicans, or lean toward the Republican Party, without necessarily liking or supporting GOP officials or approving the ways official party organs are structured and run.

For Tea Partiers these are crucial distinctions. Tea Party supporters overwhelmingly vote for Republicans, especially in general elections where Democrats might otherwise win. But not all of them will call themselves Republicans; they might say they are "Independents" and mean either that they are more conservative than they think the Republican Party is, or, far less commonly, that they are center-right people who lean toward the GOP. Labels are complicated by the fact that many Tea Partiers are skeptical, even scornful, of "establishment" Republicans. Tea Party citizens may say they are independent or refuse to fully embrace the Republican label, in order to signal their distrust of GOP elites. As the mission statement of the "Defense & Shield" Tea Party group in Ellensburg, Washington, puts it: "We are determined not to allow the status quo republican party to co-opt our organization, as it has other organizations in our venue . . . Rather, we intend to influence the republican party toward change, that it may more strongly embrace conservative values it claims to believe in, such as limited government, a culture of life, low taxes, balanced budgets, etc."[19]

Given the distinction between voting for Republicans versus supporting GOP officials, some pundits and a few scholars have been confused—or have deliberately tried to create confusion—about the right-wing political location of Tea Partiers. Some commentators have very misleadingly suggested that Tea Partiers are swing-voters, even "independents" analogous to Ross Perot voters in the 1990s.[20] The facts say otherwise, because whatever they may think about given GOP officials or nominees, Tea Partiers do not engage in swing voting in general elections. At the polls, they support the enemy of their main enemies: they vote for candidates that can displace Barack Obama and other Democrats.

Whatever their concern about particular Republican elites, Tea Party participants are right-wingers in the GOP orbit.[21] Tea Party supporters claim allegiance to the Republican Party by a margin of three to one or more.[22] Gallup found that 62% of Tea Partiers called themselves *conservative*

Republicans.[23] Virtually all Tea Partiers voted for John McCain over Barack Obama.[24] Yet Tea Partiers are more strongly and more angrily opposed to President Obama than other conservatives or Republican-identifiers. Indeed, nuanced surveys that drill down on attitudes reveal that Tea Party supporters are distinctly more right-wing than their closest political cousins. As of early 2011, non–Tea Party Republicans were closer to independents and Democrats on many issues about public spending and the role of government than they were to Tea Party–oriented Republicans, whose extreme opposition to public expenditures on education and environmental protection set them apart.[25] In the early 2011 clashes over the size of budget cuts that pitted the GOP-led 112th House against the Democrat-controlled Senate, Republican Speaker of the House John Boehner found himself suspended over a crevasse within his own party. Two-thirds of Tea Party Republicans pushed him to shut down the federal government rather than compromise over spending cuts, while majorities of moderate Republicans and independents preferred meeting Democrats partway to avoid a shutdown.[26]

Our fieldwork in Massachusetts, Virginia, and Arizona fleshes out what the best surveys reveal. In Boston, a casual show of hands at a Tea Party event showed only a single, somewhat rueful Obama voter in a room of forty people. In Arizona, *Peggy Lawrence* described one of the pleasures of Tea Party gatherings as being an opportunity to speak to "like-minded," "conservative" people. And in Virginia, *Bonnie Sims* said her parents "raised her conservative," while *James Morrow* described himself as "a conservative and a Republican." Some Virginians went even further, saying that they are "ultra-conservative" or even "on the far right." Those who do not call themselves Republicans are almost never Democrats or middle-of-the-roaders. They may instead think of themselves as Ron Paul libertarians, "Birchers" (members of the John Birch Society), or some other sort of independent situated beyond the right edge of the GOP.

Democrats have no hope of attracting Tea Party support, no matter how hard they tack toward the right—especially not while Barack Obama, virtually the Devil incarnate for Tea Partiers, remains in the White House. When Tea Partiers are faced at the polls with a choice of Republican versus Democrat, the latter can "fuhgettabouddit." Even when Tea Partiers wish they had better, more conservative alternatives to whatever GOP candidates are on the ballot in general election contests, most are savvy enough voters to know that they do not want to help the Democrats. Our interviewees did not think a third party was a good idea, even if they distrusted and disliked their local version of the GOP organizational "establishment," which they usually do. They are keeping their eye on the right-wing prize: pushing Barack Obama out of the presidency, and gaining further ground in Congress, governorships, and state legislatures. For that, Tea Partiers know they need to vote for the most conservative viable Republicans—and they will.

Economic Worries with a Political Edge

Journalists and academics have speculated that the Tea Party must be a response to the Great Recession that gathered force starting in 2008. The coincidence of popular protests with plunging economic indicators makes this seem plausible. For Tea Partiers, however, pessimism about the economy is politically tinged. Those who joined the eruption were not the most economically dislocated Americans—even if the newly minted Tea Partiers who took to the streets and started organizing in 2009 got an extra prod from the downward-spiraling economy.

Like many other Americans, many in the Tea Party work in sectors of the economy that have strongly felt the effects of the recent Great Recession. Nearly 2 million jobs were lost in the construction industry, which employs many families we spoke to at Tea Party meetings. Virginian Bonnie Sims told us that, while her husband has been lucky enough to keep his job in construction, "every Friday I look to be told they are closing the company." She has every reason to worry. In the course of the economic downturn, the national economy shed a quarter of all jobs in construction.[27] An engineer at a Massachusetts Tea Party meeting told us that since he was laid off, the Tea Party had become his "full-time job." But construction is not the only sector of the economy suffering. With little to cushion them in the downturn, small business owners are particularly subject to economic turmoil. Small business people may stay in operation but still experience reduced profits and higher uncertainty. Many Tea Party entrepreneurs say they have no plans to retire: in some cases because they love their work, in others because they have to keep going out of economic necessity.[28]

In Arizona, as one Tea Partier talked about having to close down her business, another chimed in with a story about her 401k. The Great Recession of 2009 and 2010 followed on the heels of a collapse in the housing market and a dramatic drop in stock values. From 2007 on, some suburban and exurban areas saw home values drop in response to the housing crisis and rising gas prices, while the tanking stock market dramatically decreased the value of many people's retirement savings in 2008 and 2009.[29] For Tea Partiers, like many older Americans, these economic shocks hit at two seemingly safe investments: their home values and their retirement accounts. Some we spoke to were empty-nesters who had planned to downsize to a smaller home. *Ben Jones* complained that he was now "stuck with" a house in Virginia he had been planning to sell. In rural and suburban areas, where many Tea Partiers live, there were simply no buyers in 2010 and 2011.

Tea Partiers do not come from the groups that have borne the brunt of the recent U.S. economic crisis, however. As older, middle class, white people, Tea Partiers tend to be better cushioned against economic upheaval than younger Americans, especially minorities. In mid-2010 the unemployment rate was 15.8% for U.S. blacks and 12.4% for Hispanics, compared to 8.8% for white people. Young Americans also face exceedingly high rates of unemployment, and an early bout of unemployment has been shown to affect one's entire career trajectory.[30] Older people have far lower rates of poverty than their younger peers, thanks to the Social Security system, which can be relied upon to cushion any shock to their economic well-being. The typical Tea Party participant simply did not, and does not, face the direst blows delivered by the Great Recession.

Though members of the Tea Party do not bear the heaviest economic burden, they do have some of the most negative views of the economy, and their worries bleed into broader fears.[31] After all, pensions and homes were supposed to be safe investments, the carefully tended fruit of years of work and thrift. Threats to these investments convinced many Tea Partiers that hard work is no longer fairly rewarded in America. Tea Party members we spoke to were acutely concerned that their children were not going to be able to be as successful as they themselves had been. As the April 2010 CBS News/*New York Times* poll found, six in ten Tea Partiers said that "when it comes to good jobs, America's best years are behind us." Even at that economically tough juncture for most Americans, Tea Partiers showed themselves to be more pessimistic than their fellow citizens. Overall, fewer than half of Americans said that good jobs are a thing of the past.[32] But for members of the Tea Party, it felt as though the fundamental rules about the American Dream had changed. Working hard no longer meant getting ahead.

One reason for their pessimism may be grounded in the economics of their stage in life. We need to keep in mind that people experience ups and downs, economic and otherwise, in relation to their expectations. Threats to things people think they can count on can be very frightening—and shocks to the economic assumptions of older people can seem especially worrying because they do not imagine an infinite future in which to recoup. Even though older, middle-class white Americans—the broad demographic from which most Tea Partiers come—were not the people hardest hit, they did see their economic security shaken when Wall Street went into a meltdown and economic dislocations rippled across America's communities.

Older people with some accumulated equity can find an economic downturn very menacing, not only because their retirement accounts and home values take a hit, but because governments at all levels spend more on programs to help working-age families (through programs such as unemployment insurance, Food Stamps, college aid, and publicly subsidized health care). All of these cost more public money at the very moment that government budgets are strained because of declining revenues from sales and income taxes. Will governments respond by hiking levies on the more economically comfortable? Many Tea Party people are acutely worried that the answer will be yes. UCLA graduate student Emily Ekins reports a strong fear among Tea Partiers that they may be asked to pay higher taxes in the future, a result consistent with our fieldwork experience.

Tea Partiers' dread of tax hikes even surpasses the usual level at which Republicans worry about and oppose tax increases. Eighty percent of Tea Partiers oppose raising taxes on Americans making more than $250,000 a year, a number that far exceeds the 56% of non-Tea Party Republicans who are opposed to such levies. [33] Even compared to fellow conservatives, Tea Partiers are especially worried about the political response to the economic downturn—which helps explain why the Tea Party outburst happened when it did.

Whatever their worries about jobs, home values, and retirement savings, older white conservatives flocked to Tea Party protests only when a Democratic president and Congress took office. The economic plunge starting in 2008 may have rattled Tea Partiers' sense of economic well-being, but it was the progressive policy agenda of Barack Obama that triggered their mobilization. In the worldview of Tea Party participants, government efforts at redistribution have skewed the rewards and costs that should rightly be apportioned by the free market—and the election of Obama only promised to make the economic situation worse. [34] Tea Partiers feared government responses orchestrated by a president they despise, who might spend more on the less privileged and hike taxes on people like themselves. Politics colored perceptions of the crisis, which heightened Tea Partiers' sense that they were "losing" the America they have known and cherished. Again, Tea Partiers are best understood as first and foremost *conservatives*, rather than merely as exemplars of demographic or economic categories.

How Far Will the Most Extreme Go?

Given that Tea Partiers are very conservative, are some of them beyond civil politics together? Tea Partiers and their allies on the ultra-fringe have been known to make violent threats. One sign that made an appearance at a rally opposing health care reform read simply, "If Brown Can't Stop It, A Browning Can," accompanied by a picture of a handgun.[35] "Brown" referred to the recent election of Senator Scott Brown, Republican from Massachusetts, who had promised to be the crucial forty-first vote against health care reform. Should the Senate GOP filibuster be unsuccessful, the sign implied, a violent response would be in order.

That was not the last time health care reform provoked troubling threats from Tea Party activists. As the Affordable Care Act made its way to the president's desk, a Virginia Tea Party blog posted what they believed to be the home address of Democratic Representative Tom Perriello, a strong proponent of President Obama's reform. The blog post urged fellow Tea Partiers to "stop by" for a "face-to-face chat" with a "personal touch."[36] By mistake, the address posted was actually that of Representative Perriello's brother, sister-in-law, and their four young children. Soon thereafter the gas line to their home was cut—an act that could have caused a murderous explosion, but fortunately did not. The FBI opened an investigation.[37] The Perriello incident came after months of angry and sometimes violent demonstrations at town halls convened by elected Democrats, and after repeated physical threats directed at Democrats in regions with many conservative activists—not just Tom Perriello and his kin, but Democrats in southern Ohio and parts of the West and South as well.[38]

The trouble with violent rhetoric, even if violence is eventually repudiated by group leaders, is that unhinged people can be encouraged to turn words into action. At the time of this writing, it is unclear who, in fact, cut the gas line to the Perriello home. Yet the Tea Party style of egging things on by over-hyping threats and using martial metaphors to mobilize conservative opposition to Democrats in government, is unlikely to cool any hotheadedness. The presence in the Tea Party of right-wingers previously or currently involved with radical organizations undoubtedly contributes to extremist rhetoric, even if in most instances people do not practice violence against political opponents.

Some anti-government extremists have unquestionably found their way into Tea Party groups—for example, members of the Oath Keepers, a group centered on current and former law enforcement officers. Expecting the Obama Administration to declare martial law across the country and detain citizens en masse, Oath Keepers proclaim their readiness to engage in armed insurrection to counter this supposed threat from the federal government.[39] At Tea Party events we observed in Virginia and Massachusetts, members of the Oath Keepers were in attendance. In Idaho, the Sandpoint Tea Party Patriots have reportedly joined a coalition called "Friends for Liberty" that also includes representatives from Oath Keepers and the John Birch Society. At the first public event convened by the Friends of Liberty, "Richard Mack, a former Arizona sheriff, brought 1,400 people to their feet with a speech about confronting a despotic federal government."[40] The possibility of such a confrontation is not entirely rhetorical because members of the Oath Keepers have been tied to various militia groups.[41]

Yet Tea Partiers can hail from far-right backgrounds without threatening violence. Consider *Timothy Manor*, one of the oldest of our interviewees in Virginia. Manor is not, as he puts it, "a participant in the digital revolution," but he has for more than thirty years engaged avidly in politics, mailing a regular stream of handwritten letters, plus his own newsletter, to public officials and fellow activists. Not beating around the bush when it comes to his partisanship, Timothy places himself "somewhere to the right of Attila the Hun." Partway through our interview, he informed us he was "going to make an admission." With a wry smile, he declared that he is "a Bircher," a member of the John Birch Society. During its heyday in the 1950s and 1960s, the John Birch Society strongly opposed the Civil Rights movement, which it saw as "almost wholly created by the Communists," and promoted a number of conspiracy theories, including the notion that the fluoridation of drinking water is a socialist threat.[42] The organization faded from national view in the 1970s, but it continues to have a small and devoted following. When the local Tea Party started in his area in the spring of 2009, loyal "Bircher" Timothy was one of the first to get involved. Though his ailments sometimes keep him from traveling as much as he would like, Timothy attends meetings regularly and makes sure that Birch Society literature is on the handout table. Timothy is fully accepted and well-liked by his fellow Patriots—and we could see why. In person, we found him charming and genteel. We cannot picture him cutting a gas line to a family home; he would be more likely to send a constant stream of protest letters via the U.S. Postal Service.

Whatever some in the militia movement might do, in short, elderly Tea Partiers are not going to pick up arms en masse and start attacking government officials, liberal politicians, or their fellow citizens. The views of Tea Party participants may be on the far right end of the political spectrum, but their activities and daily lives are usually quite ordinary. Tossing out the occasional emotional epithet or toting the occasional over-the-top sign is as far as they will go. Most Tea Party leaders may use aggressive language, but they do so only to foment activism for protests, electoral activities, and other appropriate venues for the expression of political views and differences.

When it comes to over-the-top political rhetoric, even rhetoric using martial metaphors, similar discourse happens all across the political spectrum and reverberates through U.S. democratic history. It is important to maintain a distinction between, on the one hand, individuals who use fighting words or images to show intensity in a debate or display determination at a rally and, on the other hand, organizations that threaten and prepare for actual violence. Real violence, or the threat of it, is truly deleterious, because in a democracy even heated arguments must proceed with all participants feeling assured that basic physical safety is not in question. But mere fighting words and images are part of the U.S. democratic tradition. Political life in the United States has never been a tea party. Insults and colorful metaphors, including martial metaphors, are part of the game, now as they ever have been.

SOCIAL CONSERVATIVES AND LIBERTARIANS

On the advice of Fox News television personality Glenn Beck, Stanley and Gloria Ames took an online test of their conservatism. Based on how you answered a series of multiple-choice questions, the test would let you know what kind of conservative you are. Stanley, it turned out, is a straight-down-the-ticket conservative. Gloria, on the other hand, turns out to be something of a libertarian. She seemed tickled by this finding. "I never knew!" she laughed. Since getting involved with the Tea Party, Gloria has read and enjoyed the free-market tome, *Atlas Shrugged*. Stanley has not yet made it through the whole book. His wife is the reader in the family, he says. But after discovering Cliffs Notes (a study tool, he tells us, that was not yet available during his academic career), he has absorbed the book's main ideas, and considers them "interesting."

Stanley and Gloria are not the only conservatives who have been introduced to libertarian ideas through the Tea Party. So far, we've seen a number of traits that mostly unite engaged Tea Party supporters, including race, age, socioeconomic class, and, above all, very conservative political views. There is, however, one major dimension along which Tea Party activists show diversity. Some Tea Partiers are social conservatives focused on moral and cultural issues ranging from pro-life concerns to worries about the impact of recent immigrants on the cultural coherence of American life, while others are much more secular minded libertarians, who stress individual choice on cultural matters and want the Tea Party as a whole to give absolute priority to fiscal issues. When it comes to hammering out shared positions or setting priorities for local Tea Party activity, there can be significant friction between these two clusters, particularly about religion and the role of government in enforcing moral standards.

We met many social conservatives in our fieldwork. Virginian *Mandy Hewes*, for instance, arrived at our interview wearing a pin reading "Don't Worry—God's In Charge!" She spoke movingly of her involvement in her Methodist church, and made many connections between long-standing social conservative goals and Tea Party priorities. Poll data confirms that social conservatives like Mandy make up a large percentage of people who identify with the Tea Party. According to one 2010 poll, almost 40% of Tea Party supporters described themselves as evangelical Christians, and about the same percentage said they attended religious services on a weekly basis.[43] In early 2011, the well-respected Pew Forum on Religion and Public Life issued survey findings documenting that "Tea Party supporters tend to have conservative opinions not just about economic matters, but also about social issues such as abortion and same-sex marriage."[44]

Meanwhile, libertarians are in the Tea Party, too. Although they arrive by various routes, most seem to have been involved with the Campaign for Liberty, a spin-off of the 2008 Ron Paul campaign. Over 300 Campaign for

Liberty groups tag themselves on MeetUp as a "Tea Party." In nationwide data, UCLA graduate student Emily Ekins finds interesting demographic differences between social conservatives and libertarians in the Tea Party orbit. [45] Libertarians are a bit more likely to be educated to the postgraduate level, and 28% of them have incomes over $100,000 a year, compared to 14% of socially conservative Tea Partiers. Libertarians are a bit younger (59 on average) than social conservatives (62 on average). And the libertarian Tea Partiers are more often from the West or Northeast, whereas social conservatives in the Tea Party more often live in the South. "The most striking difference between the two groups," Ekins reports, "is that . . . libertarians are significantly and substantially less likely to attend religious services every week"—only 18% of libertarian Tea Partiers attend that regularly, compared to 54% of social conservative Tea Partiers.

The 2011 Pew study of "The Tea Party and Religion" confirms this asymmetry in the overlap between Tea Partiers and religious social conservatives. "Most people who agree with the religious right also support the Tea Party," Pew researchers concluded. "But support for the Tea Party is not synonymous with support for the religious right," because nearly half of Tea Party supporters say they have not heard of the religious right or have no strong opinion about it—and about one in ten Tea Partiers express outright disagreement with religious conservatism. Clearly, there are quite a few Tea Party supporters who do not consider themselves religious conservatives— and while some of them are socially conservative on family issues and immigration matters, others are actually fairly secular libertarians who may want government to stay out of the bedroom. The Tea Party label has a broader reach than "the conservative Christian movement sometimes known as the religious right," even if religious conservatives are jumping on the Tea Party bandwagon.

This bigger tent presents some significant challenges to Tea Party cohesion. From abortion to drug laws to gay marriage, libertarians and social conservatives have almost diametrically opposing views—a fact that can lead to severe strain on Tea Party groups. An Arizona Tea Party blog post entitled, "Jesus Christ, Libertarian," castigated religious conservatives for their social views. The author interpreted the Biblical principle "let he who is without sin cast the first stone" to mean that Jesus did not approve of imposing one's personal morality on others. "By attempting to use the law to enforce their morality, social conservatives violate the very principles that they say that they cherish most," the author concluded. Such angry online outbursts surely reverberate into local meetings. Outright schism can be the result. We heard one remarkable story about a local leader who faced so many tensions in her flock that she split the group in two. She now meets separately with "the Christian Tea Party" and the "regular Tea Party."[46] Usually, differences between social conservatives and libertarians do not lead to organizational breakdowns, however, because members show sensitivity to one another's beliefs and leaders find a way to blend concerns.

Tea Party groups and Tea Party organizers and lecturers at all levels from local to state to nation are engaged in delicate balancing acts, trying to keep folks with very different cultural outlooks and beliefs together. In giving us a favorable review of a local candidate she had heard speak, Arizonan Peggy Lawrence made a point of telling us, "and I don't even know his views on social issues!" Those policies, she insisted, were beside the point for the Tea Party. Peggy's focus matches those of other Tea Partiers nationwide. In the April 2010 CBS News/*New York Times* poll, only 14% of Tea Party supporters said social issues were more important to them than economic issues.[47]

A note of caution is in order about surveys, however, even the very skillfully designed surveys we rely on in this book. Labels used in social surveys often skim too lightly over what individuals believe in detail, and definitely overlook a group's internal social dynamics. In our fieldwork experience, the many rank-and-file members who hold heartfelt Christian conservative views set the tone for the Tea Party as a whole. Libertarian members tend to accommodate the social conservative view, at least to some degree. One Virginia leader sent us a message the morning after we witnessed a Tea Party meeting in which strong views were expressed on pro-life issues. "Thinking back on last night's meeting," she wrote, "there is one clarification I feel I should make in an effort to give you the most accurate picture possible of our group. . . . Tea party organizations typically do not take a position on social issues such as abortion and gay rights. The conservatism that unites us is governmental and fiscal, not social. While it is rare to have discussion of social issues come up at our meetings, it will on occasion. . . ." Actually, in our observation, it is not so rare for socially conservative moral arguments to come up in Tea Party meetings.

In practice, social conservatives make up a vocal majority of many Tea Parties. At a meeting in Tempe, members circulated right-to-life materials with the headline, "40 Days for Life: Pray to End Abortion." New Hampshire Tea Party leader Jerry DeLemus speaks publicly and openly about his

Christian beliefs and his active role in his church. Even in relatively liberal Massachusetts, many Tea Partiers were on the front lines of the culture wars. The leader of the Greater Boston Tea Party also worked for a social conservative advocacy organization. And on the walk to a Tea Party protest in Boston, one woman complained about how "science has become a religion" in this country, replacing true religious faith. Others traded war stories of their own efforts to combat the dangers of science education in schools. One complained that a teacher had been converting the children to "environmentalism," while another proudly reported having petitioned the administration at their children's private school to offer a special class questioning the science of global warming. All of these anti-science views were presented in religious terms.

While social conservatives regularly take a prominent role in Tea Party discussions, the less religious or more libertarian members tended to remain on the periphery of the activist base. For instance, a man in his mid-thirties, a regular attendee at Massachusetts Tea Party meetings, brought fliers outlining a plan to get America's financial house in order, beginning with the abolishment of the Federal Reserve—an idea popular with Ron Paul followers. The man was warmly received, but his recommendations did not seem to get incorporated into the main thrust of the Tea Party group's activism, and some of his suggestions—like protesting *against* Sarah Palin at an upcoming Tea Party Express event—were immediately quashed by meeting organizers.

National spokespersons as well as grassroots leaders recognize that many Tea Partiers come to activism through their faith, and incorporate religious language along with their fiscal conservative rhetoric. Glenn Beck's "9/12" campaign, closely associated with Tea Party activism, has as its second tenet, "I believe in God and He is the Center of my Life." Senator Jim DeMint, who supported many Tea Party candidates through his PAC, has referred to the Tea Party as a "Great Awakening," and the 2010 National Tea Party Convention included a panel on "Why Christians Must Engage," led by Dr. Rick Scarborough, a Baptist minister known for his opposition to sex education.[48]

Often, leaders synthesize by adding a little of this and a little of that—or get creative by defining budget-cutting as including the removal of public funds for family planning groups, for example. A fascinating amalgamation of religious and fiscal themes occurred at a meeting in Tempe, Arizona. The featured speaker was Tom Jenney from the ultra-free-market organization Americans for Prosperity. The speaker clearly knew his audience, however, so he littered his discussion of fiscal issues with references to his own Christianity. In giving certain GOP politicians a bit of leeway for their failures to toe the hardest fiscal line, Jenney commented, "You know, we are all human. We are all fallen." Later, in an impressive theological maneuver, he invoked Biblical tenets to justify *opposition* to economic redistribution to help less fortunate people. Citing the Biblical commandment, "Thou shalt not steal," Jenney stressed that a "lot of these . . . bills are *stealing* bills." In a twinkling, opposition to taxes to help fund programs for the poor and lower-income families was transmuted into obedience to one of God's commandments.

Despite leaders' best efforts to bridge the divide, the varying values and religiosity of members and potential recruits to the Tea Party may limit grassroots momentum, as we learned in one of the Virginia groups we visited. Having outgrown several smaller, secular locations, the decision was made to move the group's meetings to the youth ministry auditorium behind a local evangelical church. According to several members we spoke to, this move, along with the decision to open meetings with a prayer, drove away Jewish and nonreligious members who had previously been regular attendees. *Sandra Asimov* tells us she was a "little bit reluctant" to get involved in the Tea Party because "there was a zealotry, a mixing of God and Country." Others reportedly left the organization entirely. One previously active member, an atheist who had been a prisoner of war in Vietnam, pulled back after things took a religious turn, and seems to be particularly missed by fellow Tea Partiers. All the same, no one suggested that the meeting site or the opening prayer were likely to change.

Members who had criticized moves toward overt Christianity felt they had not been heeded. Even though he himself is a lay preacher, Ben Jones told us that he objected to the group becoming "too churchy." "We are not a church; we are not a Sunday school class. We are a patriotic organization," he insisted. When asked about the reception his criticisms had received, Ben did not mince words. "I have been branded the Antichrist." Although some compatriots have told Ben that if participants "don't believe in God, let them quit," he continues to stress the ways in which overt religiosity can limit the Tea Party's appeal. This example attests to how tricky and delicate it can be to maintain an encompassing Tea Party tent on the right, as Christian conservatives crowd in and assert their distinctive values, priorities, and cultural style.

In the final analysis, the Tea Party cannot flourish as simply the Moral Majority reborn. To preserve its reach beyond the ranks of religious conservatives, the Tea Party has to avoid looking like merely one more Christian right organization. In an often-uneasy alliance, libertarians and other socially tolerant fiscal hard-liners have joined social conservatives in this freshly labeled effort. To make it all work, members and leaders alike must bridge differences, or fudge them. For the most part, they do, with impressive creativity.

CITIZEN ENGAGEMENT

We have poked and prodded Tea Partiers to get at their overall social and political characteristics, including crucial internal differences, but one much ballyhooed issue remains. Supporters and observers alike sometimes get so caught up in the romance of the Tea Party as a new outburst of political activism that they make a logical leap and claim that most Tea Party participants are "newcomers" to politics. Is this true? Are Tea Partiers, especially the men and women who organize and guide local Tea Parties, really neophytes?

Civic Habits

As we've seen, Tea Partiers are not suddenly aroused middle-of-the-roaders. Longtime conservatives predominate in the Tea Party. This recently created form of activism does, however, bring together experienced political activists with people of conservative mind whose previous engagement with politics was limited to voting and "yelling at the TV," as some of our interlocutors put it. Nationally, 43% of self-reported Tea Party supporters claim to have previously worked for a political candidate or to have given money to a campaign.[49] That leaves more than half who presumably have simply voted for Republicans or other conservatives. Nevertheless, we should be impressed that more than two-fifths of Tea Party supporters had previously gone beyond voting to more active engagement with politics—because only about one-quarter of all American adults report comparable kinds of engagement.[50] What is more, the 43% mark includes the broader circle of Tea Party supporters. Genuine Tea Party activists almost certainly have more experience under their belts than cheerleaders and armchair sympathizers.

In our trips to the field, we recorded higher levels of previous political experience than national surveys show—not surprisingly, because we talked to people who actually attend meetings and serve as organizers in their local Tea Parties. Some of those we interviewed told us that, before the Tea Party, they had not been politically engaged beyond voting. Others spoke of many previous undertakings, and sometimes reminisced about growing up in a "political family," where the news of the day was frequently discussed around the dinner table and made up a major part of daily life. A surprising number of the people we met dated their first political experience to the Goldwater campaign in 1964. Virginian Mandy Hewes told the story of her mother writing a song called "Let's Go Back to the Constitution" in 1963.

In terms of more recent political experiences, some Tea Party activists we met had been involved with the GOP or weighed in during elections. John Patterson, founder of a local Virginia Tea Party, told about putting out yard signs for election contests. Christen Varley, founder of the Greater Boston Tea Party, had previously worked for the Ohio Republican party and volunteered on a GOP Congressional campaign.[51] Some of the younger Tea Partiers we met had arrived via the failed Ron Paul campaign of 2008. An even more substantial number of Tea Party activists came out of conservative organizations pushing for this or that cause or set of policies. Several Tea Party activists in Massachusetts and Arizona had previously volunteered for organizations fighting gay marriage or advancing pro-life goals. Experience in organized efforts to mobilize support and get out messages about conservative policy priorities was certainly good preparation for Tea Party activism.

In short, while some Tea Partiers are new to political activism, seasoned hands turn out to be very common. What is more, when we broaden our purview beyond formal politics to include civic endeavors, even more Tea Partiers have amassed experience in the arts of democratic citizenship. Long before he helped to launch a local Tea Party, Virginian Ben Jones was actively involved in nonprofit and community organizations—from Habitat for Humanity, to Goodwill, to projects in local schools. Many other Tea Partiers told us about work in charitable organizations and churches. Mandy Hewes, for example, is active in her Methodist church. And we ran into others like her who combine church work with Tea Party involvement. Social scientists have long observed that people who take active roles in religious congregations gain skills that they readily transfer to civic and political life.[52] We saw clear examples among the Tea Partiers we met.

Some of the civic organizers we met were very savvy indeed about what it takes to get people involved and committed to a shared cause. Ben Jones worried that Tea Party meetings might become too focused on outside lectures. He did not want people to be mere "spectators" and urged his group to set aside time for discussion and decisions about joint endeavors. He had all kinds of ideas, too, about how to get people connected to one another, between as well as during meetings. A Tea Party organizer like Ben could sit down and have a very fruitful conversation about community organizing with the best leftist organizers we know. Indeed, some Tea Party members are explicit about borrowing from the left. A number of our interviewees cited the work of Saul Alinsky, the famed community organizer and author of *Rules for Radicals*.[53] Other Tea Party organizers arrive at the same sorts of insights based on lifetimes of civic experience and their own instincts about what it takes to build a vibrant local Tea Party.

Grassroots Tea Partiers turn out to be like many other middle-income senior citizens, who draw on lifetimes of previous community involvement to keep busy in public affairs after retiring from the workforce. Men and women involved in Tea Party activism tend to be people who have held leadership positions in other community organizations, whether on the local library board or directing a community nonprofit. The Tea Party is simply a new venue to apply previously honed skills, just as it is yet another channel through which to express deep-seated conservative values.

Women's Place in the Tea Party

One relatively consistent finding in national surveys of Tea Party supporters is that men outweigh women overall. Most surveys peg males as numbering 55% to 60% of Tea Partiers.[54] The overall preponderance of male supporters found in surveys is striking, given that women live longer and thus predominate in the older age ranges from which Tea Partiers mostly come. In another sense, though, the preponderance of male Tea Party supporters might be expected because men are more likely to support the Republican Party, and Tea Partiers come from the ranks of conservative Republicans and folks to the right of the GOP.

When the authors of this book earlier submitted an article for professional publication, we were urged by one anonymous reviewer to talk about "sexism" in the Tea Party. We declined the invitation because in our field observations and interviews we saw so many energetic women taking the lead in grassroots Tea Party activities. Both men and women serve as local and state Tea Party leaders, of course. We have told some of their stories already, and more are to come in later chapters where we further discuss the ideas of grassroots Tea Partiers and recount how local organizations were launched. But we need to tarry a bit on the question of women's place because from our fieldwork it appears that, although men may be more likely to support the Tea Party, women are dominating the organizing efforts.

Many of the men who tell pollsters that they sympathize with or generally support the Tea Party may be doing so from their armchairs in front of Fox News—or just sitting in the audience along with their wives at a Tea Party meeting or event. In the local Tea Party meetings we visited, women provided active leadership. Women leaders were at times the youngest people in the room. That was true in meetings in Massachusetts, Virginia, and Arizona, where women in early middle age were in charge. In other places, older women were at the helm—as in the York County Constitutionalists in Maine. Even when a man chaired the meeting, women were invariably the Tea Party members who prepared refreshments, and they were also usually in charge of the sign-up sheets and tables where literature was offered and Tea Party pins and bumper stickers were displayed for sale. Women often maintain the email lists for local groups and arrange for speakers and carpools.

We wish we had complete data to test the hypothesis that women are disproportionately active in running the Tea Party ground game. It certainly appears that some women have a great deal of influence at the local level, and some have used grassroots Tea Party activism as a stepping-stone to state and national influence. As we will discuss further in Chapter 3, the single most successful state-level Tea Party organization, the Virginia Tea Party Patriots Federation, was launched and initially led by a middle-aged woman, Jamie Radtke. Jenny Beth Martin, who helped organize the first Tea Party rally in Atlanta, Georgia, is now coordinating the national umbrella group, Tea Party Patriots. All of these and many other women in key Tea Party roles remind us of the active women who, throughout U.S. history, have done a great deal of the civic organizing in local communities and states.[55]

Indeed, if female Tea Partiers are the leading on-the-ground activists in many contemporary Tea Party groups and events, that would be nothing new in the annals of American civic democracy. Women's leadership has been well documented for the Christian Right—where, as the saying goes, female leaders travel the country to preach that woman's place is in the home.[56] Historically, U.S. voluntary associations depended heavily on women's contributions. American women built some of the most important moral and civic associations from the nineteenth through the mid-twentieth century.[57] Women mattered even in ostensibly male voluntary associations, because mixed-gender associations where men were officially at the forefront often deployed women leaders at the grassroots; and officially male-only groups, like veterans groups and fraternal lodges, relied on auxiliaries of wives and mothers to serve suppers and provide social glue.[58]

Women bustling about to organize things, and local meetings opening with a patriotic ritual and a prayer—these are age-old staples of grassroots civic activism in the United States. In these respects at least, the Tea Party of the early twenty-first century really does have elements that go all the way back to the U.S. Founding Fathers—and the Founding Mothers.

From Backgrounds to Passions

We have covered a lot of ground in this chapter—making a first flyover of Tea Party territory. We have pulled together what surveys tell us about the social backgrounds and political location of Tea Party sympathizers and activists compared to other Americans. To draw sharper portraits and suggest nuances that escape broad surveys, we have used insights and examples from our interviews and observations of local meetings. Any grassroots political undertaking will always have a bit of mystery about it. Social characteristics of age, gender, income, and education take us only so far. Much more remains to be understood, even after we locate Tea Partiers on the political spectrum, and even after we consider their outlooks and experiences in religion, civic life, and politics.

But we are just getting started. In the following chapter, we look more deeply at the substance of Tea Partiers' political beliefs, using survey findings once again, but shifting toward the words of Tea Partiers' themselves, which are much more evocative. Listening carefully to what specific people have to say is even more valuable when the challenge is to figure out what euphemistic generalities like "opposition to government spending" and "strongly negative views of President Obama" really mean. By hearing from people as well as mining tables of numbers, we can get a better fix on the ideas and emotions that, in the final analysis, prompted people like Stanley and Gloria, Tim and Ben, and many others, to say, yes, I am a Tea Party Patriot—and spurred each of them to reach out to others to build the cause.

2

What They Believe: Ideas and Passions

"This is America!" exclaimed CNBC commentator Rick Santelli in his famous February 2009 call for "Tea Party" resistance to the Obama Administration's mortgage-assistance measures. Reporting from the floor of the Chicago Mercantile Exchange, Santelli demanded of the traders working around him: "How many of you people want to pay for your neighbor's mortgage that has an extra bathroom and can't pay their bills?" His harsh words and dramatic gestures mingled with lofty patriotic rhetoric. "If you read our Founding Fathers, people like Benjamin Franklin and Jefferson, what we're doing in this country now is making them roll over in their graves."[1]

When *John Patterson* of Lynchburg, Virginia, heard Santelli's rant replayed, "I related to him," he says. "He went off . . . saying what a lot of people think." In his fifties, John is a technical writer now working sporadically as a consultant since being laid off by his former company. After Obama's election, John, a longtime Republican, had wondered what could be done. His son served in Iraq and it filled him with "seething rage" to hear Obama say the war could not be won. In Iraq, the "wrong people cheered" the night Obama beat McCain, the "same people trying to kill my son." John is "not calling Obama a Muslim," but he was glad when conservative-minded people who "love the same things" about this country started organizing Tea Party rallies and he could join the cause. John is determined to fight against "government meddling in the free market" and "big government folks" who are "taking the struggle out of normal life issues," by handing out benefits to people who have not earned them.

Stella Fisher of Surprise, Arizona, age 67, explains why she and her 69-year-old husband *Larry* gravitated to the Tea Party. "We always voted, but being busy people, we just didn't keep as involved as maybe we should have. And now we're to the point where we're really worried about our country. I feel like we came out of retirement. We do Tea Party stuff to take the country back to where we think it should be." In April 2009, they attended a Tax Day rally at the state capitol and visited several Tea Party groups before helping set up a local Tea Party in their neighborhood. States' rights is the number one issue for the Fishers: "We think the federal government is overstepping their authority. Take health care, take the education. All those things. . . . The EPA, they've shut down I forget how many timber plants in Arizona because of the spotted owl."

For *Bonnie Sims* of southeastern Virginia, in her sixties, "it's so sad the way the country is now." She points to the disturbing changes that prompted her and her husband to join the Tea Party. "We worked for everything we got," never used credit cards, and never got "in trouble with the law" or "lived a day in our life off welfare." "We had to earn our rights." But such "values are not taught anymore." You "have to select English" for daily transactions, and the streets in nearby Newport News are not safe to walk. She always voted, Bonnie explains, but her husband was "never political" until Obama "got in." Then "all of a sudden" his eyes went "wide open." They heard about the Tea Party and decided to go to a meeting in August 2009. The "young generation" is all "Obama, Obama, Obama," says Bonnie, but she dreads where he is leading the nation. "I am not a racist," she assures us, but Obama is "a socialist" who "got a lot of it from his father." Debt will burden our children and grandchildren. "Where will the money come from?" Bonnie wonders.

Fear punctuated by hope is a potent brew in politics. No one can listen to John, Stella, and Bonnie talk about what brought them to the Tea Party without hearing their sense of dread about where America could be headed, along with the jolt of optimism and energy they felt upon learning about the Tea Party. Issues and policies matter to Tea Party members, of course, as do their conceptions about American government. We will carefully consider the substance of these views. But we would be remiss not to underline, from the start, the *feelings* that came across so vividly when people spoke to us.

In mostly liberal academia, more and more scholars are crunching numbers or parsing texts to figure out the Tea Party. But nothing can replace hearing from people directly and trying to make an empathetic leap into their frame of reference. "Tell us a little about yourself and how you came to the Tea Party," was the simple question we used to open all of our interviews. We have challenged ourselves to hear the aspirations evident in Tea Partiers' reverence for the U.S. Constitution, to grasp the vision of society that underlies their comments about government regulations and spending, and to understand the worries that reverberate in their assessments of President Obama.

In their emotional response to politics, Tea Partiers are not so different from other Americans. Democratic politics, indeed all politics, deals with morally vital, emotionally charged matters such as what government can legitimately do, and what claims different groups can make on political power. Politics is about who we are—often in contradistinction to "them," to types of people that are not fully part of our imagined community. "We" want our representatives in government to speak for "us," not cater inappropriately to "them."

When George W. Bush claimed the presidency in 2001, aided by a startling Supreme Court decision, many Americans of liberal persuasions were shocked and disheartened. Citizens in more culturally secular parts of the country often felt alienated by the arrival in the White House of an evangelical Christian conservative, a Texas Republican, backed by GOP majorities in both houses of Congress. Things got worse for liberals when Republicans, despite razor-thin margins, moved with boldness and alacrity to push through long-sought contentious legislative priorities. But left-leaning Americans turned despair into anger, activism, and landslide electoral victories in 2006 and 2008.

In early 2009, conservative Americans also felt disheartened—and in many cases downright frightened—when a Democratic president arrived in Washington DC, greeted by 2 million cheering supporters on the Washington Mall, backed by big majorities in both houses of Congress, and bolstered by an apparently sweeping mandate to respond to the economic crisis. And there was also an element of shock at the personal history of Obama himself. Truth be told, most Americans of all races, backgrounds, and political persuasions were a bit surprised that a black man named Barack Hussein Obama could win the presidency. For most citizens, the surprise was thrilling, or at least comforting, if only because of the good things it seemed to say about our country's capacity to surmount its tragic racial past. But for very conservative Republicans, and others even further to the right, the Obama presidency was, and is, scary.

No wonder widely advertised calls for "Tea Party" protests felt like a godsend to U.S. conservatives—a very welcome opportunity for hope and joint action amidst a winter of Republican despair. Even if you disagree with them politically, it is not so hard to understand the stories told by John and Stella and Bonnie. As we move on to explore the political beliefs of Tea Partiers more fully, we should keep in mind the visceral fears and hopes that have spurred individuals and groups to action, feelings that run through their governing philosophies and public policy preferences.

REVERENCE FOR THE CONSTITUTION

A tour of Tea Party websites around the country quickly reveals widespread determination to restore twenty-first century U.S. government to the Constitutional principles articulated by the eighteenth-century Founding Fathers. The Lynchburg Tea Party of Virginia, for example, sums up the "principles that we adhere to" as "Constitutionally Limited Government"; "Freedom to Pursue Prosperity through unhindered Markets"; and "Liberty tempered by Virtue." Far to the north, the "About Us" page of the Maine Tea Party/Maine ReFounders website features "Pete the Carpenter" explaining that "We are fighting to preserve our Constitution, Country and hold true to the visions of our founding fathers."[2] Likewise, thousands of miles into the U.S. heartland, meeting on the third Thursday of each month at the Eagles Club in a small town in the northwestern corner of Nebraska, the Crawford Tea Party describes itself simply as "a group of concerned citizens . . . who desire to see a restoration of Constitutional government."[3] Just as Rick Santelli invoked Founding Fathers to excoriate an Obama mortgage-assistance measure, so do Tea Party groups across America link their present-day activities to a constantly restated reverence for the country's founding documents: the Constitution, the Bill of Rights, and the Declaration of Independence.

Constitutionalism in Practice

Constitutional reverence is not just in cyberspace. The U.S. founding documents are woven into the warp and woof of Tea Party routines. Pocket-sized versions of the Constitution appear on merchandise tables at Tea Party meetings, arrayed alongside bejeweled necklaces and teapot pins (made in China), "Don't Tread on Me" T-shirts, "TEA Party: Taxed Enough Already!" bumper stickers, and biographies of conservative celebrities such as Sarah Palin. Video tutorials are available to explain the Constitution and Declaration in a few easy lessons. And for Tea Partiers willing to sit still and pay good money, there are regular seminars, day-long workshops, even multiday courses, where right-wing professors or advocacy group experts go through the founding documents line by line, explaining how they apply to today's political battles. Elaborating the meaning of the U.S. Constitution, the Declaration, and the Bill of Rights is a lucrative business for many a roving lecturer looking to make a profit off the grass roots. Yet Tea Partiers also use the revered documents as gifts. In Arizona, one of the authors (Vanessa) was given a pocket copy of the Constitution as a "thank you" for her interest in the Tea Party. And when New Hampshire Tea Party leader Jerry DeLemus arrived to give a talk in neighboring Maine, he greeted one of the two women who lead the York County Constitutionalists with a warm hug and a special gift: a pocket Constitution autographed by Michele Bachmann, the Minnesota Republican who leads the House Tea Party Caucus.

"Constitution talk" bubbles through discussions in Tea Party gatherings, and is used to bolster a wide range of beliefs. *Sandra Asimov* explained that "smaller government, the Constitution, and personal responsibility" are the Tea Party's core principles, while fellow Virginia activist *Ben Jones* summarized Tea Party values as "honesty, transparency, adherence to the Constitution." References to the Constitution are often used to justify stands on particular issues; indeed, the invocation of Constitutional authority seems intended to render particular views incontestable. As Harvard historian Jill Lepore points out, Tea Partiers are "historical fundamentalists" who project directly accessible and unchangeable meanings onto past events and documents.[4] In Arizona, Tea Party members invoked the Constitution to reinforce state sovereignty and highlight the sanctity of any and all gun rights, while in Virginia, the emphasis was on the state's capacity to opt out of health care reform. Of course, whatever any Tea Partier wants to do with his or her private property is everywhere justified in exalted Constitutional terms.

Even the current priorities of religious conservatives in the Tea Party are attributed to America's founding documents. Although the Southwest Metro Tea Party in suburban Chanhassen, Minnesota, highlights apparently libertarian and fiscally conservative principles on its homepage, just one click on "Principles" reveals the group's firm refutation of "the secularist demand for separation of church and state." "Sanctity of Life" and "Traditional Marriage" are given billing equal to "Individual Liberty" and

"Religious Freedom" in the full list of group principles, all in the name of authentic Constitutionalism.

Despite their fondness for the Founding Fathers, Tea Party members we met did not make any reference to the intellectual battles and political compromises out of which the Constitution and its subsequent amendments were forged, let alone to the fact that key Founders were Deists, far from any brand of evangelical fundamentalism. Nor did they realize the extent to which some of the positions Tea Partiers now espouse bear a close resemblance to those of the Anti-Federalists—the folks the Founders were countering in their effort to establish sufficient federal authority to ensure a truly *United* States. The Tea Partiers we met did not show any awareness that they are echoing arguments made by the Nullifiers and Secessionists before and during the U.S. Civil War, or that their stress on "states' rights" is eerily reminiscent of dead-ender white opposition to Civil Rights laws in the 1960s.

For Tea Partiers, as for most people engaged in politics, history is a tool for battle, not a subject for university seminar musings. Political actors regularly invoke the past for reasons other than intellectual debate or verisimilitude. Invocations of the past are didactic and metaphorical. At the grass roots, the Tea Party is an effort at restoration, and we will need to figure out exactly what people are trying to save and "refound"—to use the telling phrase of the Maine ReFounders. But we can be sure that today's Tea Partiers are fighting about the here and now—using references to the "true meaning" of the Constitution in their struggle to shape the nation's future—rather than actually trying to return to any given moment in America's past. They are doing what every political endeavor does: using history as a source of inspiration and social identity.

Just like other political actors, past and present, Tea Partiers stretch the limits of the Constitution, use it selectively, and push for amendments. Tea Partiers have argued for measures such as restrictions on birthright citizenship, abridgements of freedom of religion for Muslim-Americans, and suspension of protections in the Bill of Rights for suspected terrorists. Some parts of the Constitution are lauded over others. In a telling aside during a question and answer period with members of the York County Constitutionalists, Jerry DeLemus mentioned that he might prefer to limit the amendments to the Constitution to the first ten, those in the Bill of Rights, omitting the rest altogether.[5] In practice, Tea Partiers are in the thick of ongoing arguments over how the Constitution is to be interpreted and how it might be amended.

Tea Partiers do not see their use of history as interpretive, however, and they are resistant to notions that historians or lawyers might be needed to make sense of the Constitution and apply it to ongoing disputes. For regular Tea Party participants, the Constitution is a clear-cut document readily applicable to modern political issues. They evince the democratic conviction that they themselves, as average Americans, can read and interpret the Constitution. "It's amazing how quickly the Constitution became a second language," marvels Sandra Asimov. At most, they might need to study the document and learn its full meaning. But Tea Party members do not doubt that they can do this.

A belief that foundational written documents are immediately accessible and obviously clear, that they can be understood by each person without the aid of expertise or intermediaries is a long-standing conviction in populist movements. The English Levellers felt that way, as did the Jacksonian Democrats in nineteenth-century America. Most fundamentally in Western history, the Protestant reformation against the Catholic Church was based on the tenet that each Believer could read and interpret the Bible, to attain a direct understanding of the Word of God unmediated by priests— let alone by ecclesiastical or secular lawyers.

Many Tea Party members are Protestant evangelical Christians who have transferred the skills and approaches of Bible study directly to the Constitution. Tea Parties across the country participate in "Constitution Study Groups," and in such groups they tackle commentaries as well as the original texts themselves. At suppertime, Jerry DeLemus requires his children to read from the Bible and the Constitution, the two holy texts in his household.[6] In a more public ritual setting, readings from the Constitution are performed at the start of each monthly Tea Party meeting in Lynchburg, Virginia.

The Five Thousand Year Leap is a book popular with many Tea Partiers for its elucidation of ties between the Bible and the Constitution. Written in 1981 by ultra-right ideologue Cleon Skousen, this book explains the U.S. Constitution and the founding of the United States in Biblical terms.[7] All but forgotten for many years, the book found new life after then-Fox News anchor Glenn Beck dubbed it "divinely inspired." Arizonan Tea Party regular *Gloria Ames*, for instance, calls the book "one of our Bibles." Tea Party websites often refer to the book's conclusions in their discussion of America's religious heritage. In South Carolina, the Greenville Tea Party's website claims that the Founding Fathers used "28 fundamental beliefs to create a society based on morality, faith, and ethics," and that "more progress was achieved in the last 200 years than in the previous 5,000 years of every civilization combined"[8]—two claims drawn directly from Skousen's book. For these Tea Party members, Skousen provides proof that America is a "Republic with Christian-Judeo influences."[9]

A splendid depiction of the fundamentally religious understanding of the U.S. Constitution prevalent in many Tea Party circles appears in a painting by Utah artist Jon McNaughton, entitled "One Nation, Under God." In the painting, Jesus Christ is shown holding up a copy of the United States Constitution, while American historical figures from Abigail Adams to Ronald Reagan stand admiringly behind him. The crowd in the foreground is divided into two groups. On Christ's right, people including a Marine, a farmer, and the mother of a disabled child look admiringly towards the Constitution and Savior. A college student is shown holding a copy of *Five Thousand Year Leap*. On the left of Jesus, however, one finds a less pious crowd, with faces turned away from Jesus and the Constitution. These figures include a liberal news reporter, a politician talking on his cellphone, a smug professor carrying *The Origin of Species*, and, dimly visible in the background, Satan.[10] Though McNaughton himself is not a Tea Party activist, his work has inspired widespread praise among Tea Party members, with videos explaining the symbolism of his painting appearing on Tea Party blogs from Michigan to Florida. As *Newsweek* reporter Andrew Romano puts it, the Constitution is for Tea Partiers a "sacred text" and a comforting "authoritarian scripture."[11]

Skepticism about Expertise

A persistent refrain in Tea Party circles is the scorn for politicians who fail to show suitable reverence for, and detailed mastery of, America's founding documents. Catering to Tea Party supporters, the GOP-led House of Representatives launched the 112th Congress by staging a public reading of the Constitution (though omitting touchy passages about slaves). Tea Partiers told us that they appreciated this ritual gesture. They are even more enthusiastic about a newly adopted rule that each piece of legislation debated in Congress must cite how it follows from specific passages in the Constitution.

Although he served for twelve years as a law professor at the University of Chicago, President Obama comes in for particular criticism from Tea Partiers for alleged irreverence toward the Constitution. In Virginia, several Tea Party members confidently told us that President Obama had misquoted the Constitution and the Declaration of Independence. In one case people found telling, Obama paraphrased one of the most famous lines of the Declaration of Independence and omitted the reference to "the Creator" as the source of man's inalienable rights.[12] Virginia Tea Party activists were very aware of this incident, and made repeated reference to it in interviews. For them, it revealed that Obama does not hold the Constitution sacred, and no doubt the incident heightens suspicions about his religious beliefs, as well.

Obama's former employment as a university professor hardly impresses Tea Party people, anyway. They do not defer to experts, and we heard many expressions of scorn about educated people who try to devise plans for regular citizens, or tell them what to do. Again and again, we heard Tea Partiers express derision about legislators who vote without reading every page and word in proposed legislation, as well as about federal officials who discuss measures they had not read. Ben Jones noted that Attorney General Eric Holder threatened to file suit against Arizona's 2010 immigration law without having read the law himself. When we asked if it was reasonable for a busy public figure to entrust the reading of a legal document to lawyers on his staff, we were told in no uncertain terms that this approach is inadequate. After all, Ben noted, the entire bill was "only ten pages." The clear implication was that the Attorney General was derelict in his responsibilities. Without having read a document personally, Tea Partiers feel that a citizen or official cannot be sure of what it contains.

Tea Party skepticism about experts is part and parcel of their direct approach to democracy, their belief in citizen activism. To guard against possible bamboozlement—and to demonstrate their own virtue and skill as informed democratic citizens—Tea Party members arm themselves for confrontations with their legislative representatives by reading particular bills themselves (and, impressively to us, many groups have formed subcommittees to track legislation, and refer to bills by their official numbers, as in "H.R. 1"). Jenny Beth Martin, national coordinator of the Tea Party Patriots, bragged that at the August 2009 town hall meetings where right-wing protestors confronted Congressional Democrats, the Tea Party participants frequently "knew the bills better" than the Representative who convened the events. With a chortle, Tea Party interviewees repeatedly offered their own stories of seeing an elected representative caught in a misstatement by a Tea Party activist.

The importance of first-hand reading dominates Tea Party discussions of health care reform. In point of fact, Tea Party members we interviewed were deeply misinformed about the Affordable Care Act of 2010.[13] One Virginia Tea Partier regaled us at length with (a completely factually untrue) account of the strong public option supposedly contained in the law, a measure she said would kill the private insurance companies. In a voice shaking with fear more than anger, another Virginia Tea Party member told us that the Affordable Care law includes "death panels" and would abolish Medicare—prospects which, she said, terrify the 92-year-old woman in her nursing care. The Affordable Care Act contains no such provisions, of course. But no matter if Tea Partiers themselves are misinformed. They are certain that the politicians who voted for what they derisively call ObamaCare were ignorant of its dangerous provisions. The Senate health reform bill, several interviewees noted, had been passed late at night on Christmas Eve 2009, when the politicians themselves could not possibly have read the thousands of pages of the final legislation.

For Tea Party activists, in short, any hint that a legislator or expert has not personally read every line of a bill is a "gotcha" moment, and a damning indictment. It is symbolic evidence of a larger truth that public officials are either out to "put one over" on average Americans, or are being tricked themselves. The constant reference to the Founding Fathers harkens back to an imagined time when politicians were seeking a higher good.

DO THEY REALLY HATE GOVERNMENT?

Americans have ambivalent, even contradictory reactions to government. Asked about it in the abstract, most unhesitatingly prefer "the free market" or "individual responsibility." But reactions to concrete public programs are quite different. Large majorities of Americans approve of public education, subsidized health care, veterans' benefits, and Social Security—and they appreciate many other specific government activities, too. Even programs to aid disabled or low-income people win broad approval, as long as the beneficiaries are seen as deserving of community support. That Americans are, simultaneously, "ideological conservatives" and "operational liberals" has been documented for as long as social scientists have been able to probe and measure public opinion.[14]

Tea Partiers are said to be different. Observers from all over the map portray them as firm and consistent in pure opposition to taxes, big government, handouts to business, and expensive social programs and intrusive regulations—suggesting that today's grassroots participants in the Tea Party are different from regular, middle-of-the-road Americans who hold mixed ideas about government.

A lazy conflation of elite and popular strands of Tea Partyism is at work in such claims. Professional ultra-free-market advocates like Dick Armey are all over the television—spouting their views about cutting taxes, privatizing Social Security, and sweeping away regulations—and claiming to speak for grassroots Tea Party members. So it is easy for observers to presume that local Tea Party members have signed on to the FreedomWorks program, when in fact they have not. Wishful thinking is also rampant, as every elite faction in and around the GOP imputes its preferences to grassroots Tea Partiers. Influential establishment GOP commentator Peggy Noonan, for example, praises the Tea Party as a supposedly new kind of Republican mass force—a consistently principled popular movement that will force the party to return to a (putative) golden age when, above all, it pursued fiscal responsibility.[15]

Reality on the ground does not fit these portrayals. In our individual interviews, and in the group discussions we heard, regular Tea Party people, like all Americans, can be quite inconsistent about government. At the abstract level, all of them, to be sure, decry big government, out-of-control public spending, and ballooning deficits. "The nation is broke. It is bankrupt," Virginian *James Rand* insisted in a typical declaration.[16] Rand expects that foreign borrowers will soon cease to accept the dollar as a reserve currency. He sees the United States as headed for a catastrophic default in the very near future—a prophesy of financial and societal Armageddon we heard quite often, interspersed with everyday chit-chat. At the abstract level, Tea Partiers claim that the United States is headed for ruin unless many trillions are instantly cut from the federal budget.

But when governmental specifics come into view, it is a different story. Queried about whether there is "anything they like" about government, our interviewees were, at first, genuinely startled: "I did not see that one coming," quipped one person. Shaken from their typical talking points, Tea Partiers often answered in ideologically "off message" ways. One woman loves the national parks (seemingly oblivious that GOP Tea Partiers in Congress were about to slash funding for them); another spoke of the importance of public health care for children through Medicaid (another kind of funding on the GOP chopping block); and still another woman remarked that when she went to Washington DC to protest ObamaCare, she was impressed by the beauty and grandeur of the government buildings. They made her feel proud as an American!

Small examples aside, Tea Partiers are not opposed to all kinds of regulation or big tax-supported spending. Rank-and-file Tea Party participants evaluate regulations and spending very differently, depending on who or what is regulated, and depending on the kinds of people who benefit from various kinds of public spending. Contrary to pundits like Noonan who imagine Tea Party passions as a fresh departure, we find them to be updated versions of long-standing populist conservative ideas. At the grass roots, Tea Partiers want government to get out of the way of business. Yet at the same time, virtually all want government to police immigrants. And the numerous social conservatives in Tea Party ranks want authorities to enforce their conception of traditional moral norms. More telling still, almost all Tea Partiers favor generous social benefits for Americans who "earn" them; yet in an era of rising federal deficits, they are very concerned about being stuck with the tax tab to pay for "unearned" entitlements handed out to unworthy categories of people.

The Purposes of Government Regulation

When fifty members of the Jefferson Area Tea Party in Charlottesville, Virginia, gathered in February 2011 to discuss their priorities for coming months, ambivalence about government regulation was on full display. People mocked business regulations and zoning rules, citing the example of a local fast-food franchise owner who was required to change the colors used in his business signs. Charlottesville Patriots talked about keeping a wary eye out for new state or national regulatory legislation, and discussed possibilities for running candidates for local boards in order to block or roll back regulations on enterprises and homeowners. Our observations around the country reinforce what we saw in Charlottesville: Tea Partiers are prickly about any use of government regulations to limit the pure autonomy of businesses and owners of private property.

From time to time, journalists suggest that Tea Partiers are just as skeptical of big business or business abuses as they are of government.[17] But there is little evidence of this. Tea Partiers speak of corruption in government and in labor unions they see as closely tied to government and the Democratic Party.[18] Business, by contrast, is idealized as a free-market, entrepreneurial force. More than one Tea Partier we spoke to told us they thought of themselves as "proud capitalists," and of course many are small business people. Like other conservatives, Tea Party members perceive small business owners and potential entrepreneurs as in the same boat with the wealthiest of corporate CEOs. They often project small business irritations about rules and taxes onto business in general. We heard occasional scorn about Wall Street or wasteful business practices but no calls for government regulations to set things right. Tea Party members resist any and all suggestions that the financial sector or other businesses need to be subject to regulation in the public interest. The market, left unhampered, will resolve any unfairnesses, in the Tea Party estimation.

But in the same Charlottesville meeting where typical Tea Party antipathies toward government regulation were aired, members took a very different view of the use of government powers to police disfavored groups with whom they do *not* identify. Speaking with visible emotion, one man insisted that local police should start checking the immigration status of everyone they encounter, including people pulled over for routine traffic violations. The local police had told him they could not afford to do this, that it would bust their limited budget, but the man said he didn't care, and urged the group to support a new law to force action. When it comes to law enforcement, Tea Party members support strong governmental authority, even at the expense of budgetary constraint.

Concern about illegal immigration is widespread in Tea Party circles, and draconian remedies are in vogue. In a national survey, a whopping 82% of Tea Party supporters said that illegal immigration is a "very serious" problem (compared to 60% of Americans overall, including the Tea Party supporters combined with all others).[19] Sealing America's border with Mexico and dealing with Latin immigrants are prime challenges for the nation to tackle, as Tea Partiers see it. A Tea Party bumper sticker boldfaces "LAW & BORDER" on top of a U.S. flag background. One Massachusetts Tea Party member said that after reading the latest immigration news on the conservative blog *Red State*, she felt like she wanted to "stand on the border with a gun." And a Virginia Tea Party member described in considerable detail a joking proposal to curb unauthorized immigration. Americans, he suggested, could be paid by the government a flat fee for every rattlesnake caught, which could then be gathered together and dropped en masse along the southern border. Jokes aside, it is clear that, when it comes to controlling immigration, Tea Partiers endorse a heavy-handed government response.

Another regulatory crackdown also evoked a wave of approval in Charlottesville—more than any other matter mentioned in the entire two-hour meeting. The assembled Charlottesville Tea Partiers were visibly elated when one woman brought up a just-enacted Virginia law that requires abortion clinics to operate as if they were full-fledged hospitals. The law may force the closure of up to two-thirds of these clinics, which offer an array of reproductive services to a largely poor and minority clientele, because the facilities are small, underfunded operations that cannot afford to widen hallways and hire additional staff. To the same group that had just decried rules for businesses, death-by-pettifogging regulation for women's health clinics sounded just fine, indeed morally necessary.

Tea Party support for government regulation of marriage and childbearing is certainly not limited to Charlottesville. Although the Tea Party includes a significant portion of libertarians who think differently, Tea Partiers are more likely than Americans in general to oppose legal recognition of gay marriages or civil unions. About two-thirds of all Americans favor one or another of those forms of recognition, but less than half of Tea Party supporters do—and 40% of them advocate "no legal recognition" of any kind.[20] Tea Party attitudes on abortion rights are similarly skewed. Whereas a 58% majority of all Americans approve of the decision of the Supreme Court to establish a "Constitutional right for women to obtain legal abortions in this country," only 40% of Tea Partiers approve of that court decision and 53% consider it a "bad thing."[21] As these national survey results show, many Tea Partiers fervently believe that government regulation and authority should be used to embody and enforce their understandings of traditional "family values," even as they grumble about regulatory "tyranny" toward business people and homeowners.

No wonder Tea Party heroes include politicians such as Virginia Attorney General Ken Cuccinelli, who makes a big deal about opposing gay rights and doing all he can to wield rulings and legal interpretations against abortion providers. Relatively secular Virginia Tea Partiers may not cheer on such doings by Cuccinelli, but they probably stay quiet in deference to the heartfelt feelings of the social conservatives who sit beside them in meetings.[22] To cover all right-wing bases, the Virginia Attorney General offers just as much red meat to Tea Partiers who place higher (or sole) priority on gutting or blocking government regulation of businesses. Cuccinelli is at the forefront of the Tea Party war against ObamaCare as a supposed threat to the "Constitutional liberties" of citizens. And he is also on the warpath against university scientists in Virginia who dare to suggest that global climate change is a real threat; the Tea Party-oriented Virginia Attorney General thinks nothing of using government powers to demand their emails.[23] Ken Cuccinelli is, overall, the perfect embodiment of the Tea Party attitude toward government regulation: regulations are *good* to harass my enemies and enforce my values, policy preferences, and preferred definitions of American social identity; but regulations are *bad* for the kinds of businesses and endeavors me and mine are engaged in. This stance is certainly not new. For generations, conservatives in the United States have supported strong restrictions on social behavior they consider threatening while opposing regulation of business pursuits they perceive as vital to America's prosperity.[24]

Public Spending—for the Deserving

Tea Partiers are thought to be even more exercised about "big government" taxes and spending than about regulatory impositions on business and personal freedom. But here again, their views turn out to be complex, ambiguous, and not so different from longtime conservative stands on public social provision. Most Americans, including conservatives, value public benefits they feel are earned by upstanding citizens, but conservatives are less willing than other Americans to countenance public spending on the "undeserving."

We confess to having felt skeptical from the start that Tea Partiers opposed major U.S. entitlements such as Social Security and Medicare, given the obvious demographic facts of Tea Party life. The contradictions between Tea Party ideology and the personal reliance of Tea Party members on government assistance were very much on display at the February 2011 meeting of the Charlottesville Tea Party. More than an hour into the supper gathering, after the group had discussed priorities, the speaker for the evening arrived—a flamboyant, pony-tailed, right-wing radio talk-show host named Joe Thomas, who came after the end of his regular local broadcast. Thomas is clearly a very popular figure among Charlottesville area conservatives. Partway through his riveting remarks, he commented on the possibility that the Republican-controlled House of Representatives might shut down the federal government to demand drastic cuts in federal spending in its budgetary war against Obama and the Democrats. "I almost hope the government shuts down," Thomas said. The sun would "rise the next day," you would "kiss your wife," and we would all "have to get on with it." Thomas is middle-aged, but he was speaking to a room full of elderly Tea Partiers, of whom many were regularly cashing Social Security checks, or soon would. Quite a few of his listeners were also enjoying tax-subsidized health care from Medicare or from programs for U.S. military veterans and retirees. Yet Thomas's claim that a federal shutdown would be of no consequence evoked not so much as a peep from anyone in the room.[25] The irony was clear to an outside observer, because most of Thomas's listeners would surely feel the effects of a federal shutdown quickly and significantly.

How can Tea Party members simultaneously benefit from the biggest taxpayer supported domestic social programs, and yet be so fiercely determined to slash taxes and federal spending? Some observers have suggested that Tea Partiers don't know that they benefit from government programs, citing a Tea Party sign reading "keep the government's hands off my Medicare." But we found no evidence of such naïveté. Tea Party people know that Social Security, Medicare, and veterans' programs are government-managed, expensive, and funded with taxes. It is just that they distinguish these programs, which they feel recipients have "earned," from other social benefits, which they feel unnecessarily run up expenses, or might run up public costs in the future—placing a burden on hardworking taxpayers to make payments to freeloaders who have not earned public support. Much of the Tea Party brouhaha about the "federal budget deficit" is a preemptive strike against funding for unworthy programs and recipients, not a call for cutting off spending on programs like Medicare and Social Security that currently benefit people like them. According to the April 2010 CBS News/*New York Times* poll, about half of Tea Party supporters say someone in their household receives Medicare or Social Security benefits, and 62% of Tea Party supporters believe these programs are "worth the costs . . . for taxpayers."[26] In part, this conviction comes from recognition of their own need and the need of others in their social orbit. As Arizona retiree Stella Fisher told us, "You don't take Social Security from someone when that's what they live on." Medicare is "in everyone's estate planning" explained Virginian John Patterson. But there is also a strong sense among Tea Party people that they have earned these social protections through lifetimes of hard work. As a Massachusetts Tea Party activist, *Nancy Bates*, explained in a typical remark,

"I've been working since I was 16 years old, and I do feel like I should some-day reap the benefit. I'm not looking for a handout. I'm looking for a pay out of what I paid into." Social Security and Medicare are seen as acceptable government expenses because benefits go to those who have contributed to the system. As Virginia Tea Partier James Rand explained, "I use the VA [Veterans' Administration health care], which I am entitled to. I earned it. I also pay for my Medicare/Medicaid and the [prescription drug] supple-ment. This is a collective entity except I have the right to choose [the doctor] who I go to or don't go to. . . . As far as SS [Social Security] is concerned I started paying into it in 1954 . . . so I have paid a very large sum. . . ."[27]

Nor do Tea Partiers apply a constitutional test. They are sure that Obama's Affordable Care Act is unconstitutional but elide this standard for their own entitlements. Virginian Ben Jones, who is "getting Social Security now," ac-knowledges that "Social Security and Medicare are interesting because . . . neither of those are in the Constitution. . . . How do you add those things up?" He left the question hanging and moved on. Others we spoke with engaged in no such ruminations. Only one Tea Party member out of dozens we engaged in interviews, meetings, and through questionnaires said that when she becomes eligible in a few years, she might not enroll in Social Se-curity and Medicare. This would be in part out of ideological principle, explained Virginian *Mandy Hewes*—and anyway, she loves her work as office manager in her family business and has no intention of retiring at all. Mandy also pushed aside the thought that tax breaks in the new Affordable Care law could help her business afford health insurance. She knew the details, and explained that she prefers a tax-advantaged Medical Savings Account to cover routine costs while bearing the risk of paying for a major illness herself.

Mandy aside, not a single grassroots Tea Party supporter we encoun-tered argued for privatization of Social Security or Medicare along the lines being pushed by ultra-free-market politicians like Representative Paul Ryan (R-WI) and advocacy groups like FreedomWorks and Americans for Pros-perity. Even *Timothy Manor*, a Virginia man who calls Social Security a "Ponzi scheme," noted that the Bush plan for the privatization of Social Se-curity, which he supported at the time, would have been disastrous for seniors in this economy. Arizonan Larry Fisher believes there is almost nothing done by government that the private sector cannot do better. But when pressed on Social Security, he stops short and gropes for a halfway point; he might privatize the administration, he tentatively suggests, but not the funds themselves.

When Tea Partiers expressed concerns to us about Social Security and Medicare, they focused on how to keep the programs solvent, even if additional taxes might be needed. Not surprisingly for regular consumers of Fox News, a number of the people with whom we spoke worry about imminent bankruptcy for beloved programs. Bonnie Sims, the Virginia private duty nurse in her early sixties we introduced at the start of this chapter, not only told us about the dread of her 92-year-old patient that "ObamaCare" will abolish Medicare; Bonnie also revealed her own sense of "betrayal" that Social Security will not be available when she retires in a few years. In truth, even with no reform at all, Social Security is fully solvent for decades.[28] But Bonnie believes that DC politicians have stolen the money. "Social Security was supposed to have been there for us. When did they start borrowing against it?" she asks.

If Social Security and Medicare run short of funds, what to do? A few Tea Partiers volunteered that they would be willing to entertain cuts to their own benefits. *James Morrow* explained that "as a Social Security recipient," he would not mind "taking a ten percent cut. That would help the system tremendously, if it stayed in the Social Security fund." Virginia physician *Ellen Zinn* took a surprisingly progressive approach, suggesting that cuts be aimed at the "upper income brackets." She offered that she "would not mind a tax increase to try to get the country right again." Only occasionally did we hear comments such as those of Arizona Tea Party activist *Peggy Lawrence*, who thought that older people who had already paid into Social Security should be protected, while "younger people" should shoulder cuts if necessary.

Indeed, broad surveys show that Tea Party supporters, like the vast majority of all Americans, prefer new revenues to sustain Social Security over the long haul. An especially pointed question on this matter was asked in January 2011 by Public Policy Polling.[29] "Currently," the poll explained to its nationally representative sample, "workers pay social security payroll taxes on up to $106,800 of their salary. To ensure the long-term viability of Social Security, would you rather have people pay social security taxes on salaries above $106,800, or would you rather see benefits cut and the retirement age increased to age 69?" The results were overwhelming: 77% of all Americans wanted the payroll tax increase, and only 10% supported cuts and an increase in the retirement age. But the most eye-catching result was for avowed Tea Party supporters. Two-thirds of them support increasing the payroll tax to sustain Social Security, just like most of their fellow citizens.

Only a fifth of Tea Partiers support benefit cuts and increasing the retirement age. Similar findings pertain in surveys asking about cuts to Medicare versus tax increases on the rich as tradeoffs for reducing U.S. budget deficits: Americans in general strongly prefer tax increases for the rich and fervently oppose cuts in Medicare; Tea Party supporters hold the same positions by only slightly smaller margins.[30]

Very similar results appeared in an unusually detailed February 2011 survey of the large proportion of South Dakota registered voters who claim to strongly or somewhat support the Tea Party.[31] South Dakota supporters of the Tea Party, like all others, are mostly older white Republicans. Forty-three percent of them reported that members of their households currently benefit from Social Security; and 31% said that family members currently benefit from Medicare (with 11% indicating receipt of veterans' health benefits). But the margins of support for major U.S. social entitlements outran the numbers who are currently directly benefiting. Fully 83% of South Dakota Tea Party supporters said they would prefer to "leave alone" or "increase" Social Security benefits, while 78% opposed cuts to Medicare prescription drug coverage, and 79% opposed cuts in Medicare payments to physicians and hospitals (a big issue in rural areas where such health providers, if underpaid, may not be available to elderly patients). The South Dakota poll did not ask specific questions about new revenues for Social Security and Medicare, but 56% of the Tea Party supporters surveyed did express support for "raising income taxes by 5% for everyone whose income is over a million dollars a year."[32]

So much for the notion that Tea Partiers are all little Dick Armeys. When it comes to sustaining existing, well-loved social programs like Social Security and Medicare—programs that go to Americans like themselves who are perceived to have "earned" the benefits—Tea Party people put their money where their affection is. They are just like other Americans in their willingness to contribute the payroll taxes it will take to sustain Social Security, one of the biggest and most effective parts of U.S. social spending. Support for Medicare is also strong among Tea Party supporters, as among all Americans, though the long-term fiscal solutions are not as easy as the fix for Social Security. Clearly, however, slashing the program itself is not going to go over well with Tea Party people. The ultra-ideological politicians and advocates who push privatization of beloved contributory entitlements are not registering demands from grassroots Tea Partiers. Like other Americans, Tea Partiers love the parts of government they recognize as offering legitimate benefits to citizens who have earned them.[33]

Tea Party support for social benefits and the revenues to pay for them goes beyond Social Security and Medicare. Bonnie Sims does not equivocate when it comes to what military veterans have earned: "I think they ought to be given the best." Mandy Hewes, says, "I don't think our soldiers make enough money. I wouldn't want to espouse anything that would cause our service people to feel it." Of course, some Tea Party participants are themselves benefiting from military and veterans' programs, and we met and talked with some of them in all the states we visited. Many of the men are Vietnam-era combat veterans who receive military pensions and government-sponsored health care, either through the government-run Department of Veterans Affairs hospital system, or through the government-funded TRICARE insurance program for military retirees. They feel very comfortable taking these benefits. In South Dakota as well, 57% of Tea Party supporters reported having immediate family members who were either active or veteran members of the military, National Guard, or military reserve—and, not surprisingly, 96% want to sustain or increase veterans' benefits.[34]

Tea Party events often include some kind of recognition of the troops serving overseas. For example, the 2010 Tea Party Express bus tour featured a Gold Star mother, Debbie Lee,[35] whose son, Navy SEAL Marc Lee, had died in combat in Iraq. However, in our in-depth interviews we did not find Tea Party support for America's men and women in uniform to be a function either of unalloyed hawkishness or of uncritical support for any and all defense spending. The wars in Iraq and Afghanistan provoked diverse and nuanced views both for and against continuing U.S. military engagement. Fiscal concerns were cited by some as a reason for pulling back (from Afghanistan, in particular), yet the rationale was also that the United States should not be trying to remake other countries. We heard only a little about the overall military budget—which, even *excluding* the wars in Iraq and Afghanistan, has increased by 80% in the decade since 2000, reaching about $530 billion in 2010.[36] Only one Tea Partier, a former military contractor, spoke caustically about wastefulness in defense contracts.

Workers versus Freeloaders

Compared to the huge chunks devoted to Social Security, health programs, and defense programs, only a tiny wedge of the federal budget pie goes for varieties of assistance for the poor that most people lump together under the label "welfare." The best-known welfare program, Aid to Families with Dependent Children (AFDC) was replaced during the Clinton presidency with a block grant to the states that left eligibility and spending decisions largely in the hands of governors and state legislatures. The basic block grant, Temporary Assistance for Needy Families, or TANF, costs $16 billion annually, a fraction of a percent of total federal spending.[37] Nonetheless, welfare spending is still a subject of much concern for Tea Party members. If Tea Partiers resemble most other Americans in holding Social Security, Medicare, and veterans' benefits in high regard, they take a harsher stance toward public aid for the needy.

Rarely did we hear a Tea Partier speak positively about a program aimed at helping low-income people. In one unusual instance, a Massachusetts Tea Party member, *Michael Pierce*, volunteered that he had been "brought up on welfare." A retired police officer, Michael did not express any shame in this childhood reliance on public assistance because, after all, he "had to work [his] way out." But Michael's experience with welfare as a stepping-stone stands in sharp contrast to the more typical Tea Party view, articulated by former social worker Sandra Asimov, who explained, "I differentiate between entitlements and welfare."[38] She and others like her paid into legitimate entitlements, Sandra believes, but welfare recipients have not earned what they receive. Ben Jones described welfare recipients as "generation after generation of people on the public dole." Reminded of the Clinton welfare reform, which imposed a five-year lifetime limit on federal welfare receipt, Ben was certain that "loopholes" continued to riddle the program, and that it required more oversight. Because of the support they have received from the government, people on welfare simply do not have the motivation to work, he concluded. "They just don't know any better."

Another Virginia interviewee, John Patterson, spoke with emotion about the disgust felt by his son, who works at Walmart, when people on welfare arrive at the beginning of each month to buy things with their benefit cards. John seemed especially upset that people on public assistance were able to act just like any credit-card holder, rather than being set apart as people who were spending without earning their pay. A well-marked distinction between workers and nonworkers—between productive citizens and the freeloaders—is central to the Tea Party worldview and conception of America. As Tea Partiers see it, only through hard work can one earn access both to a good income and to honorable public benefits.

Above all, Tea Party activists see themselves as productive members of society. Given that many in the Tea Party are retirees, productive work need not entail current employment. It can mean a lifetime of productive employment before retirement (or, in the case of the smattering of students who participate in Tea Party groups, it might mean preparation for a lifetime of employment). When we asked our interviewees to tell us about themselves and what brought them to the Tea Party, people often launched into a narrative of their lives as workers. "My husband and I worked for everything that we got," says Bonnie. *Sharon Little*'s self-description is similar: "I'm almost 66 years old and I'm still working." *Linda Gordon* calls herself and her husband "blue-collar working-class people" who have "had to work very hard." *Stanley Ames* tells us that, "to some extent, you make your own luck. We worked hard." Others offer more specifics about how they have contributed to the country. For instance, men like Vietnam veterans Ben Jones and James Morrow, and Navy retiree Timothy Manor, immediately identify themselves with reference to their military service. Others mention civic contributions as well as employment as they recount their life stories. The specific melodies vary, but the basic tune remains: Tea Party members establish themselves as worthy Americans in terms of the contributions they have made—and contrast themselves to other categories of people who have not worked to make their way in society and thus do not deserve taxpayer funded support.

This moral social geography, rather than any abstract commitment to free-market principles, underlies Tea Party fervor to slash or eliminate categories of public benefits seen as going to unworthy people who are "freeloading" on the public sector. For Tea Party people, it is illegitimate to use taxes and public spending to redistribute wealth from productive taxpayers like themselves to people who have not earned their way. "You are not ENTITLED To What I have EARNED," declares one Tea Party bumper sticker. Another maintains that "YOUR 'FAIR SHARE' is NOT IN MY WALLET!" "I am not rich," explains James Rand, "but I am working hard to get there, and when I do, I would prefer that the moocher class not live off my hard work."[39]

"Mooching" is indeed the key notion at work here. Even though most Tea Party supporters are more comfortably situated than the bulk of other Americans, they feel put upon by the governmental process—and see themselves as losing out to others profiting unfairly from government spending. "People no longer have to work for what they earn," Michael Pierce tells us, while fellow Bay State resident *Steven Clark* stresses that, "we shouldn't be paying for other people that don't work." In Tea Party ideology, redistribution transfers money from the industrious to the lazy, a process that is fundamentally unethical and un-American. As Stanley Ames explains, "redistribution of wealth is not the answer. What you do is earn your place." Instead of punishing the successful, according to a catchphrase that appeared on Tea Party signs at rallies across the country, the government should "Redistribute My Work Ethic." Because they lack the work ethic of more successful Americans, purported freeloaders are understood to have corrupted government programs—which, in turn, place an unfair burden on productive taxpayers. "Keep Working," says a caustic Tea Party bumper sticker. "Millions on Welfare Depend on You!"

Not only do Tea Party participants think that public assistance for lower-income Americans is more expensive and open-ended than it is, they are also angry about huge new handouts like ObamaCare and other expanded benefits for younger, less privileged Americans championed by President Obama and legislated by Democrats in 2010. In part, Tea Party fears are overwrought and misplaced because most of them fall into income categories that have enjoyed tax cuts under President Obama, not tax increases. But it is also true that even the slightest federal efforts to give additional social support to non-elderly Americans are likely to exacerbate generational and class fears about who gets what, and who pays. By the end of the twentieth century U.S. social programs were profoundly generationally imbalanced: generous for retired elderly Americans, but very spotty for working-age families, whose retirement and health benefits have also been shrinking in the private economy. When Obama and the Democrats arrived in Washington DC in 2009 determined to lighten the tax burden on most middle- and lower-income Americans, while providing additional federal support for students to attend college and for families to obtain health insurance, there were bound to be generational tensions. Older Americans already "had theirs," so to speak, and might not be so happy to see others helped, especially if there had to be trims to Medicare or slightly higher taxes on higher income people. Tea Party outbursts, as well as GOP campaign slogans, readily fanned the fires of generational resentment.[40]

In this vein, the Tea Partiers' assessments of the redistributive effects of the Affordable Care Act of 2010 are not entirely off the mark. *New York Times* columnist David Leonhardt has dubbed the law one of the most redistributive and equality-promoting major pieces of legislation in decades, precisely because it promises generous new public subsidies to help make health insurance affordable for lower- and lower-middle-income Americans, mainly adults and children in younger working families, while the revenues to pay for the new subsidies are slated to come primarily from new fees on health care businesses and from slightly increased taxes on wealthy Medicare recipients and high-income earners.[41] As older, relatively economically comfortable white Americans, a fair proportion of Tea Partiers are in the ranks of those who may pay slightly more—and others imagine they could be. And for what? To shift social support to a younger generation of Americans, about whom Tea Partiers are often deeply suspicious.

SOCIAL FEARS IN A CHANGING SOCIETY

Leaving aside general hostility to redistribution, can we hone in on which types of people, exactly, Tea Partiers believe are freeloaders? Who are the less productive, less successful "moochers" to whom wealth should *not* be redistributed via government programs? We listened carefully for the ways in which Tea Party people talked about the unworthy and, when appropriate, we asked directly who they thought were receiving government benefits unfairly. Most seemed surprised by the question, as if the classes of freeloaders in American society should be obvious to any observer. Their responses usually took the form of anecdotes, often invoking immigrants or young people. Among the younger freeloaders, interestingly, were "black sheep" relatives whose failings in elder eyes provoked broader generational observations.

Racism in White, Black, and Brown

As we listened to our Tea Party interlocutors talk about undeserving people collecting welfare benefits, racially laden group stereotypes certainly did float in and out of the interviews, even when people never mentioned African-Americans directly. Racial overtones were unmistakable, for instance, when a Virginia Tea Partier told us that a "plantation mentality" was keeping "some people" on welfare. These kinds of racially insensitive comments made in person were only a very faint echo of the racial slurs that appear rarely but persistently at Tea Party rallies across the country, including in signs with racial epithets and signs equating the presidency of Barack

Obama to "white slavery."[42] A sense of "us versus them" along racial and ethnic fault lines clearly marks the worldview of many people active in the Tea Party, although raw expressions of this outlook tend to occur in public political contexts more than in discussions or interviews.

At least one scholarly study suggests that problematic racial assumptions are widely held by Tea Party supporters.[43] In a survey conducted in seven states by scholars at the University of Washington, Tea Party supporters tended to rate blacks and Latinos as less hardworking, less intelligent, and less trustworthy than did other respondents. Tea Partiers' views of minorities were even more extreme than other avowed conservatives and Republicans. Statistically, conservative Republicans tend to agree more than do nonconservatives with statements such as "if blacks would only try harder they could be just as well off as whites," but Tea Party supporters are even more likely than other conservatives to believe that racial minorities are held back by their own personal failings. It is important to note that, compared to other Americans, Tea Partiers rate *whites* relatively poorly on these characteristics, too. Tea Partiers have negative views about all of their fellow citizens; it is just that they make extra-jaundiced assessments of the work ethic of racial and ethnic minorities.[44]

Grassroots activists are very aware of the charges of racism leveled at the Tea Party, and they are quick to point out evidence to the contrary. Tea Party members avidly come to hear fiery black preachers and other black conservatives on the lecture circuit. When some Tea Party attendees say or do overtly racist things on occasion, organizers and leaders try hard to eliminate such lapses. At various planning meetings, several Massachusetts Tea Party members raised concerns that outsiders might "infiltrate" their protests with racist or otherwise inappropriate signs in order to make local activists look bad.[45] Worries about racist interlopers were not limited to Massachusetts; other Tea Party websites have posted guidelines about how to cope with such a situation. Tea Party members we spoke to were very concerned to assure us that they held no animosity toward black people.

By contrast, fear and hatred of Islam and Muslims were commonly expressed. This kind of prejudice was not invoked to talk about freeloaders or public spending but about terrorism and cultural change—even when the people being discussed were American citizens. Bonnie, for instance, said she had been hearing stories about "the Islamics wanting to take over the country." An Arizona Tea Party seminar on Islam was advertised as a way to "learn about the mindset of Muslims who follow these teachings and how the Islamic movement in our country has been affecting laws, culture, workplace, and teachings in our schools." The seminar advertisement suggested that participants "START asking the tough questions about the teachings of Islam and the truth behind the acts of Islamic terrorism in our own backyard!"[46] Even relative moderates are very worried about the threat posed by Muslims in America. "Most of them [Muslims] just want to practice their religion in peace," Gloria explained to us. But she was also certain that some significant percentage wanted to impose "Sharia law" in the United States. We never got the sense, however, that any of our Tea Party informants actually knew any Muslim-Americans personally or even foreign Muslim visitors of whom they disapproved.[47] Their statements and fears in this area were highly abstract.

And that matters, because findings from statistical studies and even interviews can oversimplify the nuances of racial attitudes and relationships in real-life America, including in the lives of Tea Party members. Perhaps one of the most revealing moments in our interviews was a discussion with Mandy Hewes. We had asked her if there were any government programs of which she approved, and she responded by telling us about her son, Terrence. Terrence, she explained, was not her biological child. In addition to raising their own children, Mandy and her husband volunteered to provide therapeutic foster care for children who had been removed from abusive homes. As Mandy described it, she and her husband could be called at any hour of day or night to take in a child rescued from a dangerous situation by Child Protective Services. One child that came to their home in this manner was Terrence, an African-American child suffering not only from parental mistreatment but also from a learning disability. Though Terrence had come to their family at age 13, Mandy referred to him as her son, and was proud to report that Terrence had graduated high school, was working, and still called her every week. After telling us the background of her son, she observed that, "Terrence was born and raised in America. He wasn't an illegal child. Social services really helped him. He is one of those that I expect gets the help. I do think that is a needed thing."

The stereotype of Tea Party activists as unreconstructed racists—as people who react to politics and policy only through racial oppositions—simply does not jibe with the life story of this very conservative white woman who opens her home to minority teenagers from troubled backgrounds. Yet Mandy's defense of Terrence also reveals something that we found more generally among Tea Party participants—a sense that U.S. citizenship status should be a central determinant of access to public benefits and government services.

Burdensome Illegal Immigrants

Tea Partiers regularly invoke illegal immigrants as prime examples of freeloaders who are draining public coffers. For social scientists and survey researchers, the usual way to get at economic worries about immigrants has long been to ask whether they take jobs from citizens. In the February 2011 poll of South Dakota Tea Party supporters, for example, 64% percent agreed that "illegal aliens are taking jobs away from South Dakotans." But in our interviews, Tea Party people placed little emphasis on the threat of immigrants taking American jobs. Instead, the major concern was the illegitimate and costly use of government funds and services by illegal immigrants. Tea Party members base their moral condemnation on the fact that these are "lawbreakers" who crossed the border without permission and thus are using American resources unfairly.

Tea Partiers, like other Americans, sometimes show real sympathy for immigrants looking to work and get ahead, but they also frame their comments with stereotypical ethnic assumptions. Tensions about immigration issues run high in Arizona, for example, but Tea Partiers we spoke to there made careful distinctions. Larry launched into a comment about "illegals" before interrupting himself to explain, "the bad illegals, not the ones trying to get a job painting or in your garden." Along the same lines, Stanley expressed concern about unauthorized immigrants who were transporting illegal drugs or abusing American entitlement programs, but also mused that many are just looking for jobs. "It's not their fault they are here. I would have crossed the border, too," he explained. "They can't make a living down there. Why are they here? Because of our greed. We the people, when we hire a landscaper, or a plumbing job, an owner with Americans working there . . . they will be underbid. We foster that. A lot of people want the cheaper thing, and then bitch about the illegals." Stanley stressed that, "the Hispanics I've met are just super people. They are very family oriented, they respect their elders, they take care of their kids, they work hard. They are better than a lot of us here in a lot of respects."[48]

Concern about immigration is certainly not limited to Arizona. Tea Party participants across the United States are very worried about the receipt of public assistance or use of government services by unauthorized immigrants. Among two of those we interviewed in southeastern Virginia, Bonnie Sims worried that immigrants were being given "rights" that she and others had had to "earn," and Mandy Hewes spelled out in stark terms what these rights entail. "I feel like my country is being stolen by people who have come here illegally," she told us. "People come in and have the benefits of taxes, and the money spent on them puts a burden on the state, which makes me have to pay more."

The belief that illegal immigrants are stiffing the American taxpayer while abusing public assistance is widely held. In point of fact, unauthorized immigrants are excluded from many federal assistance programs even though most pay taxes—helping to buoy up Social Security, for example.[49] But at a local level, people who might be unauthorized immigrants are often perceived to be crowding hospital emergency rooms and public schools, without paying their share of taxes. The issue of health care is especially fraught because its cost is rising sharply and not all citizens have access to insurance. One Tea Party activist in Arizona protested immigration by holding up a sign reading, "Illegal Immigrants have better health care than I do."[50] Tellingly, Tea Party blogs were flooded with praise for South Carolina Republican Representative Joe Wilson after he interrupted President Obama's first State of the Union address to shout "You lie!" This historic breach of decorum occurred right after the president truthfully insisted that benefits under the health reform he supported would be limited to legal U.S. residents. Reform provisions became even more draconian toward undocumented people as the Affordable Care Act was finalized and passed by Congress. Not only are no benefits allowed; illegal immigrants cannot even use their own money to buy insurance on the new health care exchanges. But Tea Party people continue to celebrate Joe Wilson's outburst and claim that health reform will help immigrants without legal authorization to be in the United States.

Overly Entitled Young People

In addition to illegal immigrants, young people feature prominently in the stories Tea Partiers tell about undeserving freeloaders, and anecdotes about people in their own families sometimes stand in for larger generational tensions. The U.S. economy is changing in ways that make it harder for young adults to find jobs, form families, earn college degrees, and build careers and accumulate property according to the same formulas that once worked well for those in the older generations from which most Tea Partiers come. Younger cohorts of Americans are also more racially and ethnically diverse, and espouse different beliefs about families and sexual conduct. Older people have always been likely to find fault with "the kids." In interviews, the faults Tea Party participants ascribed to the younger generation included everything from foul language to poor penmanship. But the general tendency of older generations to nostalgia arguably takes on a harder edge when times are tough and economic, cultural, and demographic changes are happening very quickly.

After talking about her generation's commitment to hard work, Bonnie Sims concludes "I don't think those values are being taught anymore." John Patterson echoed the same theme, complaining that younger people have "lost the value of work." He told the story of a 29-year-old woman who expected to have a title at work just because she has a Master's degree; she did not realize that you have to "earn respect." His wife, a teacher, laments that all the kids now "expect to be praised" no matter how they perform.

Many Tea Partiers connected worries about the deteriorating behavior of young people directly to fears about wasteful entitlement spending. "A lot of [young] people . . . they just feel like they are entitled," *Betsy Stone* declares, as she tells the story of a nephew who had "been on welfare his whole life." The nephew now has children of his own, yet by her account was not even reliably taking them for their medical check-ups, even though the children are eligible for free care, presumably through Medicaid. "You give these people benefits," Betsy says scornfully, "and they don't even take advantage of it" in appropriate ways. Rather than learning to contribute to society, young people are being taught that they deserve support from the government, Michael says. "My grandson, he's fourteen and he asked me: 'Why should I work, why can't I just get free money?'" Michael was very concerned that his grandson was typical of the younger generation.

Young adults in college are not exempt from Tea Party suspicion. Montana GOP Congressman Denny Rehberg, a Tea Party favorite, was no doubt speaking to the choir when he recently denounced aid to college students as "the welfare of the 21st century." Tellingly, Rehberg grouped federal Pell Grants that help low-income students cover part of their college tuition with every other public assistance program imaginable. And the Tea Party GOPer claimed that recipients are not really trying to complete college anyway. "You can go to school, collect your Pell Grants, get food stamps, low-income energy assistance, section 8 housing, and all of a sudden we find ourselves subsidizing people that don't have to graduate from college," explained Rehberg as he outlined plans to slash college aid.[51] A similar point was made in an April 2010 blog posting on the Greater Boston Tea Party website, claiming that college kids are taking advantage of the Food Stamp program. "Call me crazy," the blogger opined, "but when I needed money for college, I got a job." Of course, getting a job may have occurred to some of the students ridiculed, but at the time the blog post was written there were five job seekers for every job opening available, and unemployment among those 20 to 24 stood at 17%.[52] The limited economic opportunities available to young people were not something Tea Party members mentioned to us. Nor did they express any concern about declining college attendance and completion for lower-income and lower-middle-income young people—a decline that has caused the United States to fall behind in the global higher education sweepstakes. Instead, Tea Partiers condemned the behavior of the young in moral terms.

Societal Decline and Fear of the Future

The Tea Party emphasis on the importance of work and earned benefits certainly meshes with widely held American values. Hard work is, after all, a cornerstone of the American Dream. Americans have long linked a person's deservingness to the effort he or she puts forth, and most tend to perceive poverty as a result of laziness rather than misfortune. But the current Tea Party distinction between freeloaders and hardworking taxpayers has ethnic, nativist, and generational undertones that distinguish it from a simple reiteration of the long-standing American creed. In Tea Party eyes, undeserving people are not simply defined by a tenuous attachment to the labor market or receipt of unearned government handouts. For Tea Partiers, deservingness is a cultural category, closely tied to certain racially and ethnically tinged assumptions about American society in the early twenty-first century. Tea Party resistance to giving more to categories of people deemed undeserving is more than just an argument about taxes and spending. It is a heartfelt cry about where they fear "their country" may be headed.

Tea Party worries about racial and ethnic minorities and overly entitled young people signal a larger fear about generational social change in America. To outside observers, Tea Partiers often seem disproportionately angry.

Why are they insisting on taking back their country and defending their "rights" from tyranny when all that is happening is a pussyfooting health care reform, more conservative than the version supported by Richard Nixon in the 1970s? What is so "fascist" or "socialist" about an economic stimulus bill, one-third of which was tax cuts? One often hears such musings in liberal circles, but it is a mistake to assess emotional responses as if they were policy statements. When Tea Partiers talk about "their rights," they are asserting a desire to live again in the country they think they recall from childhood or young adulthood. Their anger evinces a determination to restore that remembered America, and pass it on to their children and grandchildren (whether or not they are asking for this gift).

Many Tea Partiers talked about feeling as though they had been asleep, only to wake up recently in a new, strange country. Bonnie Sims was particularly prone to such comments. "It's so sad the way the country is now," she told us. "My children disagree with me, but they will never know the country I grew up in." Sandra repeats this concern nearly word for word: "My children will not see the life that I have lived." By understanding the societal threat Tea Partiers perceive, their sense that America is in decline and must be saved, we can better understand why they are so upset. As Stanley told us, "I've had such a good life, and I just want other Americans to have that life."

One might imagine the changes that worry Tea Partiers to be primarily economic. In the last thirty years, economic opportunity has declined. Instead of economic prosperity benefiting all Americans, it increasingly benefits only the very few at the top.[53] But Tea Party members rarely stressed economic concerns to us—and they never blamed business or the super-rich for America's troubles.[54] The nightmare of societal decline is usually painted in cultural hues, and the villains in the picture are freeloading social groups, liberal politicians, bossy professionals, big government, and the mainstream media.

Virginians worried that their children do not grow up fishing in local streams or know what it was like to feel safe walking home late at night. Arizona Tea Partiers talked about swings being taken out of playgrounds to meet persnickety safety standards, and schoolchildren suspended for carrying pocketknives. Forces conspire, Stella Fisher says, "to the breaking down of conservative society." Kids today believe "it's not so important that you get married, even if you have a baby with somebody. . . . It's just not good for America." Such generalized concerns about societal decline were

the ones we heard most frequently—far more often than we heard any explicit comments about ethnic or racial minorities.

Such fears are, of course, wrapped up with anxieties about immigration
and America's changing links to the larger world beyond the nation's borders. Telling us about her revelation that America had somehow changed,
Bonnie plaintively asks, "What's happening in this country? What's happening with immigration?" Tea Partiers see immigrants and young people
as harbingers of cultural decline. Even Stanley, whose views on immigration were among the most moderate of any Tea Partier we interviewed, felt
that immigration is a "threat to our culture." Though rates of immigration
have been high in recent decades, sociologists looking at the typical
measures of immigrant incorporation—educational attainment, language
assimilation, and intermarriage—find that the most recent generations of
immigrants from Asia and Latin America are "being successfully incorporated into American society," just as European immigrants were in the
past.[55] But this is not believable to many Tea Partiers, who perceive that
today's immigrants are unwilling to integrate as previous generations did.

For many reasons, then, Tea Party people peer out at a fast-changing
society, and they worry. The public image of the Tea Party is one of fierce
anger, but in person and in local meetings fear was the more typical emotion. A meeting in Tempe featured a speaker who recounted the kind of
stories that lead sensationalistic local TV news programs, emphasizing
nightmarish scenarios of home invasion and rape. This is why, she said, all
women should always carry concealed firearms. The speaker was herself
carrying a concealed weapon during her talk, she informed us, patting a
squarish bulge at her right hip. At a meeting in Virginia, a speaker discussed
the near-term probability that the federal government would impose martial law and force citizens into camps that would be called "five-minute
zones."[56] In the minds of Tea Party activists, the American present—and
especially the looming U.S. future—is often more than worrisome; it can be
downright terrifying.

Obviously, Tea Partiers speak constantly about an out-of-control federal budget deficit and the coming doom they think it portends for the
United States. There is real-world basis for worrying about the U.S. fiscal
situation, of course, though the United States is in reasonably good fiscal
shape, as the steady health of the bond market attests.[57] Tea Party worries
about national debt therefore refer to real problems, but magnify them out
of all proportion. Why? As we have learned, Tea Partiers are concerned that

U.S. deficits might be addressed in part with tax hikes, which they imagine would require people like them to help pay for social spending that benefits undeserving freeloaders. But the fiscal question in the Tea Party imagination is more than just a redistributive matter, more than just a set of worries about taxes and social spending. In the highly emotional telling of many Tea Partiers, the ballooning federal deficit merges into a general sense of a coming collapse for America. A Virginia Tea Party participant explained to us at length that, as the U.S. fiscal crisis unfolds, grocery stores will be shuttered and citizens who are not armed will risk falling prey to roving gangs. "The United States has squandered its wealth created over the last 400 years and is now destroying wealth," explains another Virginian, James Rand, who believes that politicians may decide to address the "debt load overhanging us" by seizing the 401k savings accounts of all private citizens. It might be best for the country to go into default, he muses, to wake everyone up to the severity of our collapse.

Fears about imminent American collapse fuel fear-driven urges to make extreme preparations. Living in a pristine retirement community in exurban Phoenix, Stanley and Gloria Ames outlined their plans for the coming Armageddon. "The forecast is we could have a crash, and the dollar could be worthless," Stanley explains. "So you barter in silver and gold, by weight. All of these things are scary out there. We didn't buy gold, we went into silver bullion. . . . We are concerned to the point that we are armed. We have a safe full of ammunition. We have food that has a date that will carry us out for almost a year and half. It's a frightening time." For this charming and friendly older couple, Tea Party politics inextricably mixes relatively routine political engagement with extraordinary efforts to save America and themselves in a looming end-of-the-world scenario.

BARACK OBAMA AT THE VORTEX

Nowhere are Tea Party fears more potently symbolized than in the presidency of Barack Hussein Obama. The policies and person of the forty-fourth President were the subject of immense suspicion at every Tea Party event or interview we attended. It is no coincidence that Tea Party activism began within weeks of President Obama's inauguration. Several interviewees dated their concerns about the country and national politics to Obama's election or the 2008 campaign. Others told us, quite credibly, about long-simmering worries, and insisted that the Tea Party is not just or only about opposition to Obama. True enough, but these people had a hard time pinning down a different catalyst for their sudden political mobilization in early 2009.

The freewheeling anti-Obama paranoia expressed at Tea Party rallies has been widely reported. Various articles have quoted Tea Party members saying that Obama is a secret Muslim, a foreigner, a Socialist, a Communist, a Nazi—or maybe all of the above! Obama the un-American is the overarching theme. Stoked by demagogues like Donald Trump, the claim about President Obama's otherness and illegitimacy reached its apogee in "Birtherist" claims that Obama was not really born in the United States. In our interviews, the tone was of course more measured than in public rallies, but we heard variations of all the possible epithets for Obama. Even in face-to-face interviews, Tea Party rhetoric veers into the territory described by historian Richard Hofstadter as "the paranoid style in American politics"—which should perhaps not come as a surprise, as Hofstadter was talking about John Birch Society members and Goldwater supporters, whose remnants have joined the Tea Party today.[58]

More typical in our encounters than the occasional reference to Communism or long-form birth certificates were frank admissions from Tea Party members that Obama is, to them, incomprehensible. "I just can't relate to him," said one man at a Tea Party meeting in Boston. Uncertainty veers into suspicion. "I think that he's actually not what he seems to be," said a Virginia Tea Partier. "He's disingenuous. I have delved into it deeply," claimed another. Several Tea Party members we spoke to described Obama simply as "scary." For Tea Partiers, President Obama is somehow outside or beyond comprehensible categories, and he has used confusion about who he is and what he stands for to his own nefarious political advantage.

A Perfectly Fearful Storm

In recent decades, Democratic presidents who have come to office with Democratic Congressional majorities quickly become the objects of all-out attacks from conservatives. Race is not the main factor in drives to delegitimize Democrats, even when it offers fuel for fear and stereotypes. Attacks on Bill and Hillary Clinton from 1992 to 2000 invoked personal misbehavior, business shenanigans, and all sorts of alleged moral horrors—to the point of suggesting that the Clintons murdered their friend Vince Foster (who committed suicide). A decade and a half later, ultra-right-wing attacks on Barack Obama do not usually imply anything wrong with his family values or sexual conduct. Instead, they use the material at hand: his race, his foreign father, and his background as a college professor and community organizer. Elites in the right-wing media and the netherworlds of ultra-conservative politics consciously play on whatever resentments or fears might be out there to undercut the Democratic president of the day.

The son of an African father and a white American mother, Obama is perceived by many Tea Partiers as a foreigner, an invader pretending to be an American, a fifth columnist. Obama's past as a community organizer is taken as evidence that he works on behalf of the undeserving poor and wishes to mobilize government resources on their behalf. His academic achievements and social ties put him in league with the country's intellectual elite, whose disdain feels very real to many Americans, and whose cosmopolitan leanings seem unpatriotic. For so many reasons, therefore, Obama's social ambiguities as well as his political stands make him easy to portray as a threat—especially in the eyes of very conservative Americans.

Asked about the President, Tea Party members connect Obama and his administration and political allies directly with those deemed undeserving—not just with African-Americans but also with illegal immigrants and criminals. Michael, the retired police officer, worries that "the people I was looking for back when I was a cop are now running the government." James Rand angrily asserts that "criminals" are in charge of the U.S. government.[59] It is widely believed, moreover, that President Obama intends to grant amnesty to all illegal immigrants in order to develop a new bloc of electoral support. An extra 10 million votes from newly legalized citizens would give the Obama Administration the electoral cushion needed to continue to ignore the interests of real Americans, several Tea Party members told us. Similar sentiments are invoked in group discussions, too. At the April 2011 meeting of the York Constitutionalists assembled in North Berwick, Maine, both the outside speaker and members of the group repeatedly characterized the current Democratic Party as an alliance of unionized public officials and people on welfare, and they speculated that the Obama Administration would soon use immigration reform to add current undocumented immigrants to the Democratic voter rolls.

With his Ivy League degrees, President Obama is also perceived as a member of a haughty, overbearing, and dubiously patriotic higher-educated elite. While the business community gets a free pass, Tea Party activists are very concerned about liberal cultural elites, who they believe scorn most Americans. As Sandra put it, "there is an elite class that loathes the middle class" and looks down on "stupid rednecks." Tea Partiers often use higher education as shorthand for the difference between the cultural elite and average Americans. In Boston, one activist dismissed people "with a bunch of letters after their name," while a Virginia activist commented that she had "lost all respect" for higher education. Discussing who might run for public offices, Charlottesville Tea Partiers stressed that expert qualifications were not only unnecessary, but might be harmful. Firm convictions and a determination not to compromise were all people needed to serve in local, state, or national government, these Tea Partiers agreed.

Although Tea Partiers dismiss intellectuals with harsh rhetoric, they are themselves usually well educated. Most of those we spoke to had a college education, and many had advanced degrees. One Tea Partier objected to a brief written survey we had provided, saying it did not allow her to list her full academic credentials. As with those deemed undeserving, the category of the "intellectual elite" is more politically symbolic than based on clear-cut empirical facts. In Tea Partyland, ideology and politics separate objectionable educated elites from other highly educated people.

Because of their supposed disdain for average Americans, liberal elites are imagined to be plotting new forms of regulation and control. They think "they know what's best for us," one Virginia Tea Partier explained. Regulations supported by liberals are perceived as a foreign moral code, an imposition of un-American ideals, although the exact impositions may range from "political correctness," as Timothy Manor put it, to health and safety rules. For some Tea Partiers, Michelle Obama's anti-obesity campaign is yet another elite judgment on the lifestyles of average Americans. Another source of acute concern is environmentalism. Tea Party members routinely dismiss climate change as nothing more than a hoax perpetrated by scientists and bureaucrats, as a prelude to extending the reach of their power.

To the extent the policy prescriptions advanced by educated elites appear to benefit the undeserving, those elites are seen by Tea Partiers as allied with freeloading groups to steal taxpayer money and subvert the proper role of U.S. government. The housing bubble, for instance, was explained in these terms. Through his purported ties to Fannie Mae and Freddie Mac, and to the now-defunct community organizing group ACORN, Obama is charged with joining other Democrats to promote an unsustainable boom in homeownership among the undeserving. James Morrow, for instance, assured us that Obama had received "the most money from Fannie and Freddie" of any senator except Senator Chris Dodd. For Tea Partiers, Obama is the epitome of the liberal elitist working in the interest of the undeserving.

Old Themes for a New Time

As we have seen throughout this chapter, most aspects of Tea Party thinking are not new; they add up to the most recent incarnation of American conservative populism. In talking to Tea Party activists, you hear echoes of Reagan-era stories of "welfare queens" and Nixonian rhetoric about the "silent majority," the true Americans for whom Tea Partiers think they speak. Like earlier rounds of right-wing activism, the activism of Tea Partiers is driven by societal oppositions more than by detailed policy logic. Tea Partiers at the grass roots are content with the parts of U.S. social provision they see as benefiting worthy people, even as they are determined to slash government assistance for those they see as freeloaders "mooching" at taxpayer expense. Tea Partiers want no government regulation of their own businesses, homes, and property, even as they are eager for government to crack down hard on immigrants and others they see as political or cultural opponents.

To say that Tea Partiers are part of a long-standing conservative tradition is to agree with many of our interviewees, who celebrate previous generations of conservatives as their political forebears. One Virginia Tea Partier told us that the "problems" the United States is now facing "go back to Roosevelt" and the New Deal. Looking back even further, many who watched Fox News anchor Glenn Beck echoed his criticisms of Woodrow Wilson.[60] Indeed, the Minnesota Tea Partiers affiliated with the large and vibrant Southwest Metro Tea Party see themselves as part of a long tradition battling American liberalism. As their "Principles" explain, the Tea Party's goal is to reverse the work of "Woodrow Wilson's Progressivism, FDR's New Deal, LBJ's Great Society, and President Obama's 'fundamentally transforming America.'"[61] The war is a long one and today's Tea Partiers are the latest soldiers.

Nor are connections across time merely intellectual and political. One of the few college-age Tea Partiers we met, a young man in Boston, wore a T-shirt emblazoned with Goldwater's bumper sticker slogan "AuH2O." It was history for him, but of course many of his fellow Tea Partiers remember that campaign firsthand. An extraordinary number dated their first political experiences to the 1964 Goldwater campaign. Mandy had served as a page at the Republican convention that nominated Goldwater; Ben described himself as an "old Barry Goldwater guy"; and a protestor in Boston said he had not felt this "excited" about politics "since Goldwater." Despite endless commentary comparing it to assorted movements ranging from Civil Rights to the Ross Perot campaign, the Tea Party is fundamentally the latest iteration of long-standing, hard-core conservatism in American politics.

Yet the ideas and passions of today's Tea Partiers are also born of this time and place; they are very much responses to the startling social changes and roiling politics that mark the United States in the early twenty-first century. Obama's election to the nation's highest office galvanized conservatives desperate to express their opposition to everything they believe he stands for—a country changing too quickly in directions they dread. The coincidence of Obama's election and broader Democratic gains with a scary financial meltdown heightened the threat for conservatives who turned to the Tea Party. But we cannot understand the ferocity of their reaction or the obsessive focus on Obama as an alien force without situating the politics of the economic crisis in the context of the larger societal shifts.

Just as liberals and many younger people perceive President Obama as a symbol of the breaking of boundaries, a harbinger of new possibilities in U.S. society and politics, so, too, do Tea Party participants perceive that new things are afoot—changing societal norms, greater ethnic diversity, international cosmopolitanism, and new redistributions aimed at younger citizens. What signifies hope for some Americans, triggers anger and fear in others. As James Morrow put it, "Barack Obama came right out and said he wanted to transform America." For the conservative-minded, mostly older people who have joined the Tea Party, this promise was—and is—a frightful threat.

3

Mobilized Grassroots and Roving Billionaires

The Panoply of Tea Party Organizations

When CNBC commentator Rick Santelli vented his anger on the floor of the Chicago Mercantile Exchange in February 2009, he launched a spectacular political brand for the next election cycle and beyond. The soon-boiling Tea Party commingled all-out opposition to the Obama presidency, cover for business at a time when Wall Street seemed culpable, and old-fashioned patriotic fervor in a populace reeling amidst an economic tailspin. From coast to coast, from local to national arenas, activists wasted no time turning a colorful tirade into widespread mobilizations.

Local activism in the Tea Party depends on the energy and commitment of conservative citizens willing to organize projects, attend meetings, travel to lobby days and rallies, study and discuss legislation, and learn government procedures and GOP rules. But local efforts are not all that is going on because generously funded political action committees and advocacy groups also take part in Tea Party efforts. A few of these national organizations were newly founded with the Tea Party label, but most simply added the moniker on top of long-standing organized efforts, or linked their offerings to Tea Party websites.

Some national organizations, most notably Tea Party Patriots, encourage and coordinate grassroots activists, while others, such as Tea Party Express, stage media events and give money to GOP candidates. In addition, advocacy groups such as Freedom Works and

Americans for Prosperity push long-standing ultra-free-market agendas. They are ideological organizations first and foremost and draw a lot of their specific legislative proposals from assorted right-wing policy institutes, including the Cato Institute and the Heritage Foundation in Washington DC. A vast network of policy-oriented right-wing intellectuals, generously funded, has been strategizing and writing for many years, awaiting the moment when political and electoral winds might shift just enough to allow their ideas to find a larger place on the mainstream agenda.

There is not, therefore, a single Tea Party organization, nor even a well-coordinated network. Instead, a gaggle of jostling and sometimes competing local and national organizations, none of them directly controlled by the institutional Republican Party, are pushing to influence GOP officeholders, candidates, and voters. Mapping the Tea Party as a set of organizations is no easy undertaking. Picking up the phone to call a few DC organizers does not suffice. Attending a few big conventions or rallies also falls short.[1]

In this chapter, we combine publicly available evidence with in-depth personal interviews and local observations to provide an overview of the organizations and networks that make up the Tea Party. We start with the efforts of the grassroots organizers who moved during 2009 and 2010 from sparking rallies to creating regularly meeting Tea Party groups across the country. Then we look in greater detail at the Tea Party–linked national organizations that operate with backing from right-wing billionaires and other wealthy interests. These top-down organizations, most of them established years ago, deserve a close look, not because they simply created or directly control the Tea Party, but because they are effectively leveraging grassroots activism to gain new advantages in durable crusades to remake the Republican Party and shift legislative agendas at all levels of U.S. government.

As we introduce the key players in the Tea Party field of organizations, we probe the many ways in which local and national actors influence one another. How do local Tea Party people tap regional and national resources to facilitate grassroots efforts? And how do national organizations use ties to popular undertakings to enhance their own clout? The advantages go both ways, yet tensions remain that raise provocative questions. What happens when wary, independent-minded grassroots organizers deal with national or regional orchestrators trying to coordinate popular activism, or when local Tea Partiers look out and see well-funded organizations and ambitious operators advocating in the name of the Tea Party as a whole?

In the final analysis, do rank-and-file Tea Partiers have any real control over the impresarios and politicians who speak so loudly in their name—and do they care?

GRASSROOTS GROUPS GALORE

After a full and varied career in business and civic endeavors, Tom Robinson, in his early sixties, was in a "semi-retirement phase" in early 2009, moving back and forth between domiciles in the Richmond area and a cottage in the village of Moon, in Mathews County on the Middle Peninsula of Virginia. After hearing about the Tea Party as a way for citizens to "rise up," Tom decided to found a group, partly as a way to connect to others in an area that attracts many newly resident retirees.[2] He tracked down Jean Casanave, who had published a stirring letter to the editor of the *Gloucester-Mathews Gazette-Journal,* lamenting that Americans were "losing our way" and urging people to "fight" for "our Constitution" as well as "small government, low taxes, [and] religious freedom."[3] On a pretty day in June 2009, about two dozen early recruits gathered on picnic benches in front of Tom's seaside cottage to found the Peninsula Patriots.[4] A news piece in the local paper indicated that people could get more information at the group's new Meetup site. Because he had previously used the social networking site to assemble a voluntary group to fight attention deficit disorder, Tom knew that Meetup can "help you get organized in a hurry." Before long, dozens of Peninsula Patriots were gathering monthly to hear speakers and plan for rallies, lobbying, and local advocacy.

In Lynchburg, Virginia, several "local ladies" got things going in spring 2009 with email and leaflets stuffed under windshield wipers in the Walmart parking lot. Lynchburg Tea Partiers participated in several more city and regional protests, and about fifty carpooled to the huge 9/12 Rally in Washington DC. Meanwhile, about an hour away in Charlottesville, two friends assembled twenty people, including sympathetic talk radio hosts, to mount stirring rallies and stage protests at the office of Representative Tom Perriello, Democrat of Virginia, fifth district.[5]

In both towns, new leaders stepped up to found regularly meeting groups. Following the big DC rally in September 2009, more of the same seemed "anticlimactic," explains Lynchburg Tea Partier *John Patterson.* He took the reins from the early rally organizers to influence local GOP committees and gear up for the next year's primary and general elections. In Charlottesville, the baton was passed in early

2010 to Carole Thorpe, a stay-at-home mother with lots of volunteer experience in community theatrical events. During 2009, Carole went from being "always in the front row" at rallies, to serving as one of four bus leaders for travel to the 9/12 DC rally. Carole had the know-how to lead the Jefferson Area Tea Party in a transition from "street organization" to a membership group that convenes at least monthly and uses subcommittees to pursue multiple projects at once.

The Southwest Metro Tea Party in Chanhassen, near the Twin Cities of Minnesota, was launched by Cindy Pugh and Mara Souvannasoth, two women who did not know each other before the effervescence of 2009. Mara calls herself a "stay-at-home homeschooling mom" and Cindy has worked in retail management and now devotes much of her time to civic activism.[6] Each was attracted to the Tea Party and active in rallies from the start, but they did not meet until a trip to Washington DC in November 2009, when three busloads traveled from Minnesota in response to Congresswoman Michele Bachmann's call to protest the imminent passage of health reform legislation by the U.S. House of Representatives.[7] Feeling a "strong desire to fully wake up and wake others up," they decided to work together, to "jump off the sidelines" and start a Tea Party. In June 2010, they convened an organizational meeting at the Chanhassen Library, and before long the Southwest Metro Tea Party became something of a powerhouse and model.[8] One of the largest groups in the state, it has moved to the more capacious American Legion hall, where it meets, not merely monthly, but every Monday night from 7:00 to 8:30 P.M. Three sessions per month are devoted to speakers and discussion; the fourth Monday is "Movie Night," where people bring family and friends to the likes of "Atlas Shrugged" or documentaries dramatizing the evils of liberalism.

The Tea Party could have been a flash in the pan, at least at the grass roots. After the Santelli rant, the first "Tea Party" rallies were mounted to colorful effect on February 27, 2009, and more extensively on Tax Day, April 15, 2009. Synchronization depended on mass media and national advocacy groups. Along with right-wing blogs and talk radio, Fox News, including colorful host Glenn Beck, created the sense that a massive "movement" was afoot. Online interactive maps let organizers combine efforts and guided would-be protestors to events. And the DC-based advocacy organization FreedomWorks posted tips on "How to Organize Your Own 'Tea Party' Protest."[9] Rally organizers were urged to prepare homemade signs with "BIG LETTERS" and pick a visible location such as a "main street at an intersection with lots of traffic." Carpools, press releases, and contacts with local talk radio, were additional parts of the recommended menu—as were sign-in sheets to generate "a big list of people that can plan the next, much bigger and louder, event." This formula certainly worked to build protests in the early weeks and months.

But then what? At the time, many observers across the political spectrum expected periodic rallies to be the sum total of Tea Party activity, with after-effects in the form of expanded email lists managed by professionally run advocacy organizations. When Chris Good of *The Atlantic* got in touch with "national-level conservative groups" to get their sense of the lay of the land in April 2009, a spokesman for FreedomWorks, Adam Brandon, told him that the right was trying to imitate the model of online networking and occasional public protests developed so effectively on the left by MoveOn. org. "Activists in general have learned a lot from the last election," observed Brandon. "You'd see 50 MoveOn.org people standing outside a gas station. We feel just as strongly about our issues."[10] FreedomWorks also planned to send people with sign-up sheets to public rallies, hoping (as the *Atlantic* reporter explained) to use protests against the Obama agenda to "fill conservative e-mail lists and coffers with new support."[11] At that juncture, no one anticipated that hundreds of regularly meeting local Tea Parties would pop up across America during 2009 and 2010.

Tea Party Organization in Perspective

Had the Tea Party turned into a glorified email list, no social scientist who studies U.S. voluntary associations and interest groups would have been surprised. Professionally run operations that involve grassroots citizens mainly via sporadic, emotional appeals to send money or take an online "action" are the norm these days.

Historically, from the nineteenth through the mid-twentieth centuries, politically and civically active Americans relied on voluntary associations rooted in local chapters where people met face to face, once every week or two, or perhaps monthly. Membership dues and people's time were the prime resources. The most effective and powerful U.S. voluntary associations were federations, paralleling the U.S. government, where thousands of local membership groups sent elected leaders or representatives to attend conventions and run state and national organizations. But this classic model of U.S. voluntary organization fell into disuse after the 1960s.[12] Thereafter, professionally run lobbying groups took center stage. If so-called members are involved at all, they are usually just scattered adherents who receive messages online or in the mail and make monetary contributions. Professional staffers run advocacy group offices, and they spend most of their time doing media appearances, lobbying officials, and raising funds at cocktail parties or via databases of potential supporters. Their unorganized followings do not pay regular dues, do not elect leaders, and have few mechanisms by which to hold the professionals accountable.

A few recently active associations on the right and left have found ways to link themselves to groups at the grass roots, usually through preexisting organizations or networks, or in close relationship to one of the two major political parties. The then more than century-old National Rifle Association was converted during the 1970s into a right-wing advocacy juggernaut, combining well-funded lobbying with links to people in localities and states who still belonged to gun clubs. Long-standing teachers' associations turned into unions and became active in Democratic Party politics. Around the edges of the GOP in the 1980s and 1990s, evangelical religious conservatives created associations rooted in church-based networks (much as the Civil Rights movement did in relation to black churches in the 1950s and 1960s). But, mostly, recent U.S. political organizations operate as what Marshall Ganz has aptly called "bodyless heads," that is, they are professionally run operations headquartered in Washington DC with no "ground game" to speak of, and certainly with no accountability to independently organized local membership groups.[13]

Hard-fought presidential contests bring temporary exceptions to this "bodyless heads" scenario because voters have to be mobilized in every state and local district. Starting in the 1980s, national and state Republican parties learned to work with Christian-right activists and tap into church networks to engage socially conservative voters. In the early 2000s, Democrats followed suit to some degree, as the presidential campaigns of Howard Dean in 2004 and Barack Obama in 2008 assembled impressive national networks grounded, at least in part, in face-to-face local meetings. The spread of Internet access made it easier both for people to join national lists and organize local house meetings. But presidentially focused undertakings always seem to lose steam after the candidate loses or wins.

Notably, the Obama for America organizing juggernaut that helped win the presidency lost energy and clout as it was relabeled "Organizing for America" and incorporated as a division of the Democratic National

Committee.[14] Ironically, following the landmark 2008 elections, Democrats fused volunteer activism into official party organs at the very same time that the Tea Party rubric inspired conservative grassroots activists to organize separately from official GOP organizations. For conservative activists in and around the edges of the GOP, early 2009 was a scary time, in that they suddenly faced a new "Democratic establishment" in Washington DC. But it was also a juncture of openness and opportunity because, in the wake of the discredited Bush presidency and failed McCain campaign, official GOP organizations were not going to be able to control what happened next—the exact opposite of what was happening on the left side of the political spectrum.

Certainly, early Tea Party protests were *not* launched or controlled by the institutional Republican Party, and local Tea Parties were not deferential to establishment GOP ideas about candidates or policy priorities. A scattering of Republican House members managed to speak at some of the early Tea Party rallies. But then-Chairman of the Republican National Committee, Michael Steele, was turned away when he tried to get involved in April 2009, and national-level GOP operatives were not engaged.[15] Some activists were previously involved with local Republican Party organs, and other Tea Partiers soon moved to take over their GOP committees. Yet from the start, Tea Party instigators expressed disdain for most existing GOP organizations and "establishment Republicans," especially at state and national levels. Even Karl Rove, operating as a GOP mastermind outside of official party organizations themselves, was not paid deference. Tea Party instigators, from local activists to professional right-wing national ideologues, were determined to act independently, and put pressure on the GOP at the same time that they attacked Obama and the Democrats.

So the very first grassroots Tea Party eruptions were not an institutional GOP creation, and national advocates were channeling energy towards protests and list-building in early 2009. A mystery remains: Why and how did Tea Party activists at the local level quickly move beyond mounting rallies and compiling email lists to organizing locally run Tea Party groups that met regularly and set their own agendas? This was a crucial step, one that set the Tea Party apart from the "bodyless" types of organizations that dominate contemporary U.S. political life (even though it remained to be seen whether local Tea Parties, once established, would be able to control what national organizations do in their name).

The Spread of Local Tea Parties

Local Tea Parties emerged in the spring of 2009, and spread through the summer and fall of 2009 and on into 2010. In the fall of 2010, a team of *Washington Post* reporters succeeded in contacting the organizers of about 650 Tea Party groups, from a list of over 1400 "possible groups."[16] We developed an even more comprehensive tally of local groups in the winter and spring of 2011, by using multiple online searches to find 804 currently active Tea Parties with some presence on the web, plus 164 more groups that appear to have held regular meetings at some point since February 2009. A few states, like Vermont, Delaware, and the Dakotas, have fewer than three Tea Party groups that we could trace. Fifteen states have more than thirty Tea Party groups; a few states (California, Florida, and Texas) have more than fifty local groups apiece.[17] Of course, bigger states have more people who could participate, so in Figure 3.1, we show where Tea Parties are most prevalent compared to the state population. The northern Rocky Mountain States have an unusually heavy Tea Party density, as do states in the Ozarks and lower Appalachian range and states along the southwestern border.

Just counting Tea Parties is not a perfect measure of Tea Party prevalence because it does not take into account how many people participate in each individual group. So we also mark on the map the Tea Parties that claim an online membership of at least 500 people.[18] Online membership is certainly not the same as the number of people who actually attend meetings, but it does give us a sense of where Tea Party groups have a deeper reach in their communities. Large Tea Party groups are found in state capitols and big cities, and beyond that, they are especially common in the South.

We believe our study caught local Tea Parties at close to the peak of their spread. There may be scattered Tea Parties that have no web indications whatsoever, but by 2011 local websites were the rule. Although local groups have continued to emerge during 2011—often because people who attend Tea Parties in a metropolitan area decide to spin off satellite groups closer to home—preexisting Tea Parties also fade away. The net result may be a wash. Even if our tally is merely in the ballpark, it underlines the scope of local Tea Party organizing. Tea Parties are far from being as widespread as local chapters of classic U.S. voluntary federations such as the Boy Scouts, the American Legion, or even the American Bowling Congress, each of which once had millions of members organized in an elaborate network of active local chapters.[19] But a stock of more than 800 regularly

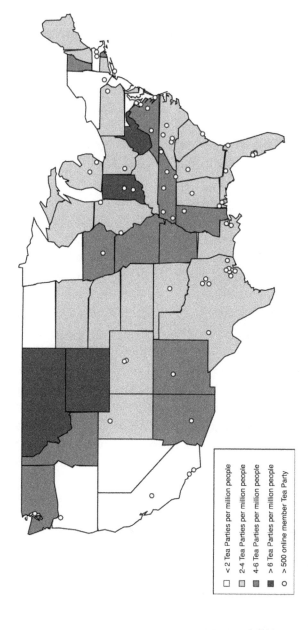

FIGURE 3.1. Local Tea Party Groups in the United States. *Number of Tea Party groups per million people in each state, and location of largest Tea Party groups. Data from nationwide survey of local Tea Party websites, spring 2011.*

< 2 Tea Parties per million people
2-4 Tea Parties per million people
4-6 Tea Parties per million people
> 6 Tea Parties per million people
> 500 online member Tea Party

meeting local groups is unusual for any U.S. political organization or network since the 1960s.

The spread of local Tea Parties was hardly anticipated in advance, not even by the right-wing media stars or national advocacy organizations trying to spur and exploit Tea Party activism in early 2009. As we have seen, FreedomWorks and other professionally run advocacy organizations were thinking in terms of rallies with television cameras and sign-up sheets to capture new adherents and donors. As we will discuss in more detail in Chapter 4, Fox News star Glenn Beck did make active efforts to build locally meeting groups through his 9/12 Project, launched in March of 2009. Though this campaign certainly got several hundred local groups mobilized, less than half of the Tea Parties we found make any reference to the 9/12 Project.[20] Whatever local organizing the national honchos expected, grassroots Tea Partiers soon accomplished more.

We can tell ourselves that local Tea Party organizing "had to happen." Rank-and-file conservatives moved toward holding regular meetings in an effort to get a handle on the many opportunities suddenly coming their way—opportunities to mount rallies and help people get to them; to debate core values like "Constitutionalism"; to develop capacities to capture publicity, pressure government officials, and take over formerly moribund GOP committees. But let's not kid ourselves: the mere presence of opportunities does not automatically mean that anyone will seize the day. People have to do the hard work and keep at it. Most local Tea Parties were *not* just preexisting groups of other kinds that draped themselves in a new label after February 2009. Remarkably, local instigators created and sustained brand-new membership groups, ongoing local parts of a nationally shared identity. This sort of thing used to happen all of the time in American civic and political life. But it is much rarer nowadays, so we have more to learn about why and how it happened.

Who Were the Local Founders—and How Did They Do It?

No national surveys pinpoint local Tea Party founders, let alone provide a window into the ideas and skills they brought to the job. Sadly, surveys today are obsessed with attitudes and individual characteristics, and pay virtually no attention to organizations or institutions. They treat individuals as isolates floating around in asocial spaces—which is not the way real people live their lives. But we can still gain some insights into what happened. From interviews and tracking local Tea Parties in public sources, we have learned that these groups were often launched by sets of organizers who did not know one another personally before they met in rallies or other protest settings. The founders of Tea Party groups acted out of like-mindedness and the desire to do ever-more-challenging things in an exciting mobilization, and they brought recognizable resources, experiences, and skills to the task.

Local organizers have important resources. Leaders who launched local Tea Parties and keep them going are usually men or women of at least modest economic means who find themselves in life circumstances where they have some flexibility in the use of their time. Retirees or semi-retired leaders often crop up—such as Tom Robinson, founder of the Peninsula Patriots whose story we briefly glimpsed in the vignette at the start of this section, or the Arizona couple profiled in an earlier chapter. Ironically, many organizers and leaders of local Tea Parties are supported in part by Social Security or veterans' pensions, and also enjoy health benefits from Medicare or veterans' health care programs. U.S. taxpayers subsidize their incomes and well-being, and hence give them the time and capacity to organize protests and Tea Party groups.

Below retirement age, Tea Party orchestrators may be small business owners free to engage in volunteer efforts while still meeting the demands of earning a living. Or they may be people who can step back from salaried employment and still get by on a spouse's salary. For example, John Patterson, the organizer from Lynchburg, Virginia, lost his salaried position and now works as an occasional consultant while doing Tea Party work. Another instance is Gena Bell, the founder of the Eastern Hills Community Tea Party in Cincinnati, Ohio, whose story is told by *Washington Post* reporter Amy Gardner.[21] Gena's husband earns a salary, and encouraged her to drop her part-time job to do more Tea Party activities.

Many local organizers are stay-at-home moms, who rely on financial support from spouses or family resources. Both Carole Thorpe in Charlottesville, Virginia, and Mara Souvannasoth in Chanhassen, Minnesota, exemplify this archetypical sort of American civic activist. Mothers who are either not wage-earning employees or who work part-time are mainstays of every kind of civic and political activism in the United States. In the Charlottesville and Chanhassen Tea Parties, the highly effective leaders are very busy women, who enjoy sufficient economic support and flexibility in daily routines to alternate motherly work with Tea Party activities.

Tea Party group founders and leaders thus seem to be reasonably economically comfortable and not tied down by demands of nine-to-five paid employment or overwhelming family obligations. But these are merely enabling factors. They alert us to the sort of folks who *could* organize Tea Parties but don't go deep enough to tell us why and how actual people took the plunge to create genuinely new organizations. A few tiny Tea Parties amount to little more than relabeled kin groups, and some are the progeny of different right-wing organizations, including the 2008 Ron Paul campaign, and the 9/12 Project, a network founded around the same time as the Tea Parties by Fox News host Glenn Beck.[22] But most local Tea Parties were freshly created organizations launched by self-appointed organizers who started out as occasional protestors.

Friends sometimes worked together as Tea Party instigators. In the central Virginia vignettes above, we note the "local ladies" who organized early rallies in Lynchburg, and the male friends who did the same in Charlottesville. In both cases, rally organizers seemed to have known each other before Santelli's rant. But as happened in Chanhassen, Minnesota, many of the leaders who stepped up to organize ongoing local Tea Parties were drawn in for the first time through public events. They were conservative-minded people who attended Tea Party rallies and only later made the transition from simple participation to organizing. People got going out of a conviction that it was time for conservatives to "get off the couch" and act, and from the sense that it would be fun to work with others who felt just as angry and threatened as you did about Obama and goings-on in Washington DC. When people told us how they got inspired, or met others with whom they could work to found a Tea Party, they echoed the same theme: how great it was to discover they were not alone in "shouting at the TV."

Prior experiences in organizing political or civic endeavors were very helpful for the men and women who took the first steps to establish ongoing local Tea Parties. We do not know how often inexperienced people tried to start Tea Parties, either with or without success, let alone how often experienced organizers tried and failed. But existing scholarship suggests, and our fieldwork confirms, that people who take it upon themselves to mount a rally or found a regularly meeting group need to have some confidence and know-how. Tea Partiers are usually well-educated, which gives them general skills to speak and write and gather information. Many have surely learned relevant skills in the workplace, or from organizing community activities for kids and parents. "'It's like being a Girl Scout mom,'" Gena

Bell told the *Washington Post*'s Amy Gardner as she recounted drumming up volunteers for rallies and fielding phone calls from fellow Tea Partiers and politicians. And many had previous political or civic experiences they could draw upon.

Previous involvement in conservative politics could be very helpful in launching a new Tea Party. When she set out to launch the Greater Boston Tea Party in early 2009, Christen Varley had social contacts as well as relevant skills from previous involvement in conservative causes. She could start emailing potential recruits at once. Yet experience in nonpolitical civic activities could also help. Tom Robinson knew how to use MeetUp to rev up the Peninsula Patriots in Virginia because he had already used that organizing website to assemble a group dealing with attention deficit disorder. Similarly, Carole Thorpe in Charlottesville, Virginia, had loads of transferable skills from her volunteer work in community theater productions, where she had not only acted dramatic parts but also pitched in to organize productions.

Because of her experience in theater projects, Carole is a whirlwind at orchestrating while delegating. She knows how to inspire and direct, yet also get other people to take responsibility as part of teams, in which each person, as she explained to us, does not feel that it "all falls on" him or her alone. When one of us (Theda) visited a meeting of the Jefferson Area Tea Party in Charlottesville, Carole's organizing skills were on full display— even if, as she later explained, she had not been active in politics prior to the Tea Party. Carole was getting her flock of about 100 Tea Partiers organized into multiple subcommittees, each with shared leadership and responsibility. Through the multiple ongoing subcommittees, the Jefferson Area Tea Party would be able to draw up a new constitution and bylaws; communicate regularly with members; do education and outreach in the community; monitor elected representatives in local, state, and national government; and mount regular rallies at the recurrent ritual peak-points in the Tea Party calendar—Tax Day in April, Independence Day in July, and Constitution Day in September.

Indeed, as local Tea Parties emerged across America, it was everywhere important for an organizing nucleus to take shape, so duties like finding appropriate meeting places, arranging refreshments, and scheduling speakers could be divvied up. A clear marker of organizational development is the formal division of labor, and we saw this happening in a number of the local groups we visited. Local Tea Party leaders told us of their efforts to recruit and encourage committee chairs and multiple participants in leadership teams, people who might or might not be elected by other members. Websites for local Tea Parties often identify multiple people as joint leaders and sometimes name different people to contact about various aspects of ongoing Tea Party activities. Sometimes the founders found themselves unhappy with the way things evolved after they formed a leadership team—that happened in one local Tea Party when more socially conservative leaders took over from a more secularly minded libertarian who started the group. But in other instances, the original kingpin(s) or queenpin(s) stayed very involved, and simply inspired others to join the leadership team.

What about money? Readers may wonder if local groups were seeded with generous grants from outside funders. Perhaps that has happened in some instances; many local Tea Party websites have "Donation" buttons and appeal for sympathetic people to pitch in. But the local groups we visited were not opulent affairs, and members were doing a lot to raise funds of their own. Members set up tables to sell costume jewelry, sweatshirts, DVDs, and books, for which they may get a bit of a take after paying the vendors. Just as in a church congregation, local Tea Parties take collections at the meeting to pay for minor expenses. A volunteer group of ladies usually sets up a refreshments counter—often with their own homemade baked goods and a donation box on the table. Meeting places are usually community halls or public libraries, or else gathering spaces connected to churches where one or more of the Tea Partiers is a member. As we noted in both Virginia and Arizona, Tea Parties that regularly meet in restaurants may use a separate room that the proprietor makes available on the understanding that many attendees will purchase meals and drinks.

To transport Tea Party people to regional or DC rallies, or to offer training to local organizers, well-funded outside groups such as Americans for Prosperity often step in. But local Tea Parties may also organize carpools or collect donations to charter their own buses or bring in a top-quality speaker. Meeting costs are usually covered by modest group efforts. And individual members often pay their own way to drive to lobbying days, protests, and meetings of governing bodies they are monitoring. The *Washington Post* survey of local Tea Parties found that most groups had only small treasuries on hand. This fits with what things looked like on the ground in the groups we visited in New England, Virginia, and Arizona.

Notably, some local Tea Parties have evolved toward establishing a regular system of membership dues, precisely in order to ensure predictable, if modest, resources under direct local control. Tea Parties in Virginia, including the Charlottesville group, instituted dues during 2011. This is a significant step toward a voluntary mode of membership-based financing that was typical in classic civic America before the era of grants from national foundations and wealthy donors. Today, civic organizers often suppose that it is "easier" on members if funding comes from outside sources. But, actually, citizen control of civic and political groups becomes stronger when members themselves finance their group's core functions—and that kind of financing is most effective when it comes through regular dues rather than occasional appeals. Carole Thorpe in Charlottesville realized the advantages that dues would bring, and made exactly this kind of case to her fellow Tea Partiers.

Are Tea Partiers Organizing States, Too?

In classic U.S. civic life, between early national times and the middle of the twentieth century, local chapters in voluntary associations were usually parts of state-level federations—and national federations, too—in which elected leaders ran conventions and orchestrated shared projects and deliberations. The American Legion, for example, once had thousands of local posts, each of which regularly sent leaders and delegates to state and national conventions; and the same was true of dozens of other political, civic, religious, fraternal, veterans', and women's voluntary membership federations that flourished in America through the mid-twentieth century. In fact, the normal pattern of growth for voluntarily organized federations in the United States involved the very early spread of federations across dozens of states. State-level organizations tended to be founded as soon as there were six to ten local lodges or clubs or posts in a given state and, once instituted, the state federation facilitated the further establishment of many more local membership units.[23] Local lodges or clubs or posts flourished within the framework of representatively governed state organizations, themselves linked to national organizations with elected volunteer leaders. State and national organizations received a small fraction of the dues regularly collected from local members. That was the formula for successful voluntary associations through most of American history.

Overall, the Tea Party does not manifest this classic pattern of federated activity, in which local groups elect higher-level leaders. As we are about to see, national organizers involved in the Tea Party are not elected or accountable; these groups are managed and funded from above. But in some states, local Tea Parties have found ways to link themselves together in coordinating arrangements. And in Virginia, the complexity of organization took a significant upward step in September 2009, when the Virginia Tea Party Patriots Federation was founded. Along with a few collaborators, Jamie Radtke, a Richmond area activist, searched local newspapers across the state to ferret out the leaders of the roughly thirty local Tea Parties that existed at the time.[24] Each local group was invited to send delegates to the gathering at which the Virginia Tea Party Patriots Federation was founded. State-level officers were elected and rules put in place to further a modicum of representative governance.

The Virginia Tea Party Patriots Federation orchestrates conference calls, now held every Tuesday night, to allow local Tea Party leaders to share ideas. It runs "lobbying days" in Richmond, convenes quarterly summits of local leaders, and maintains a professionally designed website.[25] The Virginia Federation even held its own convention in the fall of 2010. Sponsored by some big names in conservative politics, including the Heritage Foundation, Americans for Prosperity, and several Libertarian groups, the Federation convention brought thousands of Tea Partiers to the state capitol for training and seminars, and also managed to draw big-name speakers, including political analyst Dick Morris, Representative Ron Paul, former Senator Rick Santorum, and even former CNN anchor Lou Dobbs.[26]

When Virginia Tea Party Chairwoman Jamie Radtke decided to run for the GOP Senate nomination in Virginia, she stepped down as Federation Chair, and Mark Lloyd of Lynchburg was elected for 2011.[27] At the start of his term, about forty local Tea Parties were formally part of the Federation. In its maturity, the Virginia Federation is experiencing some internal tensions, including disenchantment in some local groups as state leaders move toward endorsing GOP candidates and speaking for all Virginia Tea Parties. Local leaders bristle at any loss of control. Nevertheless, Virginia stands out in the Tea Party for its relatively well-articulated local and state organization generated primarily by Virginians themselves.

Tea Partiers in other states may be trying to learn from and imitate the Virginia example. We have noted increasing state coordination starting to take shape elsewhere. The Michigan Tea Party Alliance, for instance, has a dues structure and explicit rules for member and affiliated local Tea Parties.[28] Encouraged by Tea Party Patriots, a regional alliance seems to be taking shape in northern California.[29] State-level organizers in Minnesota are encouraging coordinated efforts including lobbying the legislature. In most states, grassroots organization remains largely local or loosely coordinated across metropolitan areas. In Arizona, a dozen or so local Tea Parties cooperate through the citywide Greater Phoenix Tea Party Patriots, which acts as an information broker, sending out daily alerts about events around the sprawling city. Metropolitan coordination of this sort occurs in many states, but it is not the equivalent of a true state federation with elected leaders.

Grassroots Tea Partiers see both advantages and disadvantages from organization above the local level. On the positive side, we were told that joining the Virginia Federation was a source of pride and power for the Peninsula Patriots. Especially in smaller and rural places, one Tea Party member told us, involvement in the Federation helps people know they are part of "something bigger than your local community." But if many local Tea Partiers enjoy taking part in conference calls and conventions along with Patriots from other groups, others are wary. Local leaders may resent outside direction, or fret if higher-level leaders try to use their Tea Party's name for endeavors not approved by the flock. One Virginia leader told us that his group was contemplating withdrawal from the state federation to conserve time and protect local autonomy. And we heard hints of wariness elsewhere, too. Speaking about the array of local, citywide, and state Tea Party entities in Arizona, Larry Fisher expressed ambivalence: "We're still not sure if that makes sense . . . I'm not sure that a grassroots organization needs that much organization."

Even when association-builders in the Tea Party operate authentically from within their states, they face an uphill climb to build organizational layers above localities. Local Tea Parties were mostly well-entrenched before state-level organizers came along. Like the New Leftists of the 1960s, moreover, Tea Party participants are intensely suspicious of higher authority. They are quick to notice if other Tea Partiers seem to be using grassroots energy for their own aggrandizement or enrichment—not just at the national level, but in their own state or region. Anxious to guard local autonomy, Tea Party people can be influenced in many ways, as we are about to see, but they cannot easily be corralled into higher-level formal arrangements.

ROVING BILLIONAIRES AND NATIONAL IMPRESARIOS

The dramatic appearance and sudden spread of the Tea Party did more than energize local conservatives; it also lifted the spirits of national elites and organizations at the rightward edges of the GOP. New effervescence at the grass roots was electrifying for conservative big-money funders, political consultants, and organizations advocating free-market policy ideas.

Fresh opportunities suddenly beckoned. Organizations that lacked much of a presence in states and localities could reach out to Tea Partiers across the country, offer them support, and build contact lists for future efforts. Political action committees could use the Tea Party label to attract cash infusions and support favored GOP candidates. Advocacy organizations pushing ultra-free-market nostrums could use tableaus of grassroots Tea Partiers to give the impression that their agendas enjoy mass support. Ultra-conservatives became more optimistic about attacking the Obama presidency and reshaping the GOP.

A scramble for the head and heart of the Republican Party is an important part of the story for national conservative organizations competing to stoke and use Tea Party activism. From February 2009 on, right-wing organizations and elites scrambled to orchestrate activism where possible, and also tried to leverage the loyalties, votes, and checkbooks of Tea Partiers and their sympathizers. But that was not all. Ultra-conservative elites also wanted to prod and redirect the Republican Party.

Not Your Father's Conservatives

Scholars such as Jacob Hacker and Paul Pierson—authors of the astute books *Off Center* and *Winner-Take-All-Politics*—have made a powerful case that both major U.S. political parties, and especially the Republican Party, cater to corporate pressures and enact policies that increase inequalities of income and wealth.[30] In the pivotal decade of the 1970s, U.S. business interests created powerful new alliances and associations and learned to cooperate across industries to channel money and ideas in politics— both at election time and during months of governmental decision-making between elections. Over the past few decades, attentive and well-resourced business lobbying organizations gained enormous influence over what issues came up for debate, and they were able to block or insert critical provisions in legislation making its way through Congress and in rules taking shape within administrative agencies. In the face of this powerful lobbying force, GOP officeholders and candidates have increasingly refused to consider raising taxes, even in the sort of budgetary circumstances that prompted President Ronald Reagan to accept tax increases along with spending cuts to move toward budgetary balance.

Are today's right-wing organizations participating in the Tea Party the same as those that have been central to the GOP as it has drifted ever rightward in recent decades? In many cases, yes—which may explain why liberal muckrakers tend simply to label pro–Tea Party elites "pro-business," and leave it at that. But this characterization may not be precise enough to get at the particular sorts of wealthy kingmakers and ultra-right-wing organizations involved in the Tea Party phenomenon. They are more extreme, compared to those who counted as "mainstream" in pro-business GOP circles just a few years ago.

Both recent GOP presidents named George Bush, father and son, certainly privileged organized business interests. The same is true of Mitch McConnell, the GOP Senate leader, and John Boehner of Ohio, who served as House Minority leader before he became the GOP Speaker of the House in January 2011. Hardly insurgents, McConnell and Boehner are business-oriented good-old-boys, dull "establishment" Republicans in every way. In policy terms, they are very conservative, as were both Bushes and the 2008 GOP presidential candidate, John McCain. All of these post-1990 establishment Republicans want to gut business regulations and steadily lower taxes on corporations and high-income Americans. But at the same time, these very conservative, business-friendly Republicans believe in *some* level of responsible government in the United States. They have been wary about seeking the elimination of major entitlement programs such as Medicare or Social Security, or huge reductions in residual protections for the poor. Prior to 2011, they repeatedly supported raising the federal debt ceiling to allow the U.S. government to meet fiscal obligations. Until recently— indeed as recently as the McCain campaign in 2008—leading GOPers also espoused some interest in cap-and-trade legislation to deal with environmental threats in a market-based way; argued for health care regulations and subsidies that might extend coverage to some of the uninsured; and supported immigration reforms amounting to more than border fortifications and deportations. Establishment Republicans also believed in striking compromises to get legislation passed, and the pragmatic GOP strategists who ran their election campaigns were willing to strike an appearance of moderation. Many organized business lobbies also play complex games, supporting both Republicans and pro-corporate Democrats, and pushing for resolution of knotty issues to keep government and the economy going.

But the GOP establishment of a few years ago now looks hopelessly passé, lapped by hard-liners further to the nether-right. All along, there have been highly ideological right-wing billionaires who just do not see things the same way as regular establishment Republicans. These hard-liners are the ones seizing the Tea Party moment, pushing aside and cowing the GOP insiders. Here the context is important: wealth and income have become so amazingly unequal in the United States that a few hundred billionaire families have the means to push their own worldview in civic and political affairs.[31] The top 1% of Americans own more than a third of America's wealth, a percentage that has increased steadily since the 1970s and appears to have grown even despite the 2008 financial crisis.[32] That wealth has accrued disproportionately to the very richest of those very rich people. Especially when it comes to setting agendas for public discussion and policy debates—encouraging entire convoys of organizations or officeholders to move in one direction or another—the super-duper wealthy in America today can make quite a difference.

At the very highest levels of wealth and disposable income, resources are so stupendous that the personal outlooks, even quirks, of the super-rich matter. Billionaire philanthropists Bill and Melinda Gates are one example. Their charitable organization has done tremendous good in, for instance, combating AIDS. But the effect of their immense wealth has been to redirect vast swathes of public health policy and educational reform efforts, sometimes with unintended consequences.[33] No one elected them; they are not democratically accountable. But the Gates family is not alone in its outsize influence on policy. On the far right of the ideological and policy spectrum lurk politically active super-rich families and associated institutions named Coors, Scaife, Olin and, above all, Koch.[34]

With wealth amassed primarily in the petrochemical industry, the brothers Koch, David and Charles, add up to one of the richest multibillionaire families in America, indeed in the world.[35] They also happen to be the sons of Fred Koch, a founding member of the John Birch Society, "known for its highly skeptical view of governance and for spreading fears of a Communist takeover"—the same sort of views the Koch sons are pushing today.[36] The Koch brothers are very active in politics as well as philanthropy, willing to throw their money around to create and support policy think tanks, foundations, and university programs; to fight political enemies in the media; to support massive and sustained lobbying efforts; and to further the careers of the most extreme right-wingers that can win elections.[37]

As for *why* they are involved in politics, the Koch brothers do not so much believe in limited government as in almost no government at all: vanishing taxes on the very rich; privatization of Social Security and Medicare; defunding of all but the most residual social programs; and evisceration of regulation of industrial firms, especially in the sectors where they make their fortune.[38] In the pre–Tea Party era, the Koch brothers were not as central as they wanted to be in GOP decision-making. The policy organizations they support—such as the ultra-libertarian Cato Institute and the advocacy group Americans for Prosperity—did not have, in their view, sufficient sway in shaping public debates and legislation.

After the 2008 election, the Koch brothers and their organizational allies were determined to do all they could to limit, humiliate, and defeat Barack Obama and other Democrats in the U.S. Congress and the states, majority democracy be damned. Even after President Obama ran the successful operation to kill Osama Bin Laden, David Koch was quoted belittling the president and renewing the outlandish claim that Obama is a "socialist."[39] Blocking Obama's legislative agenda and setting up his defeat in 2012 has clearly been goal number one for the Koch coterie.[40] But the Koch brothers and their allies also want to remake the GOP, ensuring that the Republican Party does not tack back toward the middle in rhetoric or policy-making. The Koch brothers are fighting not only against Democrats, but against other GOP powerbrokers like Karl Rove and Ed Gillespie, who have their own fundraising organizations to promote their preferred brand of Republicanism. As a *Politico* article put it, Charles and David Koch aim to "reorient the conservative political apparatus around free-market, small government principles and candidates, and away from the electability-over-principles approach they see Rove and Gillespie as embodying."[41]

The Tea Party eruption in early 2009 was just what the doctor ordered for far-right ideological billionaires like the Kochs, and others of their ideological ilk roving just beyond the edge of the GOP establishment. Suddenly, prospects were better for ultra-free-market funders and affiliated idea-pushers to try to link up with grassroots Tea Partiers—and in due course to speak in their name. In fact, as we are about to see, some of the key national organizations that leapt into the fray very early, and have stayed the course most effectively, have direct or indirect ties to the Koch brothers. But not only to them, because the Kochs are indicative of a larger coterie of wealthy actors trying for some time to tug the GOP ever further toward the right.

FreedomWorks and Americans for Prosperity
Jump into the Fray

Just a day after the Santelli rant, the national advocacy organization Freedom-Works dispatched staffers and posted website tips on organizing and locating Tea Party rallies. Soon the organization's President Matt Kibbe and its Chairman Dick Armey teamed up to write a book they dubbed a "manifesto" for the Tea Party movement.[42] Clearly FreedomWorks was delighted when Tea Party protests started, and did all it could to help conservatives connect with them. But FreedomWorks was hardly some brand-new insurgent entity. Indeed, the group had been promoting the "Tea Party" idea for years.

The DC-headquartered organization by the name FreedomWorks commenced in 2004 as a professionally staffed advocacy organization devoted to training citizens and politicians at both the state and national levels on behalf of an agenda that includes reducing taxes and removing regulations on business, privatizing Social Security and reducing social-welfare programs, and furthering tort reform and school vouchers. These are key anti-government goals on the ideological right. The organization's roots went back even further than 2004—to the Koch-supported and directed think tank, Citizens for a Sound Economy, which operated from 1977 until a breakup in 2003. That breakup gave rise, in turn, to both FreedomWorks and another policy-advocacy group called Americans for Prosperity. During its lifetime, the mother ship Citizens for a Sound Economy (CSE) received at least $13 million in funding from the Koch family, along with major donations from other right-wing conservatives.[43] After the CSE breakup, Americans for Prosperity continued to enjoy direct funding and leadership through Koch Industries and the Koch brothers.[44] FreedomWorks switched its funding to other industry sources and staffed up with former lobbyists from corporate sectors interested in deregulation.[45] Both DC-based organizations continued to push the same overall anti-government agenda, and the Tea Party moment has been propitious for both organizations.

With the opening provided by the Santelli rant, FreedomWorks built activist connections. It helped to orchestrate the angry town hall protests against health reform in August 2009, co-sponsored Tea Party rallies, and gained new leverage in 2010 with GOPers elected with its endorsement or the support of other Tea Party–identified groups. FreedomWorks has, however, remained largely a national operation with only a handful of state-level staffers, while the other CSE offspring, Americans for Prosperity, appears to have gained even more ground during the Tea Party effervescence.

Riding the Tea Party wave, the AFP ballooned its contact lists from about 270,000 in 2008 to 1.5 million in 2011, while also expanding its network of coordinators to reach 32 states.[46] AFP staffers and volunteer activists often appear at Tea Party rallies, and the organization regularly pays to transport protestors across the country and even to international events.[47] AFP is also building extensive state networks. In Arizona, for example, Tom Jenney, leader of the Arizona Federation of Taxpayers, incorporated his organization as AFP's Arizona chapter. Jenney's strong local connections make him quite effective in connecting with and mobilizing local Tea Parties in Arizona. Similarly, in Wisconsin, state-level AFP staffers and adherents were involved in the rallies mounted in early 2011 to support GOP Governor Scott Walker during his efforts to push through state legislation disabling public sector labor unions.[48] As this suggests, ideological right-wing billionaires and their advocacy organizations not only want to push their own ideas and values; they want to break the organizational capacities of their political opponents. From their perspective, it is great to be able to turn out local Tea Partiers to counter pro-union demonstrators wherever such battles are afoot.

Using the Tea Party as backdrop, Americans for Prosperity is trying to reshape public discussions and attract widespread conservative support for ultra-free-market ideas about slashing taxes and business regulation and radically restructuring social expenditure programs. Speakers, videos, and articles are offered to Tea Party groups and sympathizers, as they have been provided to grassroots conservatives for many years. Back in 2008, the Wisconsin branch of Americans for Prosperity gave its "Defender of the American Dream" Award to GOP Representative Paul Ryan of Wisconsin after he developed a budget "RoadMap" that foreshadowed the radical budget he presented (and that the GOP House supported) in early 2011.[49] The Ryan budget entails huge new tax cuts for the rich; major reductions in Medicaid, college aid, and other programs for lower and lower-middle-income Americans; and the phasing out of Medicare's guaranteed health coverage for the elderly after 2021. The aim is to realize radical policy goals pushed by the Cato Institute and other Koch-funded organizations since the late 1970s.[50] Starting in the late spring of 2011, all the major national advocacy groups floating around the Tea Party pushed the Ryan budget and encouraged grassroots participants and public sympathizers to get behind it.

GOP Politicos Jump on the Tea Party Bandwagon

Just as FreedomWorks and Americans for Prosperity found in the Tea Party eruption fresh openings for pushing ideas and seeding activism, GOP-linked political action committees quickly found greener pastures, too. Political action committees (PACs) allow their sponsors to raise money and dispatch it to favored electoral candidates. It is also perfectly possible for a PAC, at the same time, to encourage assisted candidates to buy campaign services from businesses linked to the PAC itself. Money can be raised and deployed to do double duty—enhancing the PAC directors' political clout and buoying their business bottom line. Not surprisingly, Tea Party effervescence has given rise to many PACs, including entities set up in the states to let Tea Party leaders such as Jerry DeLemus in New Hampshire collect checks and wield influence.[51] We would need another book to track all of the organizations expanded or newly launched to capitalize on the Tea Party.[52] But perhaps the most visible example has been a PAC launched in the summer of 2009 called the "Tea Party Express."

Again, once we look closely, we find not a new venture run by true insurgents, but instead, a newly labeled arm of a Republican PAC called "Our Country Deserves Better," based in Sacramento, California, and linked to the GOP political consulting and public relations firm of Russo, Marsh, and Rogers. The key figure is Sal Russo, who has worked to elect Republicans all the way back to Ronald Reagan.[53] During the 2008 presidential campaign, Russo's Our Country PAC achieved some notoriety for a series of anti-Obama campaign commercials deemed misleading by the nonpartisan fact-checkers at the Annenberg Public Policy Center.[54] One ad featured actors pretending to be various foreign leaders, including Iran's Mahmoud Ahmadinejad, North Korea's Kim Jong-il, and Cuba's Fidel Castro, laughing together about Obama's willingness to meet without preconditions. The ad concluded "Barack Obama: No Match for America's

Enemies." Other anti-Obama ads trumpeted the controversial views of Obama's one-time pastor, Reverend Jeremiah Wright, and disseminated the rumor that President Obama refuses to put his hand over his heart during the Pledge of Allegiance. Obama won election anyway, leaving Russo and friends in search of new openings. When the new Tea Party label gained fashion on the right, Russo teamed up with Howard Kaloogian, a conservative GOP state lawmaker, and Mark Williams, a conservative radio talk show host, to relabel part of their PAC's activities the "Tea Party Express."

By late 2009 and into 2010, dozens of GOP office-seekers were thrilled to link their fortunes to the new effervescence. This allowed Tea Party Express (TPE) to raise and spend over $2.7 million on candidates across the country, including several of the most prominent Tea Party candidates.[55] To the tune of hundreds of thousands of dollars, TPE supported Scott Brown in his successful and pivotal January 2010 bid to win the Massachusetts Senate seat previously held by the late Senator Ted Kennedy. The Massachusetts effort notched an early scalp, signaling heft for TPE and establishing it as an electoral difference-maker. Thereafter, TPE went on to help fund Sharron Angle's campaign to unseat Senate Majority Leader Harry Reid, and also contributed to the campaigns of Tea Party–oriented Republicans who mounted primary challenges against moderate GOP incumbents. Important instances have included Christine O'Donnell's 2010 primary campaign against Mike Castle in Delaware; Joe Miller's primary campaign against Lisa Murkowski in Alaska; and primary challenges in the 2012 cycle by Tea Party candidates trying to displace Indiana Senator Richard Lugar and Maine Senator Olympia Snowe.[56] These campaigns have been good business for TPE's founders; when TPE funds Tea Party candidates, it also promotes and purchases campaign services from Russo, Marsh, and Rogers.[57]

Beyond electoral activities, Tea Party Express has sponsored bus tours that roam the country to synchronize with other Tea Party events and whip up grassroots enthusiasm among conservative voters. The first TPE bus tour coincided with the 2009 August recess, when the health care reform debate reached a fever pitch and dozens of lawmakers faced hostile audiences at local town halls. Tours continued over the next year and a half, with locations chosen to bolster other Tea Party efforts to put pressure on embattled moderate or liberal legislators in tight electoral races. One event that received a great deal of media coverage was the 2010 tour stop held in Senate Majority Leader Harry Reid's hometown of Searchlight, Nevada. The tiny town was flooded by thousands of Tea Party faithful—an event described as "Woodstock minus the LSD" by one attendee.[58] Apart from the entertainment they provide at rallies, TPE does not have meaningful ties to local activists, and there have been significant tensions between TPE and other national organizations involved in the Tea Party.[59]

An Umbrella Organization Reaches Out to the Grassroots

Last but not least in this roundup of key national players is the Tea Party Patriots (TPP), whose website was up and running within days of the original Santelli rant. Co-founders and key players in Tea Party Patriots are Jenny Beth Martin, previously employed as a GOP consultant and the former head of a Tea Party group in Georgia, and Mark Meckler, a businessman from California who had worked on conservative causes and helped organize a Tea Party in Sacramento.[60] Dubbing itself the "official grassroots American movement," TPP has developed the strongest ties to grassroots activists.

TPP was originally supported by FreedomWorks, which has launched other nominally grassroots efforts in the past.[61] Email exchanges in 2009 indicate that FreedomWorks had a lot of say about TPP activities, at least in the early months.[62] TPP also lines up in lockstep with FreedomWorks on certain issues where grassroots activists seem to have no say or involvement. In the spring of 2011, for example, the Tea Party Patriots' homepage bore a lengthy statement of opposition to net neutrality, a policy also opposed by FreedomWorks and the telecommunications industry.[63] But this issue was literally never raised in any of our Tea Party meetings or interviews. The prominent TPP stance on net neutrality is not attributable to grassroots mobilization.

Despite their ties to FreedomWorks, Tea Party Patriots presents itself as a grassroots-run umbrella group. From the start of activism in 2009, TPP steadily increased its connections to local groups and individual grassroots adherents. As of May 2011, the leaders of Tea Party Patriots claim that more than 1000 local Tea Parties are part of their flock, a number that almost certainly overstates their reach.[64] About 150 Tea Party sites in our database are clearly tied to Tea Party Patriots, using TPP branding or logos. Another 300 refer to Tea Party Patriots on their websites.

Since early 2010, Tea Party Patriots has orchestrated weekly conference-call webinars that attract the participation of as many as several hundred local Tea Party leaders in any given week.[65] Local leaders discuss problems, try to define shared issue priorities, and swap ideas about programming for regular local meetings. In early 2011, Tea Party Patriots held its first national summit, a three-day event in Phoenix, Arizona, that brought together Tea Party participants from across the country to share information and organizing strategies.[66] In addition, leaders of the Tea Party Patriots have tried to get local organizers to turn over their local contact lists to the national organization in order to increase their own nationwide capacity to orchestrate campaigns and to raise funds from Tea Party participants.[67]

Organizationally, TPP has built a staff of modest size, with various "coordinators" in different regions.[68] Finances for the organization have always been murky, and TPP evades public reporting. In September 2010, the TPP coordinators announced receipt of a $1 million anonymous donation. Local Tea Parties were invited to apply for grants to improve websites, mount educational or training efforts, and pursue other nonelectoral projects of local choosing.[69] But it is unclear how much funding ever made it to local organizers; a number of grassroots supporters, including some state coordinators who had previously been heavily involved with TPP, have distanced themselves from the organization and criticized its financial practices.[70] Like other national Tea Party–linked organizations, TPP appears to have channeled considerable sums to long-standing GOP consulting organizations.[71]

The legal status of Tea Party Patriots precludes endorsements of particular candidates in elections. Coordinators proclaim that endorsements are best left to local and state Tea Party groups, if done at all. This stance allows TPP to stay out of local and state fights over the relative conservative purity of different GOP candidates; it also protects TPP when particular candidates lose elections. Equally strategically ambiguous are TPP stands on specific parts of the federal budget. Tea Party Patriots pushes the notion of immediate, huge budget cuts, but when asked about particulars, TPP leaders mouth generalities or simply repeat the group's motto, "Fiscal Responsibility, Constitutionally Limited Government and Free Markets" (a motto nearly identical to that of FreedomWorks). Questioned about tax and health care measures at a forum at the Harvard Kennedy School of Government in April 2011, TPP Coordinator Jenny Beth Martin proclaimed that there was no need to discuss the actual content of legislation because good proposals are always to be found at think tanks such as the Cato Institute or the Heritage Foundation. GOP Congressional representatives can just adopt those, she said.

Martin's answer confirms that TPP is in the business of leveraging popular support for predetermined far-right policy proposals. Her evasiveness also underscores how assiduously national groups endeavor to keep "Tea Party" aims vague and general. "Eliminating the deficit" sounds fine to regular citizens, but specifics such as the abolition of Medicare are not popular at the grass roots, even with Tea Party people. In Congressional budget battles, Tea Party Patriots uses its national website to urge local groups to pressure GOP representatives against accepting tax increases or agreeing to lift the national debt limit, but TPP never lists specific programs to go on the chopping block. Free-market organizations supported by billionaires find it easy to urge grassroots people and GOP officials to take rigid stands. After all, these groups and their wealthy backers are not democratically accountable. Nor are they responsible for actually governing.

NATIONAL AND LOCAL IN THE TEA PARTY—A MUTUAL LEVERAGE STORY

Wednesday, April 14, 2010, was sunny and cool in eastern Massachusetts, a perfect day for a Tea Party rally. Surrounded by a ring of media vans, a crowd of a few thousand assembled on the Boston Common. The Greater Boston Tea Party had originally planned its annual Tax Day protest for April 15, but had been contacted by Tea Party Express and convinced to hold its rally a day earlier to coincide with the arrival of a multistate bus tour and a speech by Sarah Palin. The short notice ruffled some feathers in New England, but the grass roots quickly adapted. Media coverage would be assured for such a well-funded, splashy event, so local Tea Partiers provided volunteers, applauded road show speakers, and set up a booth to enroll new members.

At 7 P.M. on Tuesday, November 30, 2010, members of the Buffalo County Tea Party gathered in the Sunroom at the Northridge Retirement Community in Kearney, Nebraska, to hear a talk about legislative issues at stake in the lame duck session of Congress—the last session with Democrats in control of the House before the much-anticipated arrival of the new GOP majority in 2011. The speaker was Jeremy Jensen, a former Tea Party leader who had moved on to work as Field Director for the Americans for Prosperity of Nebraska.[72] This state branch of the national advocacy organization bills itself as "on the front line in the fight against big government" and sends regular "Action Alerts" to tens of thousands of Nebraskans to inspire them to push local, state, and federal representatives in desired directions.[73]

In the fall of 2010, the co-organizers of a local Tea Party in Maine posted an encouraging announcement on their group's blog: "Sue and Jane are happy to announce that York County Constitutionalists have received a grant from Tea Party Patriots as a result of a $1,000,000 anonymous donation" to that organization. "We will be using the grant to further our outreach and educational efforts." Months later, only eighteen people attended the April 2011 meeting of the York Constitutionalists, so the visiting speaker from New Hampshire could hardly compliment his Maine neighbors on a high turnout. But he did make a point of praising their snazzy new website and Facebook page, recently up and running with support from the grant.

At the end of a March 2011 meeting, the Surprise Tea Party in Arizona discussed various Tea Party sites and came to the consensus that everyone at the meeting should join the Tea Party Patriots mailing list. Around the same time, members of the Jefferson Area Tea Party Patriots in Charlottesville, Virginia, recommitted themselves to local autonomy. A new constitution, bylaws, and yearly membership dues would ensure that all local members have "skin in the game," explained group chair, Carole Thorpe. Dues of about $20 a year (with discounts for couples and students) will allow the group to continue its long-standing refusal to take funds or apply for grants from outsiders. Early on, Carole remembers, the Jefferson Area Tea Party was "a line" on the TPP website. But the relationship never deepened, and she does not participate in TPP conference calls or webinars.

Much ink and many keystrokes have been spent on issues of "control" in the Tea Party. Are national, billionaire-backed organizations controlling the Tea Party, or are grassroots folks in charge? These are the wrong questions to ask about a field of loosely interconnected organizations. Everyone is trying to *leverage* something they want from others in the network. The fruitful questions are: What do local Tea Partiers want from the national advocates and impresarios? What do the national organizations hope to get from various sorts of ties to grassroots groups or protesters? What tensions flare up as some actors step on the toes or offend the sensibilities of others? And are relationships shifting over time?

Loose Ties of Mutual Convenience

Consider, for example, relationships between local Tea Parties and the national political action committee called Tea Party Express (TPE)—the California-based group responsible for a media-friendly bus tour and the funding of many Tea Party candidates. Unquestionably, public rallies that gain lots of publicity can be a win-win for all concerned—including the Tea Party participants who attend, the local groups that pitch in, and of course the national organizations that help to fund and sponsor the rally. Any local irritations of scheduling and coordination, as we saw in one of the opening vignettes for this section, can usually be soothed by publicity and the potential for new members in the bargain. Tea Party Express, in turn, took control of the media imagery and content in the Boston protest, with a convenient backdrop of local, grassroots volunteers.

The relationship between big national funders and small grassroots groups appears to be one of mutual convenience, with little shared knowledge or joint investment, particularly when it comes to Tea Party Express. Quite a few of the Tea Partiers we interviewed in different places had attended events involving Tea Party Express, but no one at the grass roots reported feeling closely tied to that organization. Several people in Phoenix said they had driven north to Searchlight, Nevada, for the bus-tour rally there. But speaker Sarah Palin received mixed reviews in Arizona and Virginia, as well as in Massachusetts. The president of the Greater Boston Tea Party dismissed TPE as a group of "entertainers," and other Tea Party activists have complained that Tea Party Express is not grassroots.[74]

From the perspective of Tea Party Express, the lack of much grassroots interest and close attention may be a good thing. Grassroots supporters provide a colorful popular backdrop for TPE to attract media attention and collect more contributions to spend on candidates and affiliated business operations—without any pesky accountability to local leaders. And TPE leaders are surely content that certain aspects of their work have remained off the radar of most Tea Party activists. After a series of offensive remarks about Islam, TPE spokesman Mark Williams was eventually cashiered for writing a blog post suggesting that black people would prefer to be re-enslaved rather than have to do work.[75] Though the incident was widely covered at the time by the mainstream media, Tea Partiers we spoke to were unfamiliar with it, and thus it did not affect their views of TPE, to the degree they had any.[76] For TPE, the avoidance of close grassroots ties, and the scrutiny that might accompany such ties, may be a wise strategic choice.

Virtually all of the national organizations we have discussed have tried to link local Tea Party people with their public events.[77] The dynamics are usually the same. The local Tea Party people get added publicity when the event is nearby; Tea Parties further afield may get help paying for transportation if they are willing to take outside money. Not all groups are willing to use buses funded by FreedomWorks or Americans for Prosperity or any other outside organization. The Charlottesville Jefferson Area Tea Party took up subscriptions to charter buses of its own; and we also heard regularly about local groups putting together volunteer car-pools. But many Tea Parties take advantage of offers of resources that seem free of strings, and in return sponsoring organizations earn a measure of good will from the grassroots folks, and perhaps a few more names for their email lists.

Idea Pushers and Takers

Rallies and bus tours make for mutual back-scratching, but they do not necessarily foster deep relationships between grassroots people and the national organizations fishing in Tea Party waters. What about other kinds of relationships? Particularly fascinating to us are the ties forged to local Tea Parties by national and state-level advocacy groups pushing hard-right values and policy ideas. How do groups like Americans for Prosperity, or gun rights groups, or libertarian organizations form useful relationships with local Tea Partiers? Such professional idea-pushers want to disseminate everything from worldviews to very specific legislative plans—plans that realize free-market goals, or undo progressive policies, or defund rival groups, such as public sector unions, connected to the Democratic Party. But how do right-wing advocacy organizations manage to get local Tea Party people to listen to what are often abstruse—or implausible—ideas?

Some of the ideas of these free-market advocacy groups circulate through blog networks and get forwarded through email chains. Many Tea Party members we met are avid email forwarders, sending on to a long list of acquaintances everything from budget reports to political jokes, often several messages per day. Over time, the most successful ideas bubble to the surface through the right-wing blogosphere and into the mainstream media—a dynamic we will discuss in detail in Chapter 4. In addition, many local Tea Parties have their own well-designed websites with notices about webinars, reports, and videos disseminated by this or that right-wing advocacy group.

Indeed, by the middle of 2011, many of the almost 1000 local Tea Parties whose websites we examined in our national survey included references or links to national advocacy organizations. We define a reference broadly: some are simply links in a long list of trusted information sources, while others are reports, articles, or calls to action reposted in their entirety. Though the results are only a snapshot of Tea Party activity in the spring and early summer of 2011, they are nonetheless quite illuminating. The libertarian Cato Institute was far less popular than the more generally conservative Heritage Foundation, appearing on only 126 sites, compared to Heritage's 345. Americans for Prosperity and FreedomWorks were cited relatively equally, with FreedomWorks receiving 267 mentions and Americans for Prosperity 206. As we've already seen, Tea Party Patriots far outstrips the competition in terms of its connections to actual local Tea Parties. TPP is mentioned on 498 sites, almost half the total set of Tea Party groups we found, and almost 150 of those sites have adopted Tea Party Patriots' online branding or logos.[78]

But professionally run advocacy groups also reach Tea Parties directly. Many of them offer training sessions for grassroots Tea Party organizers and members, who may learn about policy ideas as well as organizing strategies. Several Tea Party members we spoke to in Massachusetts had taken part in workshops organized by American Majority, a conservative activist-training group founded by Republican insiders, including a former speechwriter for President George W. Bush and the former political director of the California Republican Party. Along with discussions of the Constitution, their workshops cover the typical local organizing bases, including primers on government structure, advice on "the most effective ways to contact elected officials," and guidance on using new media like Twitter. Americans for Prosperity and Tea Party Patriots have provided similar training opportunities to other Tea Party groups we spoke to.

Another dynamic to keep an eye on is the desire of local and state Tea Party groups for a constant flow of programming. Let's say you are a local Tea Party organizer interested in finding something interesting to do for each monthly meeting, and you do not have a lot of money to spend. Where to turn? Local organizers explained to us that many of their members (such as the older men and women who attend as couples) want to watch a show or hear a speaker each month. For an attractive lecture, they may show up and even put some money in the collection box. But they may be less interested if a group discussion is the only thing scheduled, or if they think the main purpose is to ask them to volunteer for tasks. Local organizers, if they are any good, want to have group discussions and inspire real participation, but they may need to make membership activities just *part* of a meeting, with an entertaining speaker or visual presentation scheduled for the rest of the event. A local Tea Party also needs to advertise programs that may attract drop-ins—to keep adding new recruits as some earlier participants drop out. After the 2010 election, one local leader explained, some people did pull back, "patting themselves on the back" for displacing Democrats from office. But others kept arriving to check out the group, enabling this local Tea Party to sustain membership and energy. Given the need to come up with attractive events months after month on a low budget, national and state organizations that offer speakers are a godsend for local leaders. In fact, a lot of ultra-conservative advocacy organizations are trying to place their speakers, so local Tea Party programmers can pick and choose. They can go with issues that seem hot in their region and engage speakers who have earned a good reputation as they make their way from one local Tea Party to the next.

These outside speakers, we think, are one way for politically consequential ideas—including some very strange ones not grounded in facts—to circulate among local Tea Parties. They are also how ideological organizations like Americans for Prosperity form closer links with local citizens—as in the opening vignette about Nebraska, where the Buffalo County group meeting in Kearney heard from a state-level organizer for Americans for Prosperity. During our visit to Arizona, that state's coordinator for Americans for Prosperity was also making the rounds, and so were speakers from the Second Amendment Sisters, a pro-gun group.

When we visited the Peninsula Patriots in Virginia in late January of 2011, the invited guest was Donna Holt, Executive Director of the Virginia Campaign for Liberty. For an audience of about sixty members, Holt presented an elaborate PowerPoint lecture connecting local sustainable planning efforts (bike paths, for example) to what she portrayed as a grandiose, decades-long, UN-hatched conspiracy to use environmentalism as a ruse for imposing a "globalist totalitarian dictatorship" on America. Conspiratorial visions of this sort may be too fantastical to survive broad public scrutiny, but they can percolate quietly in networks of local Tea Parties.[79] After listening to the Campaign for Liberty speaker, the Peninsula Patriots got a lot of takers for a subcommittee to focus on fighting sustainable development.[80] Other Virginia Tea Party groups scheduled events on the same topic in early 2011; and local groups worked together against sustainable development legislation in Richmond. The Campaign for Liberty obviously got its message out.

The need for a steady flow of programming allows national ideological organizations to provide a welcome service to grassroots Tea Parties, whose members offer a warm and largely unskeptical reception to ideas ranging from practical policies to conspiratorial visions. Often the ideas pushed by ideological elites are abstruse enough that local people will accept them uncritically. The conspiratorial talk given to the Peninsula Patriots by the Campaign for Liberty representative, like talks by other guest speakers we have heard at Tea Party meetings, provoked not a single criticism during the question-and-answer session. Instead, audience members appreciated the overarching sentiment of the presentation, which emphasized intrusive bureaucrats—a reality local people feel they understand from dealings with irritating business regulations or local zoning rules. By invoking strong feelings and providing easy-to-digest worldviews linked to specific policy goals, the national ideologues have much more impact than they likely would if they formally "controlled" local groups.

But what happens when Tea Partiers have direct, favorable personal experience of matters criticized by national ideologues? Or when grassroots Tea Partiers already have different or more mixed beliefs than those articulated by national advocates? In Chapter 2, for instance, we found that rank-and-file Tea Partiers have considerable affection for Social Security and Medicare, even as they pay lip service to extreme views about slashing federal spending. Grassroots Tea Partiers have a different take than the policy-makers at right-wing ideological think tanks, for whom Social Security and Medicare are anathema. National groups such as Freedom-Works and Americans for Prosperity have long been committed to privatizing these huge, popular U.S. social insurance programs, taking funds out of them so that taxes on business and the wealthy can be reduced. Right-wing ideologues also hope to boost for-profit businesses that manage savings for retirement. So what happens when Americans for Prosperity, FreedomWorks, and other ultra-free-market advocacy groups push these privatizing plans in the name of grassroots Tea Partiers, most of whom are either on Social Security and Medicare already, or expect to be soon? Will local Tea Partiers become skeptical of advocates claiming to speak for them—at least on matters where Tea Party people have concrete experience and views of their own?

To some degree, perhaps. The reason that Congressional Republicans backed away from Paul Ryan's Medicare voucher plan soon after the House GOP voted for it in April 2011 may have been a spreading realization in Washington DC that this plan was not playing well beyond the Beltway, even in Tea Party circles.[81] GOP leaders decided to soft-peddle the drive for privatization until the 2012 election. But no one should expect real fireworks between elite free-market advocates and local Tea Partiers. The national groups will keep their messages vague. They will continue to talk about "America going broke" and the "need to slash spending" and "cut taxes," without getting overly specific until just before they seize the chance—if one presents itself—to push through major restructurings of Medicare and Social Security. Until then, ideological advocates and GOP politicians working with them will try to fudge the truth on policy specifics and keep the focus on hatred of Obama and his allegedly "socialistic" plans. They will try to do this all the way until the critical 2012 election—when they hope to use grassroots fears and fervor to help push Obama out of the White House.

Local Tea Partiers will continue to consume ideas, speakers, and other kinds of programming from the advocacy groups, taking much of what they hear on faith. Even where Social Security and Medicare are concerned, Tea Party people may come around to ultra-free-market nostrums, if phase-out legislation includes a long timeline, so that older people today and tomorrow believe they will be held whole in federal programs, while big cuts are put in place for younger cohorts. National ideologues can make use of Tea Partiers' sense that younger Americans are not working hard enough, not "paying their dues." Generational tensions contribute to grassroots Tea Party activism, and the national ideological organizations and their DC allies may figure out how to exploit such divisions.

In the final analysis, the loose relationship between professional idea-pushers and local Tea Parties is mutually useful enough to enable advocates to set agendas and disseminate general arguments, without becoming any more answerable to local groups than Tea Party Express is accountable to the people who attend its bus-tour rallies. Free-market advocacy groups can provide programming to local Tea Parties and add tens of thousands of Tea Party members to online networks, without ever engaging in discussions or answering for the specifics of policies pushed in Washington DC and state capitols. Tea Partiers at the grass roots are not sufficiently questioning of free-market ideologues to raise tough questions. If an organization seems to be against Obama and liberals, Tea Partiers are trusting to the point of gullibility. Their outlook exemplifies that old adage in politics: the enemy of my enemy is my friend.

The Attempt to Weave Tighter Ties

Like FreedomWorks and Americans for Prosperity, the umbrella organization Tea Party Patriots reaches out very actively to local groups. From its founding in 2009, TPP adopted a folksy, volunteer pose on its national website. The national organization loudly proclaimed that it wasn't trying to control anything and allowed local Tea Parties to register themselves on the TPP website. In addition to helping manage national rallies and coordinating local groups on a weekly conference call, TPP offered some small grants to Tea Parties to enable them to upgrade their local websites and educational activities. No doubt, the applications enlarge TPP contact lists and allow for tighter links between national and local conservative organizations—and may have helped TPP raise funds from local groups.[82] Without seeming bureaucratic, TPP's activities facilitated grassroots organizing and encouraged communication about and among local and state-level Tea Party efforts.

Yet coordinating a political phenomenon steeped in the rhetoric of "states' rights" and local control remains a major challenge. Local Tea Parties and their leaders have responded in diametrically opposite ways to TPP's efforts at orchestration—as suggested by the vignettes about Maine, Arizona, and Virginia at the start of this section. With limited involvement of Tea Party Patriots, Virginia Tea Partiers launched a state federation in early 2010. Although some local Virginia Tea Party leaders now participate in TPP conference calls, others do not—and we heard suspicions from several Virginia leaders about TPP efforts at control and direction. Arguably, the success the Virginia Tea Partiers had in creating supra-local linkages through their own state federation has made local Tea Parties in that state less amenable to involvements with Tea Party Patriots. One Virginia leader was especially caustic, dismissing Tea Party Patriots as merely engaged in "building a donor base." He called three national organizations "frauds"—including TPP along with and FreedomWorks and Tea Party Express—and suggested that all three are trying to aggrandize themselves off grassroots efforts.

Tea Party groups clearly differ about the value of ties to Tea Party Patriots. Our interviews in Arizona showed that rank-and-filers could evolve favorable views of TPP in a state where it has achieved a concrete presence. In February 2011, Tea Party Patriots sponsored a summit in Phoenix, enabling us to ask for impressions from some of the grassroots people in that area. "As a matter of fact, we weren't too sure," said *Gloria Ames*. "We don't know too much about [TPP coordinators] Jenny Beth Martin and Mark Meckler." Given their "political background," Gloria was uncertain whether the two were trustworthy. In this regard, Gloria seemed to have accurate information about the careers of Meckler and Martin, both of whom had been involved in GOP politics prior to becoming coordinators for Tea Party Patriots. But Gloria's concerns were eventually assuaged. At the 2011 summit, Martin and Meckler surveyed Tea Party members on various issues, and when an issue got a mixed response from local activists, they decided not to take a position on it. "That made me feel better," Gloria concluded. *Larry Fisher*, who participates in the weekly TPP webinars, was similarly impressed with TPP's commitment to "coordinating" not "leading."

Even the most engaged local participants in Arizona were not entirely clear on how Tea Party Patriots fits into the national scene, however. In response to a question about how he came to get involved with Tea Party Patriots, Larry Fisher could not recall. "How did we find out about the national group? I don't know if I remember . . . No, they did not come around with the bus . . ." He consults with his wife, but comes to no conclusion. In short, even though Larry participates weekly in the Tea Party Patriots webinars, he could not readily distinguish TPP from Tea Party Express. Clearly, Tea Party Patriots has made headway in weaving ties to and among local Tea Parties in many states, but it has had to proceed with a light hand to avoid antagonizing locals. The result is widespread but hazy knowledge about TPP, which remains for many local Tea Partiers just one of several national organizations floating through their movement world.

The Initial Strength of Weak Ties

As we have spelled out in this chapter, the Tea Party involves loose ties of mutual convenience among vibrant actors pursuing their own purposes at local and national levels, with each set of actors trying to leverage help from the other. If this is how the Tea Party surge has worked, what is the bottom line? Have loose links among Tea Party organizations helped or hurt conservatives?

In the earliest phases—during the heady days of protest and early organizational efforts in 2009 and 2010—the Tea Party eruption benefited greatly from the loosely interrelated activism of local Tea Partiers, on the one hand, and the cheerleading of national advocates and politicos, on the other hand. Grassroots enthusiasm was encouraged by the sense that people could get their own act together—at most facilitated, but not directly controlled, by any official elites. And elite efforts to orchestrate and leverage grassroots activism, touting the Tea Party label, were not significantly impeded by the fact that national organizations rode as well as stoked grassroots activism. Loose ties were not a problem, even when various national advocacy groups went off in different directions, and even when their efforts sometimes hurt rather than helped the established Republican Party (a matter we discuss further in Chapter 5). The thrust of local and national Tea Party activism through the November 2010 elections was maximized by loosely connected organizational efforts. Tea Party efforts moved forward in mutually encouraging ways, within and across the edges of the GOP but not under party control.

The overall point, after all, was to free conservatism from the tainted "Republican Party" label in order to maximize the election of conservatives in 2010. Tea Partiers of all stripes shared that broad goal, and they were going to make greater headway through loose connections than they would through centralized management. Because there was no one center of authority and resources, the fate of the Tea Party was never inextricably linked to the political fortunes of any one candidate or organized entity. When particular candidates were defeated or particular organizational leaders discredited by scandal or racist episodes, grassroots activism was not discouraged and elites who escaped trouble could just keep operating. No one had to take responsibility for mess-ups.

But things never stay the same in politics, any more than in the rest of life. As we will see in the next two chapters, relationships have shifted over time between grassroots Tea Partiers and the national advocacy elites who maneuver to leverage and speak for the Tea Party as a whole. Once Republicans won big victories in the November 2010 elections, national actors, including in the media, wanted to see more coherence and organizational discipline in the Tea Party than there ever has truly been. Self-appointed Tea Party leaders and spokespersons attempted to fill the demand for information about what "the Tea Party wants" from Republicans in office and in U.S. politics as a whole. Leverage in the Tea Party has therefore shifted since November 2010—giving increased sway to national organizations at the expense of grassroots members.

4

Getting the Word Out

The Media as Cheerleader and Megaphone

Aired on April 6, 2009, the Glenn Beck show included a clarion call for viewers to "celebrate" the upcoming Tax Day on Wednesday, April 15. Viewers were urged either to attend a Tea Party rally or watch Fox News Channel coverage of the protests. As Beck spoke, a map of the USA splayed across the screen, highlighting the cities where Fox hosts would be present: Neil Cavuto in Sacramento, California; Greta Van Susteren in Washington DC; Sean Hannity in Atlanta, Georgia; and Beck himself in San Antonio, Texas. "FNC TAX DAY TEA PARTIES" declared the masthead across the top of the screen, unmistakably aligning Fox with the events it would cover in nine days.[1]

"Town Halls Gone Wild" screamed the headline on a July 31, 2009 article posted at *Politico*.[2] The article spoke of town halls convened by Democratic Members of Congress who faced "angry, sign-carrying mobs and disruptive behavior" from citizens angry about health care reform and other pending legislation. Half a dozen instances were mentioned, with few details on how many protesters were present or how they got there. Subsequent reports suggested that rowdy town halls were the exception rather than the rule during that August Congressional recess, and documented that protests were orchestrated and encouraged by elite advocacy organizations.[3] But the early *Politico* piece set the frame for weeks of additional media reports about grassroots Tea Partiers challenging beleaguered Democrats.

Just a little over a week after the midterm 2010 election, CNN's Deputy Political Director Paul Steinhauser—a member of the self-described "Best Political Team" on television—posted a piece on *Political Ticker* about a "two day retreat" hosted by the DC-based advocacy organization FreedomWorks at a posh hotel in Baltimore, at which newly elected GOP lawmakers would be advised on how to fulfill "the agenda of the Tea Party movement" in the soon-to-convene 112th Congress. In his article's very first sentence, Steinhauser called FreedomWorks a "leading grassroots organization"—and he proceeded to offer a populist take on the advice to be handed out. Tea Party–backed legislators would be urged to fulfill promises of "bringing change to Washington" and given pointers on how to avoid setting aside "their campaign agenda in order to compromise and curry favor with Republican House leaders."[4] Nowhere did Steinhauser mention that the advice-giver-in-chief, FreedomWorks Chairman Dick Armey, a former GOP House Majority Leader, is a longtime DC-based corporate lobbyist.

Politics depends on communication—to get messages out to potential supporters and set agendas for public discussion. When a new cause for protest is at issue, the challenges of spreading the story are especially daunting. An ongoing political party has routines for disseminating messages; corporations, advocacy groups, and universities have hefty public relations departments to craft press releases; and governments issue constant streams of official pronouncements. Reporters will usually cover such statements. But protest organizers face an additional challenge—they must get the word out to potential participants in order to draw wider public attention. People must hear that shared action is possible and that it could make a difference, or they will just stay home on their couches. If an already existing organizational network is not in place to help orchestrate protest, or if available organizations have only limited capacity, then the media's response to a protest movement's early organizing efforts becomes critical.

That is why organizers of nascent protest efforts go for dramatic, photogenic events. They have to capture the eyes and ears of the media. But would-be protest movements often fail at this undertaking because media directors have little incentive to pay sustained attention to something out of the mainstream. In recent years, for example, hundreds of thousands of Americans have mounted dramatic protests: to oppose U.S. war efforts, to call for an end to legal abortion, to support the right to organize unions, and to demand immigration reform. Most of these protests have attracted little coverage in the major media—and certainly not sustained coverage.

Even if protest events attract a day or two of attention, would-be movements usually end up a flash in the pan, as media outlets move on to the next new and controversial thing. For a protest movement to survive, it must do more. It must get leaders on television or in national and local newspapers, and garner other kinds of ongoing friendly media coverage. Again and again, protest themes must be injected into public debates to convey a sense of momentum and convince politicians and members of the general public to focus on the protestors' concerns.

Grasping the structure and dynamics of U.S. communications media will help us understand the special advantages Tea Party organizers enjoyed when so many other would-be protest efforts have fallen short of getting the publicity and media access they needed to flourish and have a major impact on governance. As we will see, the challenge of spreading and germinating the Tea Party idea was surmounted with impressive ease because a major sector of the U.S. media today is openly partisan—including Fox News Channel, the right-wing "blogosphere," and a nationwide network of right-wing talk radio programs. This aptly named conservative media "echo chamber" reaches into the homes of many Americans, buffets as well as boosts the Republican Party, and has considerable ability to set the agenda of issues that other media outlets also take up.[5] Crucially, the conservative media quickly joined and helped to orchestrate the Tea Party, breaking down the barriers between media and movement that have usually been so challenging for protestors to navigate. In this book, for good reason, we have designated the conservative media complex as one of the three main interacting forces that make up the Tea Party and give it oomph.

Still, the Tea Party impact on broader U.S. political debates depended on more than colorful rallies touted by Fox News. Tea Partiers might noisily assemble on Tax Day and Independence Day, or send dozens of people to shout at Congressional town hall meetings during the health reform debate. But how much coverage would they get—in what range of news outlets—and how would the coverage frame who Tea Partiers were and what they were doing? How quickly and accurately would news outlets get a fix on ordinary Tea Partiers themselves, their social characteristics and partisan proclivities, and what would media say about the role of elite organizations in the Tea Party universe? Would outlets check the facts of grand claims by self-appointed Tea Party spokespersons about federal spending and deficits? The media beyond the conservative echo chamber were a bit slow to leap into the Tea Party story, but once they did, the answers to these questions turned out largely as elite sponsors of the Tea Party wanted. The Tea Party eventually became the darling of a wide range of U.S. media, with reporters portraying it as a massive movement of regular Americans disgruntled with President Obama and government spending. Tea Party framings of issues were injected into the very center of U.S. public debates.

FOX AND COMPETITORS—THE MEDIA CONTEXT

Many observers of the role of U.S. media in politics as of the early twenty-first century are alarmed that partisanship has crept in. This rarely bothers very conservative pundits, of course, because (even if they constantly complain about "liberal media bias") they know that the elephants in the room are on their side. Liberals and self-styled nonpartisan critics engage in constant tut-tutting about the horrors of partisan media. They forget that American democracy was born and flourished through the nineteenth century in an environment where major newspapers, the mass media of the day, were all closely aligned with political parties. "Objective news" was not to be found; nineteenth-century editors and reporters alike presented highly selective versions of the facts, often in luridly emotional ways. Only in the twentieth century, as sociologist Michael Schudson explained in his groundbreaking book *Discovering the News*, did professional journalists gain a degree of autonomy. Journalists developed norms of objectivity and "balance," which leading newspapers and, later, television networks tried to follow, more or less.[6] Norms of objective journalism led to the convention of looking for quotes from sources on "both sides of the issue"—a practice more reflective of the fact that there were two major parties roaming the U.S. political tundra than of any law that major questions have only two possible answers. Social movements and protest efforts outside the two major parties found it harder to get a hearing in the objective-and-balanced media regime.

Today, certain major institutions—such as the *New York Times*, the *Washington Post*, *USA Today*, and National Public Radio—still follow twentieth-century norms of objectivity and balance in their coverage of politics and policy-making. They also try to cite neutral experts or authoritative sources, though often there is insufficient time to check facts thoroughly. Newsroom resources are tight and the tempo of news faster in the era of the Internet and cable news. What is more, institutions trying to practice objective journalism coexist with other kinds of outlets in a larger, raucous, and fragmented media universe.

Lots of today's outlets are frankly partisan and present news through an interpretive lens. Talk radio blares out partisan talking points, usually on the right.[7] There are influential news aggregators, such as the *Drudge Report*, and news blogs, such as *Red State* on the right and *Talking Points Memo* on the left. Towering above all others is the Fox News empire, the loudest voice in conservative media. Despite its claim to be "fair and balanced," multiple studies have documented Fox's conservative stance.[8] Even Fox News host Bill O'Reilly agrees that his station does "tilt right."[9] When Fox departs from the official GOP line, its anchors and commentators take overtly conservative stands, pressuring the official Republican Party from the right. Tensions between Fox and the Republicans do exist, but that is not because Fox anchors or hosts deviate to help Democrats, or to engage in objective or balanced coverage. Both the news and the interpretive programs on Fox are frankly and visibly on the side of Republicans and activists to the GOP right.

Conservative news reaches millions of Americans every day. Fox News averages more viewers than its chief cable television competitors CNN and MSNBC combined. In prime time, over 2 million viewers watch Fox, which carries all of the top ten most watched cable news programs.[10] All in all, a quarter of Americans report regularly watching Fox News.[11] As for radio, Rush Limbaugh, and fellow conservative radio hosts Sean Hannity, Michael Savage, Glenn Beck, and Laura Ingraham, each reach tens of millions of radio listeners across the country.[12]

Viewers and listeners respond to the partisan slant Fox and other conservative outlets present. More than half of Fox News watchers identify as politically conservative, with higher levels of conservatism among viewers of Fox News's top programs.[13] Fully 80% of Rush Limbaugh listeners identify themselves as conservatives, compared to 35% of Americans as a whole.[14] Demographics track what one would expect from the partisan skew. The average age of a Fox News Channel viewer is over 65 years, while conservative talk radio listeners average 67 years of age.[15] Less than 2% of Fox viewers are African-American.[16] All in all, right-wing media have an impressive reach into the homes of America's aging conservatives, and their audience share is unmatched by their rivals.

Given the impressive scope of conservative media, American democracy is, in an important sense, caught betwixt and between in the new media world. The frank, exuberant, all-around partisanship of the nineteenth century is not quite what we now have. True, there are both liberal and conservative bloggers, and on the tube, the Fox political slant is weakly countered by liberal-slanted shows on MSNBC. But mostly what America has right now is a thousand-pound-gorilla media juggernaut on the right, operating nineteenth-century style, coexisting with other news outlets trying to keep up while making fitful efforts, twentieth-century style, to check facts and cover "both sides of the story." Many of the outlets maneuvering for eyes and ears are commercially hard-pressed. Newspapers in particular are struggling to devise new business models, cutting news operations to the bone in the process. Most television and radio outlets are scrambling, too, trying to be colorful and fast-moving enough to attract or keep their audience. With twenty-four hours of time to fill in cable news, CNN is engaged in a losing battle with Fox to attract some of the same older, conservative viewers—the sort of people who still watch a lot of television.

Commercial competition means that issue-mongers can fan a supposedly scandalous sound bite into an uproar of intense coverage across many channels.[17] Flamboyant critics have an advantage, especially when a Democrat is in office and they operate from the right. It is easier, after all, to proclaim problems or incite controversy than to offer solutions or seek accord—just as it is easier to start fires than it is to put them out. With Democrat Barack Obama in the White House, Fox settles each day on a critical message—ideally illustrated by some controversy or scandal—certain to resonate with its viewers and listeners. Then other cable networks with 24/7 news operations try to compete with Fox—either through imitation, as CNN often does, or through a degree of partisan differentiation, which MSNBC has recently attempted. Either way, the premium is placed on magnifying or arguing with the provocative voices that first appear on Fox (or in right-wing blogs en route to Fox). In due course, even the proudest old-line media outlets allow much of their agenda to be taken up by topics launched from the right-wing noise and echo machine. The brouhaha over fake "death panels" during the health reform debate is a case in point.

Magnifying the routine dynamics that spread stories, news media sponsor incessant polls that reinforce controversial narratives by repeating hot-button phrases and turning them into questions. Citizens may be asked about nonfactual matters such as the "controversy" over Obama's birth certificate. Or they may be asked to weigh in on something they are just beginning to hear about—such as "the Tea Party" at an early stage when, truth be told, the majority of Americans had never heard of it. No matter how shaky the poll results may be, newspapers and television stations publicize results and use them to set the agendas for yet more polls, and for stories about the supposed conflicts revealed in the polls. This cycle—stories to set up polls, and polls to set up more stories—is a relatively inexpensive way to do "news" coverage because it does not require reporters to do research or travel across the country looking at actual developments.

Another critical feature of today's media is the exploding menu of options. Alongside struggling newspapers and network television channels are hundreds of cable channels and websites, all competing for the attention of media consumers. In his influential book *Post-Broadcast Democracy,* political scientist Markus Prior shows that, after the advent of widespread access to cable television, American media consumers got the power to make so many choices that many of them stopped watching any news at all.[18] Back in the pre-cable era of the Big Three networks—CBS, ABC, and NBC—there was nothing else on at dinnertime except "balanced" news, so even the least interested people saw some of it and got roughly the same version of the political facts as all other citizens. Now, uninterested people can and do flip channels, avoiding news altogether in favor of entertainment or sports.

The exploding menu not only has an impact on people willing to avoid news; it also allows Americans who care about news to select outlets that fit their partisan and value preferences. Liberals gravitate toward MSNBC while the most conservative-minded faithfully follow Fox News.[19] Because media consumers are sorting themselves out, they no longer get shared information about the world. Subgroups of American citizens can end up not just getting different slants on the same reality, but living in very different realities, believing very different things about the world.[20] This is not just a problem afflicting those with relatively little political information. The highly educated are particularly prone to misperceptions resulting from media bias since they are the people who most avidly read and watch and listen for political news.

Armed with a better sense of how U.S. news media work, we can return to the Tea Party saga. At the start, in early 2009, major outlets not only reported on events as they unfolded; a major sector of the media helped to orchestrate protests and build them into a credible political force.

THE CONSERVATIVE MEDIA HOST A TEA PARTY

As President Obama and a Democratic Congress took office and started churning out legislation, most of the ultra-free-market advocacy and political action groups that would in due course be associated with the Tea Party did not possess the communications capacities necessary to reach millions of angry and disenchanted conservatives. Try as they might to capitalize on the mid-February Santelli rant, Americans for Prosperity, FreedomWorks, and their like would not have been able to get the word out on their own. Their contact lists and field networks were far too sparse. Conservative media outlets were thus vital to the rapid launch of Tea Party activism across communities and regions.

How Messages Circulate

To trace the activity and the effects of conservative media, we focus much of our attention on Fox News because of its massive reach. But while Fox News may be the "biggest fish" in the conservative media sea, this cable channel fills only one niche in the ecosystem. Many outlets feed off one another, echoing the same messages day by day. And grassroots activists spread the messages, too. American conservatives have a powerful capacity to cycle messages between national and local sources, thereby influencing topics of public discussion every day and every week.

Ideas and news stories often pop up on conservative talk radio or on influential websites such as the *Drudge Report* or Andrew Breitbart's site before getting picked up by conservative newspapers and television. Indeed, some Fox News personalities, such as Sean Hannity, have successful radio programs where they can test and hone material that will later appear on their television programs. Once a story is up and running, hosts on local conservative radio talk shows play a pivotal role in keeping discussions going and spreading issues or controversies to every community across the land. These well-known figures are everywhere, and they don't just talk on the radio; they serve on organizing committees for public events and speak at local gatherings.

Grassroots conservatives play their part, too. Across the partisan spectrum, politically engaged Americans can gather and synthesize information, and then use the blogs, email, and social media to spread stories or action alerts. Active relaying of this sort is par for the course among U.S. conservatives. *New York Times* reporter David Barstow tells the story of the president of the Sandpoint Tea Party Patriots, a woman who was "happily retired" but is now a virtual communications whirlwind:

> Stout wakes each morning, turns on Fox News, grabs coffee and an Atkins bar, and hits the computer. She is the hub of a rapidly

expanding and highly viral political network, keeping a running correspondence with her 400 members in Sandpoint, state and national Tea Party leaders and other conservative activists. . . . Stout forwards along petitions to impeach Mr. Obama; petitions to audit the Federal Reserve; petitions to support Sarah Palin; appeals urging defiance of any federal law requiring health insurance; and on and on. [21]

As this glimpse suggests, conservatives need not be passive recipients of media output. They can also fire up their computers to talk back and spread information (or misinformation) to many others. From what we have seen, Tea Partiers are remarkably active on the Internet; indeed, we are tempted to say that the past couple of years may have brought a huge leap in computer savvy among the mostly older men and women active in the Tea Party, allowing them to use and navigate the Internet with ease, without constantly phoning their children or grandkids for advice!

On a more serious note, classic sociological work documented decades ago that citizens find news more credible if trusted people vouch for its veracity and relevance. Communications technologies and the structure of politically relevant communities may have changed since Paul Lazersfeld and his colleagues published *The People's Choice* back in 1944.[22] But the principle of "two-step communication" still has relevance. When Pam Stout contacts fellow conservatives about matters she sees or hears, that reinforces the messages others may also receive from Fox and other conservative outlets.

In at the Start

A few weeks after the Santelli rant on CNBC, Fox News was hard at work publicizing Tea Party rallies. But Fox News was not the first to grab and spread the Tea Party idea. Bloggers and talk radio hosts were first off the mark.

Once CNBC's editors posted the Santelli video to their website, the *Drudge Report* immediately linked to it, with a siren flashing alongside— Matt Drudge's code for a particularly important event.[23] Right-wing pundit Michelle Malkin responded by connecting Santelli's rant to earlier protests against Obama's economic stimulus proposals, and was soon exchanging ideas with Tea Party organizers over Twitter.[24] By the next day, the Santelli rant was enough of a story that White House Press Secretary Robert Gibbs was asked a question about it during his regular briefing.

Working alongside conservative bloggers in promoting the Tea Party idea were local talk radio hosts. Eric Von Haessler, one of the hosts on Atlanta's FM 100.5 morning show, "The Regular Guys," kicked off the February 27th Tea Party on Georgia's state capitol steps, decrying "the phalanx of academics and community organizers" in the Obama Administration and asking whether the president would represent America's "producers," "landowners," and "small business owners."[25] Mike Gallagher and his radio affiliate, News Radio 1330/950 WORD, sponsored the Tea Party in Greenville, South Carolina. "The left has to listen to us whether they like it or not, right?" this fiery radio host told the cheering crowd. "We're fed up with Barack Obama!" he continued, only weeks into the new administration.[26] So clear was the conservative media's involvement in producing the very first Tea Parties that one of CNN's earliest reports on the Tea Parties began, "Talk radio hosts are staging Boston Tea Party–style rallies across the country."[27]

Fox News soon recognized a major conservative phenomenon in the making and moved to become cheerleader in chief. Fox began to cover the April 15th rallies six weeks in advance, starting with a March 5, 2009 appearance by Newt Gingrich to talk up the protests on Greta Van Susteren's show. Scarcely a trickle of Tea Party events occurred over ensuing weeks, but that did not prevent Fox News hosts and guests from speculating wildly about the likely huge size and impact of the forthcoming rallies. Viewers watching Fox News in early 2009 were told that "Tea Party protests are erupting across the country" and assured that "these tea parties are starting to really take off."[28] Newt Gingrich went on air to make the confident prediction that the April 15th rallies would have "over 300,000" attendees.[29] By late March, Glenn Beck had not only attended a rally in Orlando, Florida. He had interviewed Tea Party activists from Houston and Indianapolis days *before* rallies occurred in those cities, featuring their plans and pitching their events. For the Tea Party in its vulnerable infancy, the mobilizing impact of such advance coverage in national prime time was invaluable. The Tea Party idea was presented as the "coming thing" to an audience primed for the message. Conservative Fox viewers across America heard that people like them were ready to stand up to Obama and the Democrats—and they were told when and where.

A week before the first annual April 15th Tea Party rallies in 2009, Fox News promotions kicked into an even higher gear. Glenn Beck told his viewers, "We're getting ready for next week's Tax Day tea parties. All across the country, people coming together to let the politicians know, OK, enough spending."[30] Sean Hannity was even more explicit: "And, of course, April 15th, our big show coming out of Atlanta. It's Tax Day, our Tax Day tea party show. Don't forget, we're going to have "Joe the Plumber."[31] At times, Fox anchors adopted an almost cajoling tone. On Sean Hannity's show, viewers were told, "Anybody can come, it's free," while Beck fans were warned, "You don't want to miss it."[32] In an ironic moment, Arthur Laffer (inventor of the Laffer Curve that was used to justify Reagan's supply-side economic theories) congratulated Beck on air for the success of the Tea Parties. "I'm just attending," Beck quickly demurred, before continuing his promotion of the upcoming San Antonio Tea Party.[33]

Indeed, during the first weeks of the Tea Party, Fox News directly linked the network's brand to these protests and allowed members of the "Fox Nation" to see the Tea Parties as a natural outgrowth of their identity as Fox News viewers. Megyn Kelly directed viewers to "join the TEA party action from your home" by going to Fox's website, which allowed viewers to find Tea Party events in their area, and the events were dubbed "FNC [Fox News Channel] Tea Parties."[34] As Glenn Beck put it on his April 6th show: "This year, Americans across the country are holding tea parties to let politicians know that we have had enough. Celebrate with Fox News. This is what we're doing next Wednesday."[35] Beck's comment was certainly an apt description since on April 15, Fox News hosts Beck, Hannity, Van Susteren, and Cavuto all broadcast their shows from Tea Party events, as promised.

Patterns of Coverage Tell the Tale

The special effort Fox made to build the Tea Party is evident from the hard data. We examined the frequency with which different media outlets referred to the Tea Party in its infancy. Figure 4.1 displays the trends in Tea Party coverage by Fox News and CNN from February to May 2009.[36]

As might be expected, CNN coverage spikes in April 2009 when Tea Party protests were held across the country. It is not that CNN ignored the early peak of Tea Party rallies; indeed, CNN coverage more than matches that of Fox News when Tea Party events are actually occurring. But coverage on Fox News has a strikingly different trajectory. Fox coverage *anticipates* Tea Party events, building up to each set of synchronized rallies. And Fox maintains coverage between those events. Clearly, the efforts at Tea Party promotion we have cited from the Sean Hannity and Glenn Beck shows on Fox were not isolated anomalies. They are part of a larger pattern

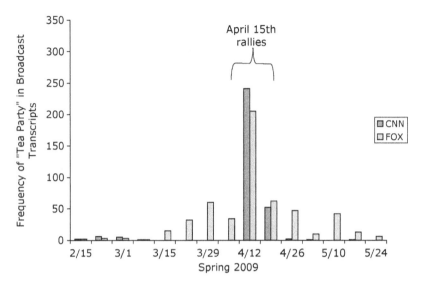

FIGURE 4.1.   Tea Party Coverage by CNN and Fox News, February to May 2009. *Data from CNN and Fox News transcripts via Lexis Nexis.*

of anticipatory coverage, practiced systematically by Fox News. And Fox kept at it. Although Tea Party coverage receded somewhat after the April 15 crescendo, it continued to be a significant part of Fox News programming. A similar big buildup of Fox coverage occurs leading into the July 4, 2009 Tea Party rallies, and again leading into the August town hall protests.[37]

These data nail down our case. Fox was not just responding to Tea Party activism as it happened. Fox served as a kind of social movement orchestrator, during what is always a dicey early period for any new protest effort—the period when potential participants have to hear about the effort and decide that it is likely to prove powerful. For weeks in advance of each early set of rallies, as the Tea Party grew from infancy to adolescence, Fox was pointing the way and cheering.

Given the loyal conservative viewership that Fox already enjoyed before the Tea Party emerged, the network's assiduous promotional and informational efforts surely made a big difference. Fox viewers are conservative Republicans who were already very upset about the election of Barack Obama. Watching Fox, they had repeated opportunities to learn about the Tea Party and participate if they should so choose. Fox urged people on and conveyed the sense that something big was afoot. The network also joined many other conservative media outlets in offering guides to find local rallies on the Fox News website.

All of this must have been quite encouraging for older, conservative viewers—many of whom were inexperienced with public protest. The Fox News imprimatur surely helped people to feel more comfortable about taking part. Many Tea Partiers told us that they had been hesitant to attend their first Tea Party, unsure whom they would meet. But as we've already seen, conservatives have great faith in Fox News. To go to an angry political protest may have seemed out of character for most of them until it was framed as an opportunity to "celebrate with Fox News." Once people got to the rallies, they found others like themselves similarly inspired. As we learned in Chapter 3, many of those who became organizers and leaders of local Tea Parties met each other for the first time at rallies, or on the bus traveling to big protest events.

The Special Role of Glenn Beck

Almost all Fox News hosts took some part in the "celebration" of the first Tax Day Tea Parties—and engaged in ongoing favorable coverage thereafter.[38] Nevertheless, flamboyant Fox host Glenn Beck deserves special credit for his role in building and shaping the Tea Party as an organized force. After taking the lead in April 2009, Beck regularly invited Tea Party organizers on-air in advance of ensuing spring and summer rallies. More than that, as the Tea Parties were getting off the ground in communities across the country, Beck was launching his own grassroots initiative, the "9/12 Project."[39] Beck's purported goal was to "bring us all back to the place we were on September 12, 2001," when the country was unified in the wake of the September 11th attacks. This unity could be achieved, Beck claimed, via adherence to the "9 Principles" and "12 Values" he laid out on-air. Beck's principles include socioreligious conservative goals as well as the fiscal tenets emphasized by national Tea Party groups. The second Beck principle, for instance, reads, "I believe in God and He is the center of my life."[40] Yet the tenor and message of the 9/12 Project overlaps strongly with that of the Tea Party. The 9/12 Project also claims to draw from the words of the Founding Fathers, and emphasizes personal responsibility and limited government.

Week after week and month after month, Glenn Beck encouraged his viewers to get together in groups and watch his show, discuss books he had recommended, and hold their elected leaders accountable for living up to the 9/12 Project's conservative aims. Though nominally a distinct formation, Beck's "9/12 Project" overlaps heavily with Tea Party activism. In

August 2010, at least 115 Tea Parties of those registered on the Tea Party Patriots website had a name including some variation of 9/12, such as the "Wyoming 912 Coalition" or "Daytona 912." And in the nationwide survey of local Tea Parties we completed in the spring of 2011, over 400 groups referred to the 9/12 Project on their site.

Beck's trademark "9/12 Project" worked with FreedomWorks and other Tea Party groups to co-sponsor the first unified national manifestation of Tea Party enthusiasm—the September 12, 2009, rally that brought tens of thousands of activists to the Mall in Washington DC.[41] Arguably, this was the moment when the Tea Party shifted into national gear, moving beyond synchronized regional rallies. Across the board, mainstream media began to agree that Tea Partiers were proving themselves to be a big deal politically, less than a year into Obama's presidency.

Beck's influence among Tea Partiers permeates far beyond people who have joined groups formally aligned with the 9/12 Project. Either deliberately or unconsciously, the people we interviewed often used phrases and arguments from the Beck show. *Stella Fisher* explained her concern with American politics in terms of a spectrum from anarchy to tyranny, as Beck often did on his show. *Stanley Ames* referred to various Washington liberals as "spooky," one of Beck's pet words; and his wife *Gloria* spoke knowledgeably about the turn-of-the-century Progressive movement, a bête noir of the Glenn Beck show.

Although some Tea Party leaders have tried to distance themselves from Beck, and a few people we spoke with expressed some doubts about him, the relationship between Beck and Tea Party organizations was eventually solidified.[42] During 2010 and 2011, FreedomWorks conducted membership drives featuring a picture of Glenn Beck and a "special offer for Glenn Beck listeners." This formalized the link between the controversial Fox personality and the national advocacy organization and pro-business lobby that has been closely allied with Tea Party Patriots and involved in spurring Tea Party protests from the start. Glenn Beck became "the cable news poster child for these tea parties," as his fellow Fox host Greta Van Susteren aptly put it.[43]

Fox and Tea Partiers Forge a Community of Meaning

After the Tea Party was up and running, Fox News as a whole moved away from direct promotion and began to integrate the Tea Party seamlessly into its ongoing conservative narratives. Along the way, the network offered a distinctive framing of what the Tea Party was all about. A community of Fox-viewing Tea Partiers came to share a powerful, widely shared political identity, and the Fox News framing, in due course, shaped national perceptions of the Tea Party phenomenon.

Of course, Fox News also continued to provide the kind of political coverage and interpretive discussion that mobilizes conservatives with information and misinformation, as the network had been doing for years before the Tea Party came into existence. Fox gave a soapbox to Tea Party politicians who, like other conservative Republicans, found a place for gentle interviews in the lead-up to the 2010 midterm elections.[44] Not only were the questions friendly, Fox programs allowed Tea Party politicians to solicit online monetary contributions.[45]

Fox News's conservative slant encourages a particular worldview. "The more we learn . . . the more we pay attention, the more disturbed we get," Stanley Ames explains. "If you watch the networks, you aren't informed about how bad off we are." Fox News provides a constant drumbeat of news that shapes the American conservative worldview and keeps people on edge.[46] This effect was true during the height of the Tea Party, as it was in the years before the Obama Administration came to office.

But in its role as Tea Party promoter, Fox News deserves special mention. So successful was the Fox News cheerleading that Fox viewers and Tea Party participants became heavily overlapping categories. According to the CBS/*New York Times* national poll taken in April 2010, 63% of Tea Party supporters watched Fox News, compared to 11% of all respondents. Among Tea Partiers, the diet of Fox News coverage was only occasionally supplemented by other television news sources. Only one in nine Tea Party supporters reported getting their news from one of the classic Big Three networks, while among all U.S. respondents, more than a quarter reported watching network news.[47] From our encounters, the rate of Fox News watching seemed even higher among true activists as opposed to mere sympathizers with the Tea Party. In Virginia, every single Tea Party member we spoke to mentioned Fox News as a prime news source. Similarly, when we asked one Arizona activist where she gets her information, she laughed and said, "where do you think?" before telling us that "of course" she watches Fox News. An Arizona couple we met reported watching at least six hours of Fox News *a day*. In Boston, too, then–Fox News host Glenn Beck was regularly cited by Tea Party participants—in the same matter-of-course way that the *New York Times* comes up in Cambridge liberal circles—as both a common currency and a cultural touchstone. Fox News's national coverage was far more popular than even local conservative media. Most Massachusetts Tea Partiers do not even bother with the generally conservative *Boston Herald*, let alone the *Boston Globe*.[48]

As Tea Party activists worked to build a major political force, Fox News played a unique role in giving their undertakings special meaning, not only among all conservatives, but for Tea Partiers themselves. Throughout 2009 and 2010, Fox News viewers were informed that the Tea Party was "grassroots," "genuine," "organic," "spontaneous," "independent," and "mainstream."[49] Fox News owner Rupert Murdoch himself said of the Tea Party, "They're not extremist. They're moderate centrists."[50] Fox News viewers were also regularly told that the Tea Party represented people like themselves. As Glenn Beck put it, "This is the tea party. This is you and me."[51] Tea Party activism was a source of hope, Beck concluded. "You're not alone, America. You are the majority. A year ago, you didn't know that."[52]

Though they touted the Tea Party as a massive and independent force, Fox News commentators also insisted that Tea Party groups would be most effective operating within the Republican Party, not outside of it. The electoral power of the Tea Party was a frequent subject of discussion on Fox, long before a slew of Tea Party candidates emerged. Between major events, viewers were reminded that the Tea Party "is far from over," and that the phenomenon had the capacity to kick "the establishment's rear end."[53] Yet emphasis on the Tea Party as independent and powerful did not mean that the phenomenon should operate outside of the established two-party system. Fox anchors and commentators persistently emphasized the dangers of "disunity" and the political impracticality of becoming an actually independent third party.[54] Instead, the Tea Party was quickly framed as a challenge to the Republican establishment that would also boost the GOP— or as Bill Kristol described it, "the best thing that has happened to the Republican Party in recent times."[55] The Fox News audience that included the vast majority of Tea Party participants was regularly encouraged to engage in the electoral process in ways that would prod the Republican Party rightward but not undercut its ability to win elections.

In Fox and affiliated conservative outlets, the Tea Party took on meaning not only as a political grouping, but also as a vital cultural force. Fox News assigned the Tea Party a starring role in what conservatives understand as a long-running culture war between coastal elites and middle Americans. As we saw earlier, Tea Party members think of the elite not primarily as an economic category but as a cultural stratum, a coterie of liberal intellectuals and bureaucrats who wish to impose ideas and schemes about matters such as economic redistribution and environmental regulation on unwitting regular Americans. Fox News coverage of the Tea Party both draws upon and fuels this potent interpretation.

In framing the social conflict between elites and middle America, Fox News adopts the rhetorical style of Richard Nixon, who, as Rick Perlstein says, "so brilliantly co-opted the liberals' populism, channeling it into a white middle-class rage at the sophisticates."[56] Speaking on Fox, Newt Gingrich announced that "the Tea Parties were a direct threat to the elite left and the elite left is going berserk."[57] In the world of Fox News, the coastal elite maneuvers in partnership with poor minority groups, and they work together through the mainstream media to denigrate ordinary Americans, including Tea Partiers. Using this map of the political world, the Tea Party is said to be reviled precisely because it is the representative of middle-class whites, the true Americans. As regular Fox News contributor Jim Pinkerton put it, "There has never been a poor minority that the mainstream media didn't gush over. [. . .] What is left out is the white, middle, and working class. To them [in the mainstream media], they're a bunch of Archie Bunkers."[58]

For the many middle-class white conservatives in the Fox News audience, such rhetoric hits home. But in case any viewers should fail to take things personally enough, Fox News hosts regularly remind them. When it comes to specifying who is targeted in criticisms of the Tea Party, the Fox News answer is always "you," the viewer at home. "The American media will never embrace the Tea Party. Why?" asked Fox host Bill O'Reilly, who had the answer ready to hand. "Generally speaking, they look down on the folks, they think *you are dumb*."[59] Glenn Beck, too, promised an exposé of mainstream media Tea Party coverage, telling viewers that they would learn "what the media said *about you* or people that think like you."[60] In another episode, Beck told his audience that Tea Party critics are "trying to belittle and dismiss *you, the viewer*."[61] At Fox News, criticism of the Tea Party is never presented dispassionately or in the abstract. It is framed as a personal attack on the audience.

Both the constant refrain of "us versus them" and the everyday flow of political information and misinformation reinforce the sense of an embattled community of conservatives—whose latest effort to fight back valiantly is embodied in the Tea Party. With such coverage, Fox and other conservative media outlets not only touted a heartening brand to help the Tea Party get off the ground; they also helped to establish and sustain it as a national political force into 2010 and beyond.

MAINSTREAM MEDIA JOIN THE PARTY

As the Tea Party gained traction and political definition with crucial assistance from right-wing media, it gradually attracted the sorts of across-the-board media fascination necessary to influence public discussions during and after the critical elections of 2010. At first, the mainstream media's coverage tracked public protests and reacted to the level of attention being paid by conservative news outlets. But by 2010, most media outlets decided that the Tea Party was a major ongoing story—the next big thing in U.S. politics. Reporters spent months parsing polls and field reports to figure out who Tea Partiers were and where they fit in the overall political spectrum. Intense and often misleading media coverage provided an enormous boost in publicity for what was portrayed as a mass movement. After the November 2010 elections, yet another media-influenced dynamic took hold, as coverage shifted to featuring national elites who claimed to speak for "the Tea Party" as a whole. Suddenly, the grassroots faded and the likes of Representative Michele Bachmann, Senator Jim DeMint, and Dick Armey appeared even more front and center.

Initial Wariness

In the early months of the Tea Party, Fox News's wall-to-wall coverage, more than the protests themselves, caught the attention of the mainstream press. Outlets covered the most spectacular public events. But eyebrows were also raised, with some editors and commentators wondering if the whole thing was a Fox-manufactured chimera. In the days before the April rallies, CNN contributor Howard Kurtz concluded that Fox News "practically seems to be a co-sponsor" of the planned Tea Party events, and asked, "Is it OK for the gang at Fox News to join those April 15th tea party protests?"[62] As David Carr commented in the *New York Times*, "the news media are supplying both the pictures and the war."[63] Ironically, this coverage of Fox's coverage was at least tangentially a source of publicity for the Tea Party protests themselves. But it also suggests that many in the media were at first suspicious of the Tea Party phenomenon and alert to the role of the conservative media in its development.

Even as they voiced concerns about Fox's coverage, journalists on CNN became defensive about their own coverage—and significantly upped attention to the Tea Party. On April 13th, still two days before the protests, CNN not only reported on the upcoming protests but discussed whether their coverage was adequate, and promised that there would be more coverage to come "as the protests draw closer."[64] They kept their word, featuring the Chicago-based Tea Party organizer Eric Odom on April 14th and providing extensive coverage of the spring and summer Tea Party rallies. CNN also moved toward what would become an increasingly close relationship to Tea Party Express, the Republican-led political action committee that relabeled its activities to cater to the Tea Party. Starting in the fall of 2009, CNN sent reporters to travel along on Tea Party Express bus tours, sending periodic dispatches from the road. CNN would later work out an arrangement with Tea Party Express to co-sponsor an early GOP presidential primary debate.[65]

Spectacular coverage of protests happened again around the time of the August 2009 Congressional recess, when grassroots Tea Partiers were portrayed as expressing widespread popular anger about health reform and other legislation pushed by President Obama and the Congressional Democrats. The July 31, 2009 article by *Politico* on "Town Halls Gone Wild" was influential in keying reporters to that angle.[66] Angry protestors yelling at Congressmen and Congresswomen made for great theater, and a few dramatic town hall episodes got a lot of television time.[67] But the coverage was at best partial. The roles of elite GOP operatives and free-market advocacy organizations in facilitating town hall protests did not get much play in early mainstream media portrayals of the Tea Party.

In late 2009, Fox News explicitly goaded other major networks to increase their coverage. Following the September 12th 2009 Taxpayer's March on Washington, Fox News ran a full-page color ad in the *Washington Post*, with an aerial picture of the rally and the headline "How did ABC, CBS, NBC, MSNBC, and CNN miss this?"[68] CNN reporters responded angrily on air, running a montage of various reporters covering the September 12th event. CNN anchor Rick Sanchez concluded: "Here's the fact. We did cover the event. What we didn't do is promote the event. . . . That's not what real news organizations are supposed to do."[69] Wolf Blitzer went so far as to call Fox's allegation "false"—a rarity on a show that tends to cushion factual assertions with phrases like "some people say."[70] But the ad may have had an impact, prodding CNN and other outlets to cover the Tea Party more assiduously. As Jeffrey Toobin put it, "when FOX News decides that the tea parties and the rally in Washington by the tea party people is a big story, some people followed that."[71] There certainly have been many instances when stories leap from conservative media circles to mainstream news outlets. Political scientists and media scholars have found that Fox News and other conservative media outlets have significant power to amplify conservative viewpoints and reshape public debate.[72]

Whatever the impact of Fox's goading, coverage of the Tea Party was comparatively judicious in 2009—at least, as we will see, compared to the lavish attention paid in the following year. CNN featured extensive coverage of eye-catching events, but also skepticism of the Tea Party phenomenon as a whole. The network also offered relatively clear-eyed assessments of the participants' conservative leanings, pointed to the involvement of conservative media as event promoters, and raised occasional questions about the funding behind the phenomenon. In print and online media, less able to take advantage of flashy imagery, the first Tea Parties passed largely unnoticed. The very first Tea Party protests received only very marginal coverage in the *New York Times*, a mention in an article about CNBC's place in the cable news standings.[73] Rick Klein, writing for ABC News's *The Note*, cited the support of major funders on the right and cautioned "not to read too much" into the protests, but argued that the "populist anger" the protests unleashed was a significant political phenomenon.[74]

When attention was paid to Tea Partiers, it often focused on the Tea Party's extremism. Gail Collins described the town hall protestors as "people who appear to have been sitting in their attics . . . listening for signs of alien aircraft."[75] Even when articles aimed to provide a balanced view of Tea Party participants, the assumption was often that the Tea Party was dominated by crackpots. An article in the Fort Worth *Star-Telegram*, for instance, commented that, though a local rally was scheduled to feature local Texas secessionists, "not all Tea Party events are run by cultists and conspiracy hobbyists."[76] In late 2009, the mainstream media's almost universal assumption was that extremist views hold a significant place in the Tea Party. In the following year, however, that assessment was turned on its head.

The Next Big Political Thing

Starting in early 2010, the Tea Party became a fashionable subject deemed deserving of rapt and continual media attention. As one indication of more general trends, Figure 4.2 shows the same kind of data we presented earlier on the frequency of the phrase "Tea Party" in CNN's transcripts. In this figure, we have "zoomed out" to show the rhythms of CNN's attention to the Tea Party over the entire eighteen-month span from the birth of the Tea Party through the summer of 2010. Clearly, coverage boomed starting in early 2010, about a year into the Tea Party phenomenon.

Why did early 2010 mark a sea change in the quantity and quality of coverage associated with the Tea Party? Electoral politics certainly helped to spur the shift, as two somewhat surprising electoral challenges by GOP politicians were attributed in large part to Tea Party influence.[77] In mid-January 2010, in a Massachusetts special election to fill the Senate seat of the recently deceased Edward Kennedy, previously little-known Republican Scott Brown surged to victory; and in the Florida GOP contest for nomination to the Senate, conservative Marco Rubio's campaign overtook the candidate originally backed by the establishment, Governor Charlie Crist. Although both Brown and Rubio were to the right of the norm in

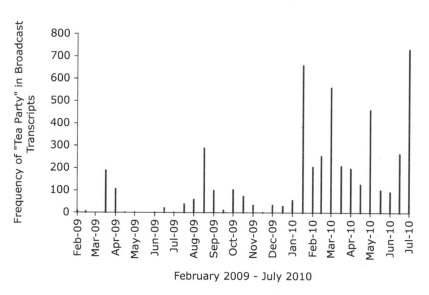

FIGURE 4.2. Tea Party Coverage by CNN in 2009 and 2010. *Data from CNN transcripts via Lexis-Nexis.*

their respective states and enjoyed significant contributions from national Tea Party funders, their ties to actual local Tea Party groups were tenuous. During the Florida Senate primary, local Tea Party members expressed concerns about Rubio, alleging that he ignored their requests to meet with him.[78] As for Scott Brown in Massachusetts, he participated in a fund-raiser with local Tea Party members in the last weeks of his campaign, yet claimed eleven days later to be "unfamiliar" with the Tea Party.[79] Such ambiguities got lost in the media translation, however, as both Brown and Rubio were touted as "Tea Party candidates" who won their respective elections with grassroots support against long odds. On February 1st, a *New Yorker* profile described the Tea Party as "the social movement that helped take Ted Kennedy's Massachusetts Senate seat away from the Democrats."[80]

Whenever a movement or interest group seems to have big clout in elections, journalists sit up and take notice—and this is what clearly happened for the Tea Party in 2010. With newfound credentials as an electoral force and kingmaker, the Tea Party was suddenly something all sorts of media outlets felt they had to probe, characterize, and feature.[81] Investigative reporters were dispatched, some of them far into the hinterlands to do virtually anthropological investigations.[82] Mainly, though, media-funded pollsters were set to work devising ways to characterize Tea Partiers and get a fix on what Americans in general thought about them. Simultaneously, political writers and pundits geared up to report survey findings and speculate about the impact of the Tea Party on primary and general election contests throughout 2010. In previous electoral cycles, "Reagan Democrats" or "Soccer Moms" were the big story. This time it was going to be "the Tea Party."

As media outlets rushed to respond to the apparently underreported Tea Party, journalists moved away from early mainstream assessments, which had rightly pegged the Tea Party as a conservative anti-tax, anti-Obama force within the Republican Party. In the spring of 2010, the mainstream media began to portray the Tea Party as a full-fledged independent political movement, and speculated about whether it might even be an alternative to the two major parties. That storyline depended heavily on interpretations of polling that we dissect below—and it was eventually overtaken by events, as the alignment of Tea Partiers with Republican goals and their engagement in Republican primaries became unmistakable.

The Use and Misuse of Surveys

A sure sign that the Tea Party was not at first taken very seriously by the mainstream media is the paucity of poll questions asked during early months. Many national political polls are commissioned by media outlets, and even those that run independently tend to set agendas in close tandem with national political coverage. Tellingly, a search of the database at the Roper Center for Public Opinion Research—the world's largest repository of survey data—finds fewer than ten poll questions asked about the Tea Party in 2009. Reporters were not yet obsessed with pinpointing Tea Party supporters. Although outlets like CNN took advantage of the Tea Party's TV-friendly spectacles—not only covering nationally synchronized rallies, but also sending a reporter to travel with the Tea Party Express bus tour in the fall of 2009—the hoopla was seen more as a sideshow than as central to serious politics.

By contrast, as media interest in the Tea Party skyrocketed during 2010, at least 300 poll questions asked explicitly about the Tea Party.[83] The Tea Party was the subject of more questions than were asked about Wall Street, though 2010 saw the passage of a major piece of financial reform legislation. More questions were asked about the Tea Party than were asked about the Iraq War, despite the fact that the conflict continued to cost the United States $5.5 billion a month.[84] By any standard, that is an extraordinary level of attention.

These polls then helped to drive yet more media coverage. Each new poll was the subject of multiple articles and opinion pieces, as journalists attempted to have the last word on the exotic and fascinating new political development. As Jonathan Martin and Ben Smith commented, "findings have been unveiled with the earnest detachment of Margaret Mead reporting her findings among teenage girls in Samoa."[85] This flurry of national surveys was used to assess the size of the Tea Party, the characteristics of its supporters, and its likely electoral implications.

But poll questions have to be designed and worded, and how they are designed influences the results obtained. In the earliest phases of intensive polling about the Tea Party, the nature of the poll questions, and dubious interpretations of the results, fed an overinflated and imprecise narrative about the Tea Party as a large mainstream movement. For much of 2010, polls and media interpretations fudged the limited scope and the deeply conservative nature of the Tea Party, making it seem more broadly popular and centrist than it really was.

Starting in the spring of 2010, a top question on reporters' minds was the scope of the Tea Party phenomenon. More than half of the 301 Tea Party–related poll questions put into the field during 2010 asked respondents whether they "support," "agree with," or "feel favorable" towards the Tea Party. Results were breathlessly reported. On the right, the Tea Party was persistently portrayed as a grassroots movement with a wide and growing base of support. *New York Times* columnist David Brooks went so far as to make the extraordinary assertion, in February 2010, that the Tea Party movement was "equally large" as the movement that brought Barack Obama to the presidency.[86] On the left, some contested this claim, but others engaged in handwringing about the apparent breadth of the Tea Party's popularity. Adele Stan of the progressive online news-magazine *Alternet* deemed the Tea Party a "profound threat," citing a poll showing 37% of Americans viewing it favorably.[87] Controversies could go on and on because there were wide deviations in poll results. Between February and December of 2010, levels of Tea Party support appeared to shift wildly from poll to poll, sometimes showing participation as low as 2%, and at other times suggesting that as many as a third of Americans were Tea Party supporters. Absent consensus or clear trends, each new poll resulted in a fresh round of tea-leaf reading by pundits.

Rarely discussed was how much of an effect the wording of questions had on whether respondents reported supporting or being involved with the Tea Party. Figure 4.3 summarizes the results of 45 polls from the major polling and news organizations, including Gallup, ABC/*Washington Post*, CBS/*New York Times*, NBC/*Wall Street Journal*, Quinnipiac, McClatchy, and CNN, among others.

Questions are divided into three types, depending on the type of support or involvement they specified. Asked a broad question such as "Do you consider yourself to be a supporter of the Tea Party movement?" between 18% and 31% of respondents said yes (with an average across polls of 26%). But when respondents were asked if they "consider themselves a part" of the Tea Party, the percentages drop to around 13% (with a range between 11% and 15%). Finally, in the six polls that query Americans about active participation in the Tea Party—for instance, donating money or attending a Tea Party event—involvement drops even lower, averaging about 8% (for all kinds of active participation combined).

The sense readers get of the level of Tea Party activity clearly varies depending on how the question is asked—and, not surprisingly, active involvement is

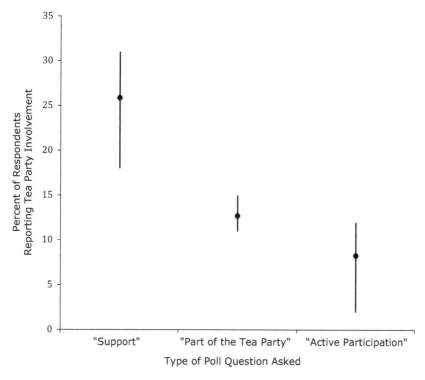

FIGURE 4.3. Survey Questions and Levels of Tea Party Support. *Results include 45 poll questions from the Roper Center on Public Opinion database.*

much less common than generalized support. All of the results are probably high-end estimates. Scholarship on surveys has established that people tend to overstate their involvement in all kinds of arenas, ranging from whether they voted to how often they attend church. As poll analyst Mark Blumenthal explains, "respondents often exaggerate their true levels of activism."[88] In Chapter 1 we explained our estimate that about 200,000 people were active participants in local Tea Parties in early 2011, a tiny fraction of American adults. Of course, polls were capturing broader circles of participation and sympathy. People could have read an email, visited a website, or dropped in on a rally and come to consider themselves active Tea Party participants. And it is certainly the case that many conservative Republicans, at least half of all GOP identifiers, are actively supportive of or sympathetic to the Tea Party.

The point about journalistic coverage of the Tea Party in 2010 is that editors and story-writers tended to put the broadest possible face on the Tea Party, and did not clearly distinguish levels and types of support. As

Washington Post columnist E.J. Dionne put it, the Tea Party in 2010 was a "tempest in a very small teapot."[89] But it could be made to seem massive. Expansive definitions based on the most general poll questions implied that a broad swath of Americans were deemed Tea Partiers, even if they had never attended a Tea Party meeting or rally, made a donation, or even visited a Tea Party website. As a result, the traits that made Tea Party activists unique—particularly their advanced age, lack of racial diversity, and their deep conservatism—were diluted in reports of survey findings. As late as April 2010, Gallup summarized their newest poll results with the headline "Tea Partiers Are Fairly Mainstream in Their Demographics."[90] And reporter Glynnis MacNicol followed a similar interpretive line in her discussion of the Gallup results. "Turns out no matter how in the habit the media is of using 'Tea Partiers' as a byword for crazy, fringe, offensive sign-bearing Americans," she wrote, "they are actually the opposite. Namely, everyday Americans."[91] Other polls would soon provide much more accurate and detailed takes on core participants in the Tea Party, but early, misleading results such as these helped bolster the case that the Tea Party was a popular, mainstream phenomenon.

Locating the Tea Party Politically

The framing of poll questions also ascribed to the Tea Party a level of independence and organizational strength that the phenomenon simply did not have. Even in 2009, the fledgling Tea Party was quickly dubbed a "movement," a term typically associated with broad and sustained surges such as Civil Rights, the Christian right, women's suffrage, and the labor movement. Other protest groups of recent years (even those that mounted larger rallies than the Tea Party, such as supporters of immigration rights) were neither described as movements, nor followed as closely in the media.

Terminology aside, people in the mainstream media dallied with the notion that the Tea Party was a novel, viable alternative to the major parties. One version of this notion migrated from conservative circles into the mainstream. Starting in the spring of 2009, right-wing strategists, including former House Majority Leader Newt Gingrich and Glenn Reynolds of the conservative blog Instapundit, argued that the Tea Party could turn into a third-party movement.[92] Early poll questions took up this notion and ran with it—going so far as to ask Americans to choose among imaginary tickets of candidates from the Democratic Party, the Republican Party, and "the Tea Party." The first analysts to use this question were conservative-leaning pollsters for Rasmussen (in December 2009) and the *National Review* (in January 2010).[93] Indeed, Scott Rasmussen later co-authored a book claiming, unbelievably, that the Tea Party movement was "fundamentally remaking the two-party system."[94] Soon enough, mainstream outlets, like CNN, NBC, and Quinnipiac, followed Rasmussen's lead. Results from such poll questions made news across the country—and pundits regularly implied that Tea Partiers were a force different from Republicans, or even from conservatives. Washington insider publications like *Frum Forum, The Hill,* and *Plumline* cited the Rasmussen poll's findings, and David Brooks claimed that the Rasmussen poll was evidence that the Tea Party was "especially popular among independents."[95]

The wrong-headed notion that the Tea Party appealed to centrist independents was bolstered by another misreading of poll data. Several polls conducted in early 2010 asked about respondents' party identification with a simple question, something along the lines of: "Generally speaking, do you usually think of yourself as a Republican, a Democrat, an Independent, or what?"[96] This seems like a straightforward question but, in fact, it got pollsters misleading answers because a lot of people who generally vote for either Democrats or Republicans tend to say they are independent when first asked. Pollsters have come to understand this, so most use a standard follow-up question about whether respondents "lean" towards one party or another. Study after study has found that "leaners" typically behave like party faithful.[97] Polls that ask only that first question without the follow-up often find that large percentages of respondents are political independents, though many of those surveyed actually vote regularly for one party or the other.

In fact, Tea Partiers are conservative Republican voters. But in the early going, single-question polls mistakenly recorded very high levels of political "independence" among sympathizers or supporters. For example, the April 2010 poll done by the Winston Group concluded that 40% of Tea Partiers were Democrats or independents. These results were widely and uncritically reported, making headlines at the *LA Times* and *The Hill,* and through the McClatchy News Service, and getting coverage on CNN.[98] Perhaps media outlets should not be faulted for a lack of familiarity with the intricacies of party identification survey questions. But given that the Winston Group is run by David Winston, a lifelong Republican strategist and former advisor to Newt Gingrich, these poll figures should certainly have provoked more scrutiny than they received. Instead, media outlets that had in 2009 consistently and correctly referred to the Tea Party as a movement of conservatives, now trumpeted it as part of a "growing cloud of political independents," akin to the Ross Perot movement in 1992.[99]

In the real world, political developments in and around the Republican Party steadily undermined any narrative of the Tea Party as a bunch of centrist swing-voters. Tea Party voters and funders weighed in during GOP primaries, sometimes knocking out incumbents. One key electoral event after another, in short, revealed Tea Party forces to be kingmakers, boosters, or spoilers for the GOP, even as quite a few pollsters and analysts persisted in debating whether it was a nascent third party. Only in the latter part of 2010 did the preponderance of poll questions ask about the influence of the Tea Party on the Republican Party—and, in due course, about whether respondents saw a difference between the Republican Party and the Tea Party.

We might conclude that pollsters and their media sponsors and commentators eventually got it right, so it does not matter that they were slow to get an accurate bead on the Tea Party's true political location. By the time they did, the flood of Tea Party candidates running in Republican primaries made any claims of political independence implausible to even the most casual observer. But it probably does matter that, for six months or more, claims of the Tea Party's mainstream appeal and political independence were reinforced by an approach to polling and interpretation of survey results that was fundamentally misleading. Credulous reporting—and perhaps some eagerness among reporters and editors to tout an interesting story about a supposedly mainstream populist uprising—misled regular American media consumers for months. The misrepresentation was also a shot in the arm for local and national Tea Party groups seeking to build followings, collect checks, and influence public discussions. It could only help the Tea Party to be portrayed as "mainstream."

Overall, between mid-2009 and mid-2010, the pendulum of media coverage of the Tea Party swung from comic derision to solemn portentousness. No longer (mistakenly) portrayed as a trivial collection of crackpots, the Tea Party came during much of 2010 to be (misleadingly) portrayed as a formidable, independent political movement that threatened to overturn the two-party system.

A more accurate portrayal would have stressed the Tea Party as a force aiming to remake as well as boost the Republican Party, a force that involved both ideological elites and big money funders on the one hand, and genuine grassroots protestors and organizers, on the other hand. Does it matter that the Tea Party was portrayed as too large, popular, and centrist? We cannot rerun history during 2010 to find out. But it was an important election year, when Americans in general were trying to make sense of raging debates over the economy, the effectiveness of government and the Obama administration, and the alternatives offered by Democrats and Republicans. A better understanding of what the Tea Party was really about—pushing the GOP to the right, and fiercely opposing all things Democrat or Obama—could only have helped the majority of citizens to more effectively think through their options.

The Growing Leverage of National Advocates

The penultimate phase of mainstream media handling of the Tea Party came after the November 2010 elections—which, as we will learn in greater detail in the next chapter, were a triumph for the GOP in part because Tea Party activists and funders played significant roles. Right now, let's look at what happened after Tea Partiers appeared to influence electoral outcomes in a big way, as they did during special elections and GOP primaries and, even more spectacularly, in the November 2010 general elections.

Once editors and reporters realized that the Tea Party was not only an anthropologically fascinating clump of activists and voters, but also a force helping to shift party balances in elections, they became preoccupied with finding "Tea Party leaders" to quote and put on the air. The hunt for such spokespersons happened all along. But it became more intense as Tea Party–linked candidates won elections. Sending cameras to rallies, even writing about national surveys, was no longer enough once the GOP—apparently riding a Tea Party wave—won control of the House of Representatives and was poised to redirect policies about taxes, spending, hot-button social issues, and major federal programs like Medicare, Medicaid, and Social Security. What did "the Tea Party" think about these issues? What would it demand from the newly elected GOP legislators engaged in fierce debates with President Obama and the (still barely) Democrat-controlled Senate?

One instance of the media's hunt for easy answers appeared in an opening vignette for this chapter, where we saw that immediately after the November elections, former GOP honcho and corporate lobbyist Dick

Armey, chairman of the DC-based, business-funded advocacy organization FreedomWorks, was rebranded a "grassroots" leader by CNN's Paul Steinhauser. Another even more startling instance occurred on January 25th, 2011, following the President's State of the Union address and the traditional response from the opposing party. President Obama duly delivered his address, and the officially designated GOP spokesman, Representative Paul Ryan of Wisconsin, delivered his party's rebuttal. But then CNN teamed up with Tea Party Express to broadcast *yet another* response to the President— by Representative Michele Bachmann, Republican from Minnesota and the self-appointed chair of the House Tea Party Caucus! CNN's broadcast could give a casual viewer the false impression that the Tea Party was something apart from both major parties; consequently, in the aftermath, the network drew criticism from the right and the left for airing what was essentially a second GOP response to Obama. But CNN defended its choice, claiming that the Tea Party "has become a major force in American politics." [100] This did not explain, however, why one GOP politician was an appropriate mouthpiece for the entire complex phenomenon.

The pressing need to find media spokespersons for the Tea Party was, of course, awkward, given that the actual Tea Party has never been more than a disunited field of jostling organizations. A lot of Tea Party activism goes on in localities, states, and regions—and even at the national level there are no true chieftains of any global Tea Party entity. Alas, if such realities were bravely acknowledged, reporters would have a hard time figuring out "Tea Party demands," let alone conveying the complexity to readers and viewers. Instead, media outlets looked around for easy-to-contact spokespersons. And, naturally, there are always ambitious national politicos and advocacy elites who, in this particular case, like to see themselves as "Tea Party leaders." After the 2010 elections, especially, a lot of self-designated Tea Party leaders were happy to make themselves available for public statements or performances. Supply met demand.

Writing for the *Columbia Journalism Review*, Joel Meares nicely captures the symbiosis that has played out in the "Tea Party spokesperson" game. As 2011 dawned, explains Meares, "Tea Party Patriots co-founder and national coordinator Mark Meckler was the lead quote-giver in the major *New York Times* and *Los Angeles Times* stories" that first weekend of the New Year, as reporters tried to get a sense of what would happen with the new GOP House majority. Meares explains how the stories were framed and what their commonalities tell us about media practices:

The themes of both pieces are near identical: the Tea Party is displeased with what it views as GOP capitulation in the lame duck session that ended in 2010, and, as such, will be keeping its eye on the new class of Republicans entering Congress tomorrow. Meckler—as a kind of figurehead for the Tea Party movement in the stories—led the charge on both claims, in both outlets. The problem with both stories is that, to varying degrees, like many reports on the still amorphous movement, the writers for the most part treat the movement as uniform and un-conflicted. Both posit Meckler as a kind of movement leader, when he is but one of many vying for that position—a position still some way off from viably existing. Without a more nuanced treatment of this not-monolithic movement, readers are left with the impression, encouraged by each new report of this nature, that the Tea Party is something it isn't.[101]

As the Tea Party became an electoral and national lobbying force—and was portrayed that way in the media—the balance of leverage between top-down and bottom-up actors shifted within the Tea Party itself. Changes in the internal dynamics of the Tea Party started with early electoral victories and sped up after the Republican Party won smashing triumphs in November 2010, bringing many Tea Party–aligned legislators and governors into office.

Even before the 2010 elections, self-designated Congressional Tea Party leaders appeared on the scene, with Minnesota GOP Representative Michele Bachmann founding a "Tea Party Caucus" in the House, and South Carolina GOP Senator Jim DeMint founding a similar, though less effective, caucus in the Senate. Both caucuses grew after the 2010 elections. Once the legislative caucuses formed, media outlets could follow—and quote—supposed Tea Party spokespersons who are in fact elected officeholders from very particular places (a conservative Minnesota district, the ultra-conservative state of South Carolina, and so forth).

More broadly, as the Tea Party gained celebrity, various paid professionals and staffers outside of public office gained chances to speak on behalf of the whole amorphous protest effort. Designation by the media has raised the profiles not just of the coordinators of Tea Party Patriots, but also of flacks from free-market think tanks and advocacy organizations, and of directors of political action committees funneling funds to Republican candidates deemed "Tea Party endorsed." After November 2010, delegates from inside-the-beltway advocacy organizations ramped up appearances in the media and at forums, anointed as mouthpieces for a mass "grassroots movement." Honchos from the national and state units of Americans for Prosperity popped up on television and in the newspapers to tell us "what the Tea Party wants"—which turns out to include things like the privatization of Social Security and Medicare that such organizations and their ideological funders have been pushing for decades. And of course spokespersons from political action committees like Tea Party Express stepped forward to tell us which moderate GOP Senators "the Tea Party" is targeting for primary defeats in 2012.[102]

There is an ironic counterpart to the growing visibility of elite spokespersons. The Tea Party, as we have seen, originally captivated the mainstream media because it was seen as a mighty grassroots force. But the needs of media outlets themselves increasingly privilege the parts of the Tea Party panoply that are anything but truly grass roots. With national spokespersons such as elected officeholders and paid professionals gaining clout, grassroots Tea Partiers tend to lose visibility.

As of mid-2011, local Tea Party groups were still perking along in many places (as we have seen earlier and will further see in the next chapter). Following the big election victories for the GOP in 2010, grassroots Tea Parties geared up as persistent "watchdogs" monitoring and pressing elected officeholders. But such activities at the grass roots are not flashy, and national media only occasionally notice, even when they continue to give disproportionate play to rallies that are not where the real grassroots action is anymore. After November 2010, the frequency and size of regional and national Tea Party protest rallies diminished. Tax Day rallies in 2011, for instance, were much smaller in many cities than they were in 2010, though they still attracted a lot of press.[103] Similarly, the turnout for DC rallies to pressure Congress has been pitiful by past Tea Party standards, even when the press still flock to cover rallies where protestors barely outnumber the reporters and camera-people.[104] These shifts at the grass roots toward local organizing rather than rallies have not diminished the national media presence of "the Tea Party," however. Media outlets can run a bit of footage showing people in costumes with signs—and then proceed to feature the likes of Michele Bachmann and Jim DeMint from Congress, or Dick Armey from Freedom-Works, or Mark Meckler and Jenny Beth Martin from Tea Party Patriots. The mass movement portrayed in 2010 can simply be reassigned to the role of backdrop for pronouncements from such elite soothsayers.

Loosely interconnected all along, the Tea Party has evolved from a field of organizations where much of the élan and initiative rested in hundreds of local groups, into a much-publicized political faction where national organizations have the advantage. Conservative media, as we documented in this chapter, played an indispensable role at the start, helping the nascent Tea Party mount visible protests and achieve ongoing political clout. Then media outlets across the board trumpeted all sorts of Tea Party undertakings in a critical midterm election year. Media outlets from giant to tiny have been part of the Tea Party story all along. And, naturally, they are also pivotal to the most recent shifts in visibility—as elite spokespersons for "the Tea Party" hog the cameras, while grassroots citizens and local Tea Parties fade into the shadows.

5

How the Tea Party Boosts the GOP and Prods It Rightward

The Tea Party includes grassroots activists, conservative media ideologues, and billionaire-backed free-market advocacy groups, all jostling for attention and power. With the Republican victories in the 2010 midterms, Tea Partiers from each of these arenas have felt free to call the shots: to demand immediate measures to slash public spending and taxes, abolish the rights of public sector unions, and eliminate business regulations. Wherever they can weigh in, Tea Partiers loudly tell Republican officeholders to do what they want or else face challenges from the right in the next election.

For the Republican Party, the Tea Party cuts both ways. Certainly, its enthusiasm and resources fuel the GOP. But the story is more complex because the Tea Party is not just a booster organization for Any-Old-Republicans. Tea Party activists at the grass roots and the right-wing advocates roving the national landscape with billionaire backing have designs on the Republican Party. They want to remake it into a much more uncompromising and ideologically principled force. As Tea Party forces make headway in achieving this ideological purification, they spur movement of the Republican Party ever further toward the right, and align the party with a label that principally appeals to older, very conservative white voters.

As we have learned throughout this book, Tea Party activists, supporters, and funders are not middle-of-the-roaders. With very few exceptions, they are people with long histories of voting for and giving money to Republicans. Even those who have stood apart to the right of the GOP—organizing as Libertarians, for example—certainly have not helped Democrats. At the grass roots as well as in national advocacy circles, Tea Party people aim to defeat Obama and Democrats, and want to curb taxes and government activities at all levels from localities to states to the federal government. To these ends, Tea Partiers reject any notion of organizing a separate third party that would divide forces on the right and clear the way for Democrats.[1] Maneuvering at the rightward end of the GOP, Tea Party participants aim to elect staunchly conservative Republicans. They enjoyed considerable success in 2010, and they aim to do more of the same in 2012.

Yet Tea Partiers also vex "establishment" Republicans. Funders and television hosts and radio jocks brandishing the Tea Party label have undercut longtime Republican officeholders in primaries, including some conservatives who initially enjoyed virtually unanimous backing from Republican Party officials and strategists. Between elections, Tea Party activists are moving in and taking over Republican Party committees in many places. And because Tea Party grassroots participants and elites distrust moderate GOP officeholders, they appoint themselves watchdogs to keep officials "honest," pushing Republican candidates and officials to be more staunchly ultra-conservative.

Above all, Tea Partiers want Republicans in office to refuse compromises with Democrats over the scope and funding of government. They "go nuclear" when GOP officeholders take any steps toward moderation and negotiation. If Tea Party–oriented Republicans have even tiny margins of control, they are expected to ram through maximalist programs. If GOP officials have to coexist with Democrats and moderates, well, as the Tea Party sees it, they should just suck it up and hold firm, until they get their way, or most of it.

Such pressures from the Tea Party can put Republican officeholders and candidates in a bind. What happens if compromises must be made to keep government in operation? Or if candidates looking toward the next election are worried about attracting support from moderate Republicans and middle-of-the-road independents as well as from hard-core GOP conservatives? This question is especially acute for politicians facing election or reelection in the presidential election year of 2012, when voter turnout will be higher, younger, and more diverse than in 2010.

To explain how and why the Tea Party both boosts the GOP and prods it toward right-wing overreach, it helps to keep the key insight of this book front and center. Several interacting forces are at work in the Tea Party: grass-roots activism, media hype, and the interventions of national advocacy groups channeling funds and endorsements. Most of the time, all these forces push in the same direction and boost the Republican Party in its bottom-line competition against Democrats. But not always. At times, ultra-free-market advocates operating in the name of the Tea Party press for policies that may hamper the efforts of GOP officials and strategists to build majorities in election contests. What is more, ideological advocates leveraging the Tea Party may go further than the grass roots—for example toward calling for legislation eliminating Medicare or privatizing Social Security. The chief aim of the national advocates is to push GOP candidates and officeholders toward the ideological right—above all, to hold their feet to the fire for big cuts in taxes and public spending and the removal of regulations that in any way limit the prerogatives of business or the super-wealthy. The national billionaire-backed advocacy groups that manipulate funding and endorsements in the name of the Tea Party are not merely trying to win the next election for the GOP. Nor are the ideological advocates giving priority to grassroots concerns. Instead, they aim to remake the Republican Party into a disciplined, uncompromising machine devoted to radical free-market goals.

This chapter focuses on three phases in the intricate and unfolding relationship between the GOP and the Tea Party. We start with the role of the Tea Party in the 2010 elections, and then examine the ways in which elite and grassroots Tea Party forces have prodded newly empowered GOP officeholders. At the end, we weigh prospects for the Tea Party to help and hurt Republicans in the run-up to 2012.

THE TEA PARTY AND THE GOP IN 2010

The Republican Party scored commanding electoral victories in November 2010—and in the process, the party experienced internal tensions and lost some key opportunities, especially in races for control of the Senate. Tea Party forces were at work in both the smashing successes and the missed opportunities. Yet, as we are about to show, from the perspective of Tea Party actors themselves, the bottom line may be very good—or at least good enough and headed in the right direction.

Did Tea Party Enthusiasm Fuel Republican Victories?

The big picture is clear enough: the growth of the Tea Party in 2009 and 2010 coincided with an electoral turnaround for Republicans. In the late fall of 2008, pundits were marveling at the huge victories just scored by Barack Obama and Democratic candidates for Congress and state-level offices, wondering if America was on the verge of a second New Deal and permanent Democratic majorities.[2] The Republican Party and its leaders were in bad shape with the public. But just two years later the Republican Party roared back to life, with Tea Party voters flooding the polls to support its candidates, and self-appointed Tea Party spokespersons crowing about America's turn to the right.

In November 2010, resurgent Republicans gained sixty-three seats to take control of the House of Representatives, and won six additional seats in the Senate to greatly reduce the previous Democratic margin of control in that body. GOP gains were even more astounding in states across the country, as Republicans gained around 700 seats in state legislatures and added six governorships, to bring their total to twenty-nine (with Democrats holding on to just twenty governorships and an Independent elected in Rhode Island).[3] With electoral redistricting in process following the 2010 U.S. Census, Republicans can jigger district boundaries to try to protect incumbent Republican officeholders and force out some Democrats where population losses dictate fewer districts. Equally important, Republican governors backed by like-minded legislatures now call the tune in states such as Florida, Michigan, Wisconsin, and Ohio that will be pivotal in the 2012 presidential contest. President Obama rightly declared that his party took a "shellacking" in November 2010. The results crimp his style as president and complicate his campaign for reelection.

The role of the Tea Party in the GOP voter upsurge in 2010 is a matter of some debate. For many commentators, it seems obvious that the rising GOP tide that crested well beyond Democratic shoreline defenses in November 2010 was significantly propelled by the Tea Party efforts that burst onto the scene right at the start of Obama's presidency and built momentum through 2009 and 2010. Even before the November election, the *New York Times* proclaimed the "Tea Party set to win enough races for wide influence."[4] Right after the election, major outlets announced, as ABC News put it, that "candidates backed by the Tea Party scored major victories in Tuesday's midterm elections"—though a few high-profile losses were noted, especially among Senate contenders.[5] Fox News trumpeted Tea Party victories nonstop, of course, and other outlets got carried away, too. An NBC affiliate in Montana proclaimed the Tea Party one of the "biggest 2010 election winners. . . . Once dismissed with little chance of having lasting power, the tea party's effect on the midterm elections can't be viewed as anything other than immense."[6] Before long, a conventional wisdom jelled, so thoroughly that by March of 2011 a routine *New York Times* news analysis about budget maneuvers in the GOP House could nonchalantly refer to "the Tea Party ideology that catapulted Republicans to the majority in November and made . . . [John Boehner] House speaker."[7]

Not everyone agrees with the dominant storyline, however. A *Washington Post* investigatory team raised questions in late October 2010 about whether Tea Party activists really did amount to an electoral juggernaut. Reporter Amy Gardner and her colleagues tracked down 647 local Tea Party groups and interviewed their leaders. Most Tea Party groups claimed fewer than fifty members, had tiny budgets, did not officially endorse political candidates, and did not report high levels of involvement in organized get-out-the-vote efforts or other electioneering activities.[8] How could such scattered and relatively small groups have a huge electoral impact, especially when their leaders reported that members mostly just attended meetings to hear lectures and educate themselves as voters?

Two additional skeptics are Harvard political scientists Steve Ansolabehere and Jim Snyder, who crunched some numbers to see what happened to Tea Party Congressional candidates "in an election year that favored Republican politicians because of the prolonged economic recession and stubbornly high unemployment."[9] "Tea Party candidates" in this study were those formally endorsed by Tea Party Express, FreedomWorks, or both. The authors found that these national advocacy groups spent only a fraction of the huge sums of money directed to GOP candidates by all kinds of business and conservative fundraisers. And they stress that, especially in the House races, Tea Party–endorsed candidates won their races no more frequently than other GOP candidates did. Although Tea Party endorsed candidates usually won, the national advocacy groups "played with a stacked deck, tending to support Republican candidates in Republican-leaning districts more than in Democratic-leaning districts."[10] Ansolabehere and Snyder suggest that Tea Party Express and FreedomWorks merely rode the GOP wave of 2010, and did not propel or shape it.[11]

While the conventional wisdom about the Tea Party as driver of the GOP victories sometimes gets carried away, we think the doubters underestimate the impact of combined Tea Party forces on GOP momentum going into November 2010. Most basically, grassroots Tea Party protests and local network-building helped the Republican Party escape the defeatism that pervaded party ranks after the massive defeats Republicans suffered in 2008. After that election, conservatives and the Republican rank-and-file continued to hate Obama and wanted to renew the conservative movement. But they were discouraged. They could not hark back to the unpopular George W. Bush, and many never liked John McCain that much. And by the end of 2009, the Republican National Committee was in near-complete disarray, struggling from financial mismanagement and serious failures of leadership under Michael Steele.[12] With the "Republican Party" tarnished, the emergence of the Tea Party raised the spirits of conservatives and gave them a place to channel energies. As Nate Silver aptly puts it, the Tea Party ended up serving as "an end-around for Republicans," allowing them to escape the consequences of "a party brand which is badly damaged."[13] The various Tea Party funder groups also served the purpose of directing money to conservative candidates without it having to be filtered through the bumbling Republican Party machine—an approach taken by other Republican advocacy groups as well, particularly in the wake of the Supreme Court decision striking down significant campaign-finance limitations.[14]

Moreover, the huge media coverage for Tea Party complaints about "big government" spending and bailouts—not to mention the coverage of dramatic protests about ObamaCare and cap and trade legislation—helped Republicans and conservatives to reset national agendas of debate. People stopped talking about Obama and "change we can believe in" and started talking about government tyranny. As the economy continued to be in the doldrums and unemployment remained high, the GOP, buoyed by Tea Party hoopla, made the upcoming elections about approval or disapproval of Obama and the Democrats.

To be sure, most voters who went to the polls in November 2010 told exit pollsters that their primary concern was the economy and jobs.[15] Democrats held the presidency and the formal leadership of both houses of Congress, so naturally, voters held them more responsible for the down economy. But voters did not express a lot of positive, forward-looking faith in the Republican Party, and most of those who went to the polls in November 2010 did not profess to be Tea Party supporters, either. Still, anyone who turned on the television in 2009 and 2010 had heard and seen much about Tea Party complaints and GOP messages claiming that Washington DC was hurting rather than helping economic growth. Obama and the Democrats were not given credit for economic recovery measures and reforms they enacted, not even when experts pronounced the measures effective in staving off a second Great Depression in the United States. How could some droning economic report compete with pictures of protesters carrying provocative signs?

The academic political science profession includes an industry of number-crunchers who create models to predict election outcomes. These models aren't perfect, but they do give us some important rules of thumb.[16] Down economies and prior gains by an incumbent party that controls both the presidency and Congress are the two best predictors of big election *losses* for that party the next time around. So, Tea Party or no Tea Party, Democrats were bound to suffer losses in November 2010 according to conventional academic wisdom. But of course the Democrats suffered *even* bigger losses than many political science modelers expected. We think much of the reason lies in the parallel between who Tea Party people are and who goes to the polls in midterm elections, and did so especially in 2010.

In the presidential election year of 2008, 63% of eligible U.S. voters went to the polls. Younger voters, minorities, and women all participated at high rates and delivered disproportionate support to Democrats across the board.[17] But in 2010, the electorate shrank to just 40.3% of eligible voters— that's right, less than half of the voters who could have showed up at the polls actually did.[18] As is usually the case, those who voted were markedly older, whiter, and more comfortable economically than those who stayed home. Midterm voters usually lean toward Republicans. And in 2010, this was even more the case than usual because Republicans and older people were revved up to go to the polls, while younger voters and those who might have voted Democratic were unenthusiastic and stayed home in droves. The demographic categories that are more Democratic-friendly were the ones hardest hit, overall, by the 2008–09 Great Recession and the lingering high levels of unemployment. But younger people and minorities did not, on balance, vote their frustrations; instead, they often stayed home.

GOP constituencies, including independents who swung toward the Republicans in 2010, were angry and afraid more than disappointed, and they went to the polls to "throw the bastards out." It might be a coincidence that Tea Party supporters overlap with the older, white, middle-class

Republicans who turned out enthusiastically and disproportionately in 2010, but probably not. Older white Americans were, all along, the ones least happy about Obama's presence in the White House. Some small fraction of them organized the hundreds of Tea Party groups that met and protested across the country during 2009 and 2010. But that Tea Party minority surely had an effect far disproportionate to simple numbers.

Social scientists have established something that makes intuitive good sense: when people get together in groups, even just to socialize with one another, they are more likely than their isolated fellow citizens to also get themselves to the polls on election day.[19] People who attend meetings or otherwise get together with others are more likely to think they know what is going on politically, more likely to think it could matter if they vote, and more likely to feel obligated to vote in order not to let their friends down. So the *Washington Post* study was perhaps too quick to dismiss the electoral relevance of local Tea Party efforts. Even when grassroots Tea Party groups did not report being engaged in formal election activities, hundreds of revved up clusters of like-minded people getting together regularly across the United States certainly did matter (and not just because television and other news outlets constantly trumpeted Tea Partiers' angry and fearful claims: their attacks on "ObamaCare"; their scorn at the "bailouts"; their claim that federal regulations and spending were killing the economy and squandering the nation's future). Even if most local Tea Party groups could not rival the efforts of millions of mainly youthful 2008 Obama for America people in getting out the vote, the older Americans who attend Tea Party meetings have lots of friends and contacts. Tea Party grassroots participants were themselves highly motivated to vote in 2010, and they likely influenced other Republican and GOP-leaning voters, especially other older people like themselves.

November 2010 was an election that expressed, above all, the fears and anger of many older citizens. Older white Americans not only voted in high numbers—making up a substantially bigger part of the electorate even than they usually do in midterm elections—they swung hard against the Democrats. Before Obama burst on the political scene, back in the 2006 midterm election, voters 65 and older essentially split their party support, giving 52% to Democratic House candidates.[20] But older voters, especially whites, had relatively little enthusiasm for Barack Obama as he gained political traction in 2007 and 2008. In 2008, the GOP, led by John McCain, won the 65-and-over vote by an 8% margin (53% to 45%).[21] Thereafter, the age gap opened even further, so that in the 2010 midterm elections the GOP thumped Democrats among voters 65 and older by an amazing 21% margin, 59% to 38%.[22]

Almost certainly, the agitation and anger of older Tea Party sympathizers had something to do with this swing. Tea Partiers hate Obama and decried health reform starting in the summer of 2009. Both of these messages resonated with older voters in general. Older Americans, for example, have been the demographic group most opposed to the Affordable Care Act of 2010, with many of them telling pollsters that they fear "death panels" or think that health reform for all Americans will result in sharp cuts to Medicare.[23] Such fearful messages, aimed at the elderly, were pushed nonstop by the Tea Party and other GOP-related groups during 2009 and 2010. Fearmongering among the elderly, a group wary of Obama in the first place, surely helped to ensure that Congressional Democrats in 2010 not only experienced a negative swing but suffered a devastating set of electoral setbacks.

The bottom line, then, is that Tea Party forces—especially grassroots participants and the favorable media attention they got—may not have made the difference in November 2010 between GOP victory and defeat. But the Tea Partiers and their adoring media surely helped re-inspire grassroots conservatives, set a national agenda for the election, and claim a Republican-wave election as vindication for a particular, extreme conservative ideology.

Not Always Hand in Glove

Not everything came up roses for the GOP partnership with the Tea Party in 2010. Just seven weeks before the critical midterm elections, Karl Rove was flummoxed and of two minds—uncharacteristic for a man routinely dubbed "The Architect" for his plotting of winning strategies for fellow Republicans. Rove's discomfiture was sparked by the results of the September 14, 2010 primary elections, particularly in the tiny, typically overlooked state of Delaware. The master GOP strategist was suddenly looking at the results of Tea Party interventions that might cost his party control of the next Congress in an upcoming November election that otherwise looked like a slam dunk for sweeping Republican gains.

On Fox television that primary-election evening an obviously chagrined Rove raised questions about the "nutty" statements and "checkered background" of Christine O'Donnell, a 41-year-old Tea Party–backed upstart who had surged from far behind to win the Delaware GOP Senate nomination.[24] O'Donnell was a little-known social issues activist, a woman of questionable career achievements and dubious personal finances, who had roundly lost both elections she had previously contested.[25] But in the final weeks before the September 14 primary, she was the beneficiary of high-profile endorsements from two self-appointed Tea Party impresarios, Sarah Palin and ultra-conservative South Carolina GOP Senator Jim DeMint, and at the same time was buoyed by the sudden infusion of hundreds of thousands of dollars in campaign cash from the California-based Tea Party Express.[26] Also backed by the National Rifle Association, the Concerned Women for America, the Family Research Council, and assorted anti-abortion groups, O'Donnell aroused passionate populist enthusiasm from right-wing GOP voters in two out of three Delaware counties, Kent and Sussex—counties that are more rural and socially conservative than the more populous New Castle County surrounding Wilmington.[27] Boosted by an extraordinarily high turnout for a Delaware GOP primary, especially from Christian evangelicals, O'Donnell claimed a 53% to 47% victory over her establishment rival Mike Castle, a nine-term GOP House incumbent and popular former governor.[28]

This was perhaps the most surprising of a number of Tea Party upsets in GOP primaries during 2010. Well-liked by many Delaware voters of all political persuasions, Mike Castle was a moderate conservative backed by state and national Republican Party leaders. Just weeks before the September primary, he had seemed a "sure thing" to win the GOP nomination and go on in November to win the Delaware Senate seat long held by Democrats (indeed, until 2009, by Vice President Joe Biden). On primary election eve, Fox's Sean Hannity tried to get Karl Rove to agree that O'Donnell's conservative victory over a RINO ("Republican In Name Only") was a good thing. Although Castle had toed the GOP line in opposing Obama's 2009 stimulus legislation and 2010 health reform, Hannity cited the things right-wing Republicans disliked: Castle supported abortion rights and gun control, he had voted for the bailout of Wall Street banks, and he was one of only a few GOP House members to vote in favor of cap and trade legislation during the 111th Congress. These stances were not ideal, Rove agreed, but he explained to Fox's overwhelmingly Republican viewers that prior to the Delaware primary, "we were looking at eight to nine seats in the Senate"—enough, perhaps, to flip control from the Democrats to the GOP—but "we are now looking at seven to eight in my opinion," because with O'Donnell rather than Castle as the GOP nominee, the November 2010 general election in Delaware "is not a race we're going to be able to win." "At the end of the day . . . we are going to find ourselves with somebody who says conservative things, but doesn't have the character that the people of Delaware want. . . ."[29]

Within hours a firestorm of conservative anger pushed back against Rove's reluctance to cheerlead for O'Donnell. National advocates renewed and amplified the support they orchestrated for her before the primary. A day later, Rove stopped criticizing and got with the program. He pledged his support to O'Donnell and declared that he had sent a check to her campaign.[30]

O'Donnell's war chest was brimming, in any case. For the November election, she greatly outraised her Democratic opponent, New Castle County Executive Chris Coons. To be sure, Coons did very well, raising over $3.8 million, about half from in-state sources and the rest from national Democrats thrilled at their chance to hold the former Biden seat. But O'Donnell hauled in an amazing $7.5 million, 90% from national conservatives and other interests outside Delaware.[31] Similarly, while O'Donnell only sporadically campaigned on the ground in Delaware, she was a sensation in the national media. In due course, the Pew Project for Excellence in Journalism would conclude that O'Donnell got more media coverage during 2010 than any other figure except President Obama.[32]

Still, Rove had been right about Christine O'Donnell. Her past was picked apart, and she was a constant font of controversial, silly statements— some recorded long in the past (for example, she had acknowledged dabbling in witchcraft and once led a campaign against out-of-wedlock sex) and others delivered off-the-cuff during the campaign (such as her inability to identify any Supreme Court justices, her confusing statements about the theory of evolution, and her assertion that the U.S. Constitution does not enshrine the separation of church and state). From the day after the primary, O'Donnell trailed Democrat Coons in polls of prospective Delaware voters. Despite a relatively high turnout on November 2, O'Donnell lost to Coons, gaining only 40% of the vote to 57% for him.[33] The remarkable amounts of campaign money O'Donnell raised netted her only five percentage points more in the final vote balance than she won in 2008, when she got 35% running against Joe Biden as a little-known candidate with modest, primarily in-state funding.[34] Her national Tea Party funders could leverage a 2010 primary victory and much notoriety. But in a state not safe for the GOP, they could not deliver that extra Senate seat that Karl Rove had been counting on.

The 2010 Delaware story reminds us that the Tea Party is not just about grassroots activists who get themselves and their neighbors to the polls to vote for Republicans in contests against Democrats. The Tea Party also includes billionaire-funded national organizations and self-appointed national spokespersons whose impact on 2010 and beyond we also need to highlight. Urged on and glorified by Fox News and other conservative media outlets, grassroots Tea Partiers helped to set the issue agenda and probably increased the enthusiasm and determination of many older whites to vote against Obama and the Democrats. Yet Tea Party funders and king-makers were also roving the landscape during the run-up to November 2010. They, too, influenced national discussions by funding issue ads and making endorsements and fiery pronouncements. For the national funders and advocates, the primary goal was not just to help any old Republican get elected in a favorable year.

Wielding endorsements and sending checks, self-appointed Tea Party politicians and organizations like Tea Party Express and FreedomWorks, and their ilk were trying to increase their dominance within the Republican Party, and to make sure that moderate, compromise-oriented Republicans did not get nominated at all. No wonder Ansolabehere and Snyder found that formal endorsements and funding made little difference to whether a House Republican beat a Democrat in November 2010, and also found a slight negative effect of Tea Party endorsements on GOP versus Democratic Senate races in 2010.[35] Mere GOP general election victories were not really what the ultra-free-market billionaire Tea Party funding fronts were after—and not what self-declared Tea Party impresarios like Sarah Palin and Jim DeMint were aiming for, either.

These national actors were trying to cull out moderately conservative Republicans and replace them with ultra-conservatives. Their goal was to solidify their own power-base within the Republican Party by increasing the party's stock of new, loyal, and ideologically driven politicians. In this, the elites involved with "Tea Party" activism were not unlike previous advocates for Christian conservatives. "The Christian Coalition . . . basically collapsed since the departure of Ralph Reed," Michael Franc, vice president for government relations at the Heritage Foundation told a *New York Times* reporter. "There was a vacuum and Armey and some of these other economic conservative groups have filled it" by engaging conservative voters on the ground and pushing a purer ideological agenda.[36] Thus, the real action for them was in the GOP primaries. And as the Senate races of 2010 show, sometimes the ultra-free-marketers went so far in replacing regular conservative GOPers with far-right alternatives that they jeopardized otherwise excellent Republican prospects to win in November.

Christine O'Donnell in Delaware was not the only case of national Tea Party overkill. There were additional states where ultra-right-wing GOP candidates not likely to appeal to moderate voters were nominated with help from some combination of outside funding from Tea Party Express (or other national Tea Party groups) and endorsements from kingpins.[37] These instances included Sharron Angle in Nevada, Ken Buck in Colorado, Jim Miller in Alaska, and Carl Paladino in New York. In all these cases except perhaps the last, the ultra-right candidates, endorsed and helped by national Tea Party backers, displaced less extreme GOP conservatives who had established track records in their states. After Miller nudged out Murkowski in the Alaska primary, she still hung in there and won a remarkable comeback as a write-in candidate. Republicans kept her Senate seat, even if Murkowski is now a bit soured on Jim DeMint and Tea Party billionaires who tried to push her out. But in the final analysis, the Republican Party in 2010 forfeited potentially winnable Senate races not only in Delaware but also in Nevada and Colorado; and the party reduced its chances to compete for the governorship in New York.

Does it matter from the perspective of the roving billionaire Tea Party advocacy groups? Not clear. After all, in other GOP nomination races they helped along very conservative nominees who ultimately won Senate seats in November even after displacing slightly more centrist GOP competitors. Those key nomination victories included Mike Lee in Utah, who displaced longtime incumbent Bob Bennett, a GOP Senator who had shown too much of a proclivity to compromise with Democrats; Rand Paul in Kentucky, the ultra-libertarian who can be depended upon to bash the federal government much more thoroughly than Trey Grayson, the establishment-preferred GOP candidate, might have done; and Marco Rubio in Florida, who as a charismatic ultra-conservative Latino is much more useful to pro-free-market conservatives than Charlie Crist, the middle-of-the-roader who had official GOP backing at the start of the 2010 election cycle. In all of these states, Republicans were probably going to win in 2010 before Tea Party national advocates intervened in the GOP primaries to make sure that it was their kind of Republican who won.[38]

Looking ahead to 2012, there are so many Senate seats held by Democrats at risk (twenty-three Democratic Senate seats are up in 2012, compared to only ten seats for the GOP to defend) that the Republican Party is very likely to claim leadership control of that chamber in the near future. For ultra-free-market national advocates who started working years before the "Tea Party" label came along, it makes little difference if they overshot a bit in 2010 because their long-term crusade to remake the Republican Party as an ultra-right juggernaut remains on schedule.

OFFICEHOLDERS AND IDEOLOGUES

New infusions of Republican lawmakers arrived in Washington DC in January 2011—and many hard-edged GOP governors and legislators also took office in key states like Wisconsin, Ohio, Florida, Michigan, and elsewhere. Freshly elected Republicans often gained office with overt support from Tea Party backers, who expected quick and decisive action on their priorities. In Washington, the GOP-led House delivered symbolism at first: a ritual reading of the Constitution, and a quixotic vote to repeal the Affordable Care Act (which, of course, cannot happen with a Democratic Senate and Obama in the White House), along with anti-abortion legislation designed to appeal to social conservatives. It would take some weeks to get GOP troops lined up to start fighting consequential budget wars with the Democrats.

Quicker off the mark were Tea Party–aligned governors backed by large legislative majorities. GOP governors in Wisconsin, Ohio, and Florida cut taxes, eliminated business regulations, reduced benefits for schoolteachers and other public workers, attacked the bargaining rights of unions, and canceled federally funded rail projects.[39] In Maine, the Tea Party–aligned Governor Paul LePage (who won office with just 38% of the vote after his two opponents split the rest of the returns) not only pushed for abrupt policy shifts, but also made a point of publicly insulting the NAACP and ordering the removal of murals at the Maine Department of Labor that depicted scenes of working people in the state's past and honored figures such as Frances Perkins, the first female Secretary of Labor in America.[40] Along with fellow right-wing governors such as Scott Walker in Wisconsin, John Kasich in Ohio, and Rick Scott in Florida, Maine Governor LePage projects an in-your-face image that thrills his Tea Party backers. Similar pugnaciousness has been on display from many GOP Representatives and Senators in Washington DC. Style reflects substance in this instance, because the kinds of Republicans who won in 2010 are more extreme on policy issues than even the very conservative Republicans who inhabited Congress and statehouses before Obama.

The 112th Congress Lunges Rightward

Determining the degree to which every Republican officeholder across the country is aligned with the Tea Party would be an intricate and protracted challenge. But the Tea Party impact in the 2010 elections comes into sharp focus when we measure shifts in the ideological composition of the House of Representatives from the 111th Congress (of Obama's first two years) to the 112th Congress that arrived in January 2011 and will be in office through the end of 2012. Political scientists use quantitative indices to locate legislators on the left-right spectrum and measure the size of gaps between the two major parties. Adam Bonica has developed a new twist on long-standing measures to provide a clear picture of the Republican-led House installed in DC in January 2011. This GOP House contingent turns out to have ushered in a new phase in the extreme ideological polarization of U.S. politics.[41]

Figure 5.1 locates the ideological proclivities of legislators who carried over from the 111th to the 112th House of Representatives on both sides of the aisle, and also indicates the proclivities of those who departed or were

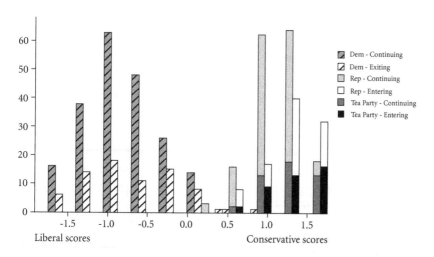

FIGURE 5.1. Partisan Shifts in the House of Representatives from 2010 to 2011. *Member Ideology in the 112th Congress Prepared by Adam Bonica, Stanford University.*

newly elected in 2010. Bonica's scale runs from less than -1.5 for extreme liberalism to more than 1.5 for extreme conservatism. On the Democratic side, to the left of the figure, we see what happened with Democrats who stayed in office from the 111th House to the 112th House, versus those who were booted from office by the voters. So many Democrats lost in 2010 that moderates and liberals alike departed. The Democratic contingent in the House became only a smidgen more liberal after 2010.

But the story is very different among Republicans tallied on the right side of the figure. Republicans who stayed in office from the 111th to 112th Congress are all more conservative, mostly much more conservative, than the Democrats. Yet the Republicans newly elected in 2010 are even further to the right than their GOP predecessors. An amazing 77% of the newly arriving Republicans, including dozens of Tea Party–backed Republicans, are to the right of the typical Republican in the previous Congress—and many are to the right of *almost all* continuing Republicans. For both continuing and newly arrived Republicans, Figure 5.1 indicates how many in each ideological location are aligned with the Tea Party.[42] Clearly, the Tea Party–aligned Republicans are bunched toward the right, and many of the Tea Party solons are new arrivals in the freshman class of the 112th Congress.

The ideological shift from the 111th to the 112th Congress was extraordinary—indeed, larger than any previous shift from one House to the next, including the change that occurred in 1994, when Republicans displaced Democrats from control of the majority for the first time in decades.[43] It is also important to realize that the rightward lunge of the House GOP in 2010 greatly extended a previous rightward trend for House Republicans. Ideological sorting out between the two parties in Congress has been going on for decades, but in recent years virtually all of the incremental polarization comes from Republicans moving ever further rightward while the Democrats mostly stay put. This trend was exacerbated, big time, after the 2010 elections.

Some long-term perspective can be helpful.[44] Back during the New Deal, World War II, and the immediate postwar period, there were moderates and liberals in the Republican Party—just as there were many conservatives, particularly southern conservatives, in the Democratic Party. But after the Civil Rights revolution of the 1960s, activists and voters started sorting themselves out—with the Democratic Party becoming more liberal and Republicans becoming more consistently conservative. For a while, some middle-of-the-roaders remained in each party—moderate Republicans and conservative Democrats. A handful of them are still there in the Senate (for instance, Susan

Collins of Maine on the Republican side and Ben Nelson of Nebraska on the Democratic side). But for decades, moderates have been disappearing, especially from the ranks of House Republicans. Recent ideological polarization in the House has been driven primarily by the steady movement of the Republican Party toward the anti-government right.[45] That movement has happened in part through the arrival of more radical right-wing GOP officeholders, and in part because Republican incumbents have shifted their votes toward the right—especially on the key issue of taxes.

Back in the 1980s, President Ronald Reagan dealt with federal budget deficits much as fiscally cautious Republicans before him had done, by arriving at compromises with Democrats that included tax increases as well as spending cuts. President Reagan's approach is currently favored by Democratic President Barack Obama, but today's Republicans insist that all conceivable tax increases must be "off the table" in Congressional discussions about how to tackle federal deficits. Remarkably, GOPers take this extreme stand in lockstep, even though ballooning budget deficits are largely driven by the after-effects of GOP policies and tax cuts pursued during the presidency of George W. Bush from 2000 to 2008.[46] Republicans caused most of the currently projected federal budget problems, but they take a no-compromise stand on how to fix them, demanding that Democrats essentially eviscerate Medicare, Medicaid, and Social Security, so that Republicans can maintain, indeed increase, big tax cuts for businesses and for millionaires and billionaires. Contemporary Republicans are, for the most part, not truly conservative, and not really interested in fiscal probity. Their goal is to dismantle much of what the federal government does.

Plutocrats Against Taxes

Why would Republicans today take such an extreme stance—and do so virtually unanimously? The answer lies in the ideological and punitive pressures that come from vigilant wealthy interests in the orbit of the GOP. Since 1999, a key plutocrat-funded GOP advocacy group, the Club for Growth, has made it clear that it will fund a right-wing primary election challenger to any GOP officeholder or candidate who dares even speak about tax increases, let alone vote for them. The Club for Growth and other like-minded anti-tax groups have little trouble raising huge amounts of money to back up their stance—after all, the super-wealthy in the United States only get richer and richer with every passing year, so investments in politics amount to "rounding errors" on their fabulous fortunes.[47] A powerful coalition of anti-tax GOP elites is orchestrated by Grover Norquist of the lobbying organization Americans for Tax Reform. And what this coalition wants is clear: *more* tax cuts for the wealthy, whenever the chance to push them through Congress arises.[48] Anti-tax elites most certainly will not countenance increases that hit wealthy families or businesses, even if wars or other major undertakings come along to increase public spending, and even if the costs of Social Security and Medicare are bound to go up as the American population gets older.

Alignment with Tea Party activists is the latest elite maneuver in the war against taxes and the associated push to dismantle costly popular social programs like Medicare and Social Security that must be paid for if they are to remain in place for future generations of Americans. Well before 2009, the Club for Growth and other elite GOP advocacy groups were quite effective at disciplining GOP politicians. Still, they did not have much of a "ground game." That is, the Club for Growth and its far-right allies could spend big money to influence elections and policy debates, and they could lobby legislators, governors, and federal agencies. But they were not directly connected to grassroots networks focused on anti-tax, small government issues. Like the institutional Republican Party itself, far-right advocacy organizations tended to ally with separately organized Christian conservatives to build broad popular support. That could be awkward, because Christian conservatives have their own values and priorities, and are not even 100% reliable when it comes to extreme free-market policies, such as phasing out popular social programs. Consequently, the Club for Growth and other like-minded groups were delighted when grassroots Tea Party activism came along in 2009. Now the anti-tax mantra would have some popular oomph behind it, enthusiastic backing from the ranks of ordinary middle-class conservatives attending Tea Party rallies and meetings.

Indeed, the Tea Party erupted at just the right moment to cut Obama and the Democrats off at the pass in the never-ending war to reduce regulations on business and free the U.S. wealthy from having to pay taxes to sustain social supports for their fellow citizens. That is how the situation looks to right-wing interests. With dozens of new Tea Party legislators and governors taking office in early 2011, perhaps political groundwork could be laid to push Obama out in 2012. In the meantime, GOPers loyal to ultra-right agendas can roll back government spending, smash unions that are politically aligned with Democrats, and—above all—block tax increases on the privileged.

Ideological Elites Set the 2011 GOP Agenda

Elite and grassroots Tea Party forces were confident after November 2010 that they could call the tune for newly empowered Republicans.[49] The word "compromise" never appears in public statements from Tea Party spokespersons—nor did we hear that word from grassroots Tea Partiers in early 2011. Tea Party people are adamantly opposed to any give and take with Democrats, or with moderate Republicans for that matter. Most Tea Party groups are willing to go so far as to push the United States of America into a massive default on previously legislated obligations. In the summer of 2011, they pressed Republicans in Congress to vote against raising the debt limit, a fiscal housekeeping step that used to be routine.

To block compromises and enforce discipline on Republicans in office and running in 2012, a predictable Tea Party division of labor took shape very quickly after the 2010 elections. Policy proposals for GOP legislators were put forward by idea-pushers and lobbyists with ties to the elite advocacy organizations in the Tea Party world—by Americans for Prosperity and FreedomWorks, as well as by think tanks like the Heritage Foundation and the Cato Institute. At the same time, the grass roots dug in to monitor GOP legislators and give them a push from below if they seemed to stray toward compromise or halfway measures.

As we glimpsed in Chapter 4, before the Republicans elected to the 112th Congress could even officially convene, many were "oriented" by wealthy organizations claiming the Tea Party mantle. Right after the November election, Dick Armey, head of FreedomWorks and former GOP Majority Leader from the 1990s, convened a Tea Party retreat in Baltimore to instruct incoming GOP House members on how to stay true to their small-government principles and avoid being co-opted by current GOP House leaders steeped in the ways of Washington DC.[50] One might expect the "ways of Washington DC" to refer to such staples as cozying up to business lobbyists and holding constant fundraisers to solicit checks for the next election. But, no, the threats stressed by elite ideologues speaking for the Tea Party were the perils of doing business as usual through compromises with Democrats. Leaders from FreedomWorks feared that Speaker John Boehner might ask freshman Republicans and Tea Party veterans to participate in such deals, and they wanted to head off the temptation. "Don't be dazzled by plum committee assignments and other enticements from Republican leaders," or tempted by special spending targeted on local districts—not if such goodies stand in the way of the right-wing priorities of tax cuts and huge reductions in spending.[51] In effect, FreedomWorks head Dick Armey appointed himself the shadow Speaker of the House for 2011; he told rank-and-file GOP legislators to refuse exactly the sort of cooperation with Republican Congressional leaders that Armey himself had routinely orchestrated back in the 1990s, when he served as GOP House Majority leader under Speaker Newt Gingrich and put together complex deals involving perks and targeted spending.

Similarly, the Koch-supported advocacy organization Americans for Prosperity (AFP) jumped into the game of pressuring and instructing Republican officeholders. Soon after the FreedomWorks retreat in November 2010, AFP assembled a rally on Capitol Hill to tell legislators "We're watching!" as the crowd chanted, with AFP leaders vowing to work to unelect GOPers next time should they fail to toe the ideological line.[52] Again in January, as the 112th Congress convened, Americans for Prosperity representatives, including one of the famed billionaire Koch brothers, David, dropped into the Capitol to greet and lobby GOP leaders and incoming representatives, bending their ears on such ultra-free-market priorities as gutting the Environmental Protection Agency and promoting the privatization of Social Security and Medicare.[53] Koch-supported Republicans were appointed to the key House Energy and Commerce committee dealing with environmental and energy legislation, in which Koch Industries has a huge stake.[54] Many other committees were also now led by Republicans with close ties to the industries touched by legislation those committees would adjudicate. Prominent Tea Party Republicans were reported to have hired longtime lobbyists to help run their offices.[55]

The Radical Ryan Plan

The all-important House Budget Committee for the 112th Congress is chaired by Congressman Paul Ryan, a longtime favorite of Americans for Prosperity and strongly backed by its Wisconsin arm. Right at the start of the 112th Congress, House Republicans voted to give Ryan authority to draw up a budget with targets to meet for draconian spending cuts. By early April, Congressman Ryan released a radical budget plan, drawing ideas and partisan fiscal estimates from the Heritage Foundation and other right-wing sources.[56] Dubbed by a liberal critic a plan to "repeal the 20th century," Ryan's budget outline called for extending all previous tax cuts tilted toward the very wealthy, and it proposed to add yet more tax cuts for business and plutocrats.[57] To pay for all of this and maintain some faintly plausible claim that, after twenty years, the federal budget would move toward balance, Ryan proposed massive cuts in everything the federal government does for the health and safety of the U.S. population, including huge cuts in education funding and college grants and loans, as well as in Food Stamps and Medicaid. In addition, Ryan proposed to get rid of the Affordable Care Act of 2010 and eliminate Medicare as it has been known since 1965, starting with Americans who turn 65 years old in 2021. Until then, retired Americans would enjoy, as they do now, health care largely covered by public funds, even if they become very sick or disabled in old age. After that, older Americans would have to absorb thousands of dollars per year in higher costs because the Ryan plan would merely give them vouchers of dwindling value to try to buy insurance on the private market. Private insurance companies, needless to say, are not anxious to sell reasonably priced health plans to older people.

Despite the sudden, sweeping changes embodied in the Ryan budget plan, the rightward-leaning GOP Representatives in the 112th House voted for it almost unanimously only one week after it was proposed. House Republicans held no hearings and spent virtually no time in deliberation before voting to dismantle decades of popular and effective U.S. social spending on health care for senior citizens—and on many other social needs for children, the disabled, and young adults. It is doubtful that Republicans in the 112th House fully understood the ramifications; they simply did what House GOP leaders told them to do. Those GOP leaders, in turn, took their policy cues from extreme ideologues in the think tanks and billionaire-backed advocacy organizations that surround today's Republican Party—groups whose real interest lies in maintaining and increasing tax cuts for the wealthy. Quite aptly, the Ryan budget, featuring the abolition of Medicare, has been labeled a "radical" instance of "right-wing social engineering." These damning phrases came not from liberal sources, but from the lips of the very conservative Republican Newt Gingrich, who mounted a campaign for the 2012 GOP presidential nomination.[58] Gingrich is a 1990s-vintage GOP conservative who led the rightward charge starting in the Reagan era. That he thinks today's GOP policymakers are going too far toward the ideological right is very telling.

At its debut, the Ryan plan to eliminate traditional Medicare was described in the media as a "Tea Party proposal." But it would be more accurate to call it a "Koch proposal," an ideological scheme to realize long-standing ultra-right hopes to privatize and radically shrink a major national social program. There is no evidence that ordinary American citizens who sympathize with the Tea Party were clamoring for the elimination of Medicare in early 2011. We heard no such thing from our interviewees, and a respected national survey completed right after the Ryan plan appeared revealed that 70% of Tea Party supporters, along with even higher percentages of other Americans, oppose cuts in Medicare spending.[59] The only thing about the Ryan Medicare scheme that might be considered a sop to rank-and-file Tea Partiers is his specification that the current Medicare guarantee would stay in place for people now 55 or older. No doubt Congressman Ryan and his advocacy allies understand the age groups from which most grassroots Tea Partiers come—and they have tried to target their radical restructuring to hit people just under the age of most current Tea Party participants.

Overall, the Ryan budget includes many specifics unpopular with Americans of all ages and partisan persuasions. Additional tax cuts for millionaires and billionaires run directly counter to the preferences expressed repeatedly by substantial majorities of Americans, who want shared sacrifice and higher taxes on the wealthy instead.[60] The fact is that grand calls for "eliminating the deficit" and "cutting taxes" sound good in the abstract, but budget realities make carrying through a plan like Ryan's blueprint a formula for gutting just about every specific part of the U.S. government that middle-class and low-income Americans care about.

With the launch of Ryan's budget in the spring of 2011, the abstract ideas promoted by ideological elites who have latched on to the Tea Party label began to run into concrete popular views. By voting for such ideas, the new GOP House walked itself far out on an ideological limb, and the possibility opened that many of its members would be on the part of the limb that gets sawed off in 2012. Respected electoral analyst Charlie Cook was one of many who started to suggest that "it's not inconceivable that Republicans might start seeing things go against them in the court of public opinion."[61]

Republican leaders and spokespersons know this, so from the late spring and summer of 2011 onward, they waged highly abstract media wars about "the federal debt limit" and the overall size of budgets for 2012 and beyond. Rather than focus on exactly what might be cut from government's menu, GOP leaders spoke about overall targets for vague cuts, and about gimmicks such as a balanced budget amendment to the Constitution or

automatic ceilings that would supposedly go into effect without any representative or senator having to explain a cut to any particular program.
Amidst ongoing theatrics, actual budget-writing proceeded quietly in ways
that allowed the GOP House to try to satisfy industry lobbyists and shift as
many cuts as possible toward measures helping lower-income people. All
the while, Republican Congressional leaders staged recurrent, dramatic
clashes with the White House and Senate Democrats, making bold declarations about "America going bankrupt."

Theatrical threats and last-minute brinksmanship have become the
order of the day and will likely remain so until voters go to the polls in
November 2012. "Hysterical stunt governing" is how journalist Juan Williams aptly summed up the GOP approach in the Tea Party era. He attributed the approach to the Republican leadership's need to propitiate Tea
Party–backed freshman legislators and other Tea Party sympathizers
inside and outside of DC, who veto compromises and "want to see"
Speaker Boehner and other Republican Congressional leaders "attacking
the President and calling out the Democrats in Congress as big spenders."[62]
Using dramatic threats accompanied by a lot of public chest-thumping,
the Republicans of the 112th Congress will see how often they can get
President Obama and Congressional Democrats to cave in—see if they
can push Democrats into making big cuts in programs vital to Democratic Party constituencies, such as Medicaid and Pell Grants. Republican
leaders will also use the threat of derailing national economic recovery by
refusing to pay U.S. obligations to try to get President Obama and Democratic leaders to sign on to right-wing ideological plans to eviscerate
Social Security and Medicare—because if Democrats sign, that will enable
GOP leaders to claim that such unpopular steps were taken in a "bipartisan" way.

GRASSROOTS TEA PARTIERS DIG IN

Even as elite Tea Party organizations teamed up with Republican Congressional leaders to push extreme policy agendas, grassroots Tea Partiers also
took steps to reap the fruits of right-wing GOP victories in 2010. Big rallies
lost steam, but local Tea Party participants threw themselves into serving as
watchdogs over legislators and, in many cases, exerting new muscle inside
the Republican Party itself.

Starting in the spring of 2011, some observers opined that the Tea Party was losing popular traction, pointing to sparse turnout at DC rallies such as the one called on March 31 to pressure Congress during the first big budget battle.[63] True enough, the focus inside the Beltway—and in the national media that hangs on events in the nation's Capitol—did shift after the 112th Congress took over. Media coverage of "the Tea Party" became obsessed with self-appointed Tea Party spokespersons like Dick Armey and the coordinators of Tea Party Patriots, the Tea Party Express, and even, at times, leaders from truly obscure groups. An event at the National Press Club in May 2011, for example, featured William Temple of the Tea Party Founding Fathers, dressed in colonial attire. Likewise, some of the media gave regular airtime to self-declared Tea Party legislators in Congress. After 2010, rallies in the Capitol, when they occurred at all, became less grassroots affairs than sparse backdrops to the spokespersons the media really wanted to cover; and quite often, the press just attended events featuring those spokespersons directly.

Watchdogs Barking at GOP Heels

But the upward shift of media interest did not mean that grassroots Tea Partiers stopped doing politically consequential things. Instead, as we saw clearly in the visits we made in various regions, local Tea Partiers are digging in locally for the long haul. As passels of new GOP legislators took office in local and state governments as well as in Washington DC, local Tea Party activists turned toward watchdog activities. National advocacy groups like FreedomWorks offered local Tea Partiers new tools, by setting up websites where they could track legislators in real time and fire off complaints about things they do not like.[64] The umbrella group Tea Party Patriots also took it upon itself to distribute freshman legislators' personal email addresses and cellphone numbers so that people could contact representatives to "show them that you won't tolerate politics as usual and show them the power of the Tea Party."[65]

During our field work, we saw local groups embracing watchdog functions with enthusiasm. In Arizona, Tea Partiers were concerned that they could not adequately track all the legislation moving in Washington DC, and they were looking for some reliable assistance. In Tempe, as we have already noted, Tea Partiers took careful notes on a draft "scorecard" from Americans for Prosperity and readied themselves to contact their local representatives.

In Surprise, Arizonan Tea Partiers were reporting the results of visiting various national "Tea Party" websites, looking for those worth joining or visiting regularly. In each case, the emphasis was on ensuring that relatively conservative Republican legislators were in lockstep with Tea Party principles. Democrats, and even some moderate Republicans, were written off as "lost causes" to be ousted, if possible, in the next election.

Similarly, when New Hampshire Tea Party leader Jerry DeLemus visited Berwick, Maine, in April 2011, he explained how New Hampshire activists were keeping up pressure on the legions of GOPers they helped elect (including more than 100 overtly Tea Party–affiliated representatives in the 400-person New Hampshire House). A former Marine, DeLemus punctuated his speech with insistence that he and his fellow Tea Partiers won't "retreat" or "back down."[66] With vivid martial imagery, he described ongoing efforts to get Republicans to toe the line and gave vivid examples of face-to-face confrontations with representatives tempted to stray from Tea Party orthodoxy. They "represent you," he told his audience, explaining that elected GOP officials must do what they promised in advance to do and not adjust their views once in office. DeLemus urged his Maine listeners to press Republicans in the Maine legislature, too, as firmly as he and his Tea Party compatriots had done in New Hampshire. We Tea Partiers, DeLemus maintained, need to be as "resolute" and "aggressive" as liberals who are "trying to destroy this country." The aim, he summed up, should be to make Republican officeholders more "afraid" of the Tea Party than they are of Democrats.

One of the two women who co-chair the York County Constitutionalists echoed DeLemus's tough stance. During the discussion period, she spoke scornfully of eight GOP Maine state senators who had publicly criticized Governor Paul LePage for taking down the labor murals and for the governor's rudeness to political opponents. That such public criticism of LePage could come from other Republican officeholders incensed the York Tea Party leader. We need to "call them on it," she said with evident anger. The incident proved to her that Maine Tea Partiers need to "take over the GOP" and "discipline" elected officials, just as leftist "radicals in the Sixties" once did.[67]

In the Jefferson Area Tea Party of Charlottesville, Virginia, the approach was a bit less pugnacious. A watchdog subcommittee was formed in the spring of 2011 with an intricate division of labor. Members doled out assignments, with some tasked to track happenings in local government in both Charlottesville and Albemarle County, while others planned to track legislation in the Virginia Assembly and monitor the positions taken by representatives from their area, and still others would keep an eye on what Virginia senators and newly elected fifth district GOP House member Robert Hurt are doing in Washington DC. Anytime a tracker sees something worrisome, he or she is to alert the entire Tea Party group. Meanwhile, the group was discussing big issues, like the debt limit. With little angst, they agreed it should not be raised—and planned to pressure their Congressional representatives accordingly. In the summer of 2011, national surveys showed that Tea Party sympathizers were especially likely to oppose raising the federal debt limit, despite the financial crisis that might follow.[68] As we've seen, Tea Partiers believe that the United States already faces economic Armageddon, so a further step in that direction does not provoke much concern.

Remaking the Republican Party

Not only are Tea Partiers warily watching GOP representatives considered theirs to direct. In many places, Tea Partiers have taken over chunks of the Republican Party apparatus, the local and state committees that determine nominating procedures and deploy resources in each election cycle. By grabbing GOP beachheads in late 2010 and 2011, if they had not already done so earlier, Tea Partiers could more effectively make good on the "or else" part of their message to Republican officeholders—"or else" we will challenge you in the next primary.

We heard some disagreement about how much effort local Tea Parties should put into directly taking over GOP committees, especially if that were to be a prelude to endorsing Republican candidates for election. Some local activists, such as those in Charlottesville, felt it would be better to stick to watchdog roles. But others espoused the position taken, for example, by Jerry DeLemus in New Hampshire, who teamed up with other Tea Partiers in New Hampshire to stage what he himself called a kind of "coup" in the election for GOP state chair that took place right after November 2010. New Hampshire is a state with many moderate as well as conservative Republicans. An establishment GOPer of the traditional middle-of-the-road New Hampshire variety was expected to win, a protégé of former Republican Governor John Sununu. But New Hampshire Tea Party activists were greatly fired up after the November 2010 elections in which they helped propel Republicans to victory in a Senate race and two House races, as well as in many state-level contests. Tea Partiers figured out the complex GOP party voting rules, packed the relevant meetings with "boots on the ground," and elected their guy, Jack Kimball, instead of Sununu's candidate. Moderate New Hampshire Republicans were shocked, just as they were by many radical-right measures pushed through the New Hampshire legislature with the support of Tea Party Republicans starting in January 2011.[69] "Many moderates now say they are resigned to having little sway in shaping the state's agenda. . . . 'We know we don't have much of a chance of convincing anybody of anything,' said Representative Priscilla Lockwood, a moderate Republican."[70]

Moderate New Hampshire Republicans fear that having Tea Partiers running the GOP apparatus could make it more difficult for 2012 GOP presidential contenders to appeal simultaneously to Republican and independent voters in a state where presidential primaries are open to all voters, not just to registered Republicans. By contrast, the state's Tea Partiers are delighted to exercise leverage in the GOP primary. Every Republican presidential hopeful who passes through speaks to a Tea Party rally and schmoozes with local group leaders; some GOP presidential contenders, like Tim Pawlenty, have even sent staffers to local meetings.[71] Tea Party leaders we spoke to enjoyed the attention, and hope to be arbiters in the 2012 primary.

Tea Partiers also believe that their sway inside the New Hampshire GOP apparatus will shift the state-level party in directions they favor. "Jack's election is frosting on the cake," an activist told the *Boston Globe*, explaining that the election of Kimball as a Tea Party chair of the state GOP "gives people hope that the Republican platform will be reinforced and that people will start acting like Republicans."[72] In Tea Party eyes, all too many GOP moderates in New Hampshire have *not* acted like genuine Republicans. Not surprisingly, analogous Tea Party sentiments and organizational tactics have contributed to takeovers of local GOP committees in different parts of Virginia, as well as to makeovers at the statewide level in Arizona and the state of Washington. "The 'outsiders' of 2010 are now moving to the inside," observed ABC News reporter Amy Walter in her January 2011 overview of Tea Party efforts to reorient Republican Party organizations in various states.[73]

Often, local Tea Party activists discover GOP committees to be virtually moribund, run by a few "good old boys" who are easy to displace. We heard stories from widely scattered places about ensconced party officials who were startled when, one night, a crowd of well-organized Tea Partiers turned up to vote them out, leaving them to slink away in bemusement. At other times, moderate Republicans are somewhat forewarned and push back at least a bit, as in the New Hampshire competition for the GOP state chairmanship. Either way, the Tea Party usually can prevail, at least in states where there are many local groups with people who can be mobilized—just as a couple of decades ago, locally organized Christian conservatives took over GOP committees, the better to nominate friendly candidates and block wishy-washy moderates the next time around.

When Tea Partiers do prevail, the look of GOP committees changes, as several of our interviewees vividly described to us. The made-over GOP bodies become less buttoned down, and no longer operate like routine, sleepy gatherings of the local Chamber of Commerce. Suddenly, there is energy in the room, with people who dress and act in not-so-professional ways. The Tea Party Republican committees adopt a more fervent, populist tone. With Tea Partiers in charge, GOP committees become much more purposive and demanding.

From our perspective as political scientists, local Tea Party takeovers of GOP committees are likely to matter—along with local Tea Party efforts to exert watchdog pressures on elected representatives. GOPers who want to run for election or reelection to state legislatures and Congress will think twice—or three times—before ignoring the stated policy preferences of even relatively small Tea Party minorities in their districts, if they think those folks are closely following what they do and will turn out in primary contests or weigh in on crucial procedural or endorsement decisions taken by GOP committees. As Jerry DeLemus stressed when explaining New Hampshire Tea Party achievements to his Maine neighbors, it helps to get a "reputation for effectiveness." Ongoing organization matters; turning out for meetings matters; repeatedly contacting legislators matters. And so does taking direct control of GOP organs.

From one angle of vision, the entrenched localism of grassroots Tea Partiers reduces their clout; it is easy for national political reporters to make that surmise. But from another perspective, steady local activity allows Tea Partiers to put sustained pressure on GOP officeholders from below. Tea Party Express chair Amy Kremer may therefore have been correct when she declared to a *National Journal* reporter in May 2011, that it "absolutely is not true" that the Tea Party is losing clout. "You're not seeing the great big rallies that you did before, because people are engaged on a local level doing things."[74]

The bottom line for the Tea Party's impact on Congress—and on state legislatures—lies in its capacity to *coordinate* national pressures from wealthy funders and ideological advocates with contacts from grassroots Tea Partiers who have a reputation for clout in local districts. When coordinated pressure can be mounted—as it has been in budget battles—the Tea Party delivers a loud and clear absolutist message to legislators, a message that comes both from advocates in DC and from local districts. Tea Partiers tell the GOP legislators they helped to elect that they are watching them and will withdraw money and votes next time if the legislators do not vote as Tea Partiers want. The ongoing credibility of such threats remains to be seen. But many GOP legislators worry when they hear statements like one from Darla Dawald, national director of the Patriot Action Network, who told a reporter, "we will remove as many incumbents as we can that do not do the job they were hired to do."[75] Dawald's group is part of a dense network of national and regional conservative organizations linked to the Tea Party brand. Her words alone might not matter—but words like hers get through to GOP representatives when they are echoed by local groups active in their districts.

WHAT NEXT FOR REPUBLICANS AND THEIR TEA PARTY?

By now it should be obvious that Tea Partiers have a self-centered understanding of democracy. Tea Partiers consider themselves to be the true, patriotic Americans, and they believe that elected Republican representatives are "hired" to do pretty much exactly what Tea Partiers themselves say should be done. Government by and for the Tea Party, could be the motto. Little thought is given either by local activists or by national advocacy groups to discussing vital national issues with people outside the Tea Party. When we spoke with grassroots activists and observed discussions in meetings, we never heard anyone acknowledge the need for two-way dialogue with other Americans who think differently from Tea Partiers. The talk was all about getting GOP representatives to do as they had "promised" Tea Party voters, with no acknowledgement that other kinds of voters also supported successful GOP candidates, let alone any acceptance that Democratic representatives, elected by other constituencies, also have legitimate roles to play in Congress and state legislatures.

When non–Tea Partiers came up, they were portrayed as people who need to be "educated" about Tea Party points of view—unless the others were Democrats, in which case they were scornfully dismissed. At the April 2011 Tea Party meeting in North Berwick, Maine, for example, both the speaker and members of the audience described the Democratic Party as an unholy alliance of dependents on "welfare," public sector employees leeching from taxpayers, and immigrants trying to vote illegally. Such conceptions of Democrats are widespread among Tea Partiers. The bottom line is that talking with Democrats would be a waste of time, and compromises or bargains with them verge on the illegitimate.

The Republicans who gained seats in the Senate and took control of the House of Representatives in 2011 include many persons of this mindset, legislators who believe they are in office to do what the Tea Party demands with little discussion and no dickering. GOP Representatives and Senators may hold this view of their duty by conviction, as is surely true of many freshmen who came directly out of Tea Party circles and have little previous government experience. Or GOP Representatives and Senators may feign this outlook out of some sense that a blustering, demanding style will propitiate Tea Party constituents. Either way, the Tea Party understanding of GOP representation—that legislators should function as conveyor belts for pre-cooked right-wing policy ideas backed by emotional popular pressure—suffuses the workings of the 112th Congress, especially in the House of Representatives where all budget legislation originates.

In the past, budgets have been occasions for legislators to compromise, but Tea Party Republicans do not look at them in this light. As the United States heads into yet another high stakes presidential election, the Republican-led House of Representatives and many GOPers in the Senate are loaded for bear to pick one fight after another with the Senate Democratic majority and the Obama White House. In those fights, there are dozens of Tea Party–endorsed House members—and quite a few Tea Party–endorsed GOP Senators, too—who do not want to compromise at all with people whose ideological preferences they do not share.

As long as Tea Party grassroots activists and elite free-marketers remain determined to block compromises, even Republican officeholders and candidates who want to be flexible will fear challengers from their right. Veterans who in the past have reached across the aisle to forge effective or popular legislation—for example, Senator Richard Lugar of Indiana, or Senator Orrin Hatch of Utah, or Senator Olympia Snowe of Maine—hesitate to do so now, lest roving Tea Party billionaire groups, joining ranks with the Club for Growth and social conservative advocates, decide to go all out against them. All three onetime moderates know that Tea Party candidates might challenge them in 2012.[76]

Of course, the fact that Republicans in office worry about such challenges is a source of pride for Tea Party political action groups and roving billionaire Tea Partiers. If Tea Party funders can frighten and discipline more moderate GOP officeholders into suppressing any willingness to compromise, they will not actually have to throw them out of office. On critical questions about taxes, especially, feigned adherence to the hard-line right position is just as good as sincere adherence.

In the final analysis, compromise in Washington DC will be inevitable, at least to some degree—and a lot of what we see on television or read on the Internet or in newspapers amounts to GOP Congressional leaders trying to square circles. Republican leaders in the 112th Congress have to propitiate the absolutist demands of elite and grassroots Tea Partiers while edging toward compromises with the Obama White House and the Democratic-controlled Senate, if only to keep government functioning while policy battles rage. In the months marching toward the critical elections in November 2012, we will repeatedly see Republican Congressional leaders trying to persuade GOP legislators to say no, at least in part, to the most extreme Tea Party demands. But each time a reluctant compromise is struck, it will happen only at the very last minute, after a lot of public posturing and high-wire brinksmanship, some of which surely is dangerous to the economic well-being of the country. As the conservative *Washington Post* commentator Michael Gerson puts it, there "are always compromises in governing. But they are harder to make when one element of a political coalition views compromise itself as the problem."

Theatrical posturing, maximalist demands, and refusals to budge until the last minute (or even beyond)—this formula works to a degree for the Republican Party and its Tea Party allies. Already, national debates have moved far to the right, as most DC officeholders and pundits debate how much to slash from the federal budget, rather than focusing on job creation in a sluggish economy. Nevertheless, even as they gain ground in battles to shape public discussions and cut government, Tea Partiers also risk putting the Republican Party at risk, in two important ways.

In the first place, business interests are increasingly nervous about maximalist, uncompromising stances in budget battles. Very early in the

112th Congress, demands to slash spending on infrastructure and transportation projects aroused pushback, not just from labor unions, but also from the Chamber of Commerce, speaking for businesses looking forward to profitable contracts on publicly financed projects.[77] Businesses may love the GOP when it guts regulations and cuts taxes, but eliminating funds for public projects that reward contractors is another matter.

An even more spectacular tussle broke out several months later, when GOP Congressional leaders deferring to Tea Party demands threatened to let the United States go into default if they did not get their way in budget negotiations with Democrats. Alarmed by the consequences for credit and the threat to a nascent economic recovery, leading business and industrial associations, including the U.S. Chamber of Commerce and the National Association of Manufacturers, banded together to write a letter to Speaker Boehner urging against such brinksmanship with the U.S. financial system.[78] In the final stages of the debt ceiling battle, business leaders sent another petition to Congress, and even the *Wall Street Journal* editorial board called for a procedural compromise. [79] In short, GOP business allies do not always see eye to eye with the ideological elites and grassroots populists arrayed in the Tea Party. Whenever two different wings of the usual GOP coalition are at odds, legislators and candidates are sure to be caught awkwardly in the middle.

A second risk for the GOP lies in public opinion and the struggle to attract moderate voters going into 2012. Tea Party extremism exacerbates already considerable public disillusionment with the Republican Party. Not only will many younger, more diverse, less economically well-off voters go to the polls in 2012, "independent" voters who truly are in the middle are also more likely to vote in a presidential election year. Will the Tea Party turn more voters off about the Republican brand? There is significant social science research to suggest this is a serious possibility.[80]

National surveys reveal increasingly negative public evaluations of the Tea Party—with the percent of Americans who tell survey researchers that they are opposed to the Tea Party now surpassing those who say they support it, in some polls by a wide margin.[81] Over the past two and a half years, Americans have gradually firmed up their views of the Tea Party, following an initial period in which many were uncertain about what it was, or undecided in their assessments.[82] As the picture clears, the proportion of Americans saying they like or sympathize with the Tea Party has remained relatively steady at about 25%–30%. (In one surprising poll, from none other than Fox News, the Tea Party's popularity failed to beat out that of the much-maligned Internal Revenue Service![83]) By contrast, the percentage of Americans saying they do not like, or oppose, the Tea Party has increased. Familiarity, in short, seems to have bred dislike. This is a troubling trend for the Republican Party going into 2012 because the party has become so closely identified with Tea Party activism.

During the 2010 election cycle, the GOP strategy was openly to encourage Tea Party activism, on the theory that the party would benefit from highly motivated potential voters and from new infusions of money. No doubt, many GOP leaders still hold this perspective. On the other hand, other GOP leaders and strategists understand that hard-core conservative Republicans who identify with the Tea Party cannot provide enough votes to win all elections, certainly not in swing states and districts, or in the 2012 presidential contest. Many GOP candidates—including eventually the 2012 presidential nominee—will need to appeal not just to Tea Party supporters, but also to non–Tea Party Republicans, independents, and wobbly Democrats.

Consequently, it has to be worrisome for GOP strategists that the views of Tea Party constituents are parting company on many issues with the views of moderate Republicans and independents. American voters can be slow to figure out complicated policy issues, especially when they are fed misleading information by major media outlets. Sooner or later, however, most voters get a bead on things, particularly when real-life matters such as college aid and health care are at issue. As Americans figure out the real choices about the future of social spending and taxes for the United States, the Republican Party may not be in a good place if it continues to defer to the most ideological elements of the Tea Party. Surveys also show that even many Republicans support tax increases along with spending cuts to tackle U.S. budget deficits, a plan anathema to many of the national advocacy organizations stoking Tea Party fervor.[84] When survey-researchers issue reports declaring that the "Tea Party's Hard Line on Spending Divides the GOP," trouble may be brewing.[85] Add to that the likelihood that the style of Tea Party politics—angry, demanding, and absolutist—may be increasingly at odds with the preferences of other citizens. To the degree that Americans want government focus on what works for the economy, the tenor of Tea Party rhetoric wears thin.

For all the hype about the impact of the Tea Party on the fortunes of Republicans versus Democrats, the bigger story, as we have seen, is the impact of the Tea Party on the GOP. The Republican Party has been moving toward the right for some time, and that movement only quickened after the advent of the Tea Party. Although the symbolism of "the Tea Party" is already fading in popularity, the power of hard-right ideologues consolidated during the first years of the Obama Administration is likely to continue to drive Republican politics, crowding Republicans into an ultra-right corner. As American politics marches on, the Tea Party, even if it doggedly persists, will not be able to call all the shots—and Republican leaders will have to decide how far they want to go in the directions Tea Partiers are urging. Before long, the Tea Party ideology and its adherents may shift from an asset to an albatross for many in the Republican Party.

6

The Tea Party and American Democracy

Where is the Tea Party headed? The question was posed to Senate Majority Leader Harry Reid, Democrat of Nevada, when he appeared on the NBC program "Meet the Press" on January 9, 2011. Just a couple of months earlier, Reid had surmounted a well-funded and nationally touted challenge by GOP senate candidate Sharron Angle. "She was Tea Party backed, a Tea Party candidate," observed the NBC host David Gregory. "Do she and others, as part of this Tea Party, represent a lasting force in American politics?" Reid was characteristically blunt in response. "The Tea Party will disappear as soon as the economy gets better," he declared. "And the economy's getting better all the time."[1]

Harry Reid was a bit too glib, according to the analysis developed in this book. Even if the U.S. economy recovers more quickly and completely than most analysts anticipate, the political forces operating through the Tea Party are unlikely to go "poof" in direct relation to a rising Gross Domestic Product. The U.S. economic plunge that started in 2008 was at most an accelerant to the Tea Party explosion, which was in essence a *political* reaction by very conservative Republicans alarmed by the presidency of Barack Obama and the threat that Democrats in Washington DC might reshape U.S. policies for the longer term. Conservatives dreaded that Obama and the Democrats would use the national crisis to tighten regulations on business, raise taxes on the wealthy, and further social programs benefiting younger

Americans who are increasingly racially diverse. The older white activists of the Tea Party joined conservative ideologues and business interests in dreading what might be done by the new Democratic president and Congress—and the fears of all these groups persist. As long as Barack Obama remains in the White House, and as long as landmark Democratic achievements such as the Affordable Care Act of 2010 remain on the books, the grassroots and elite forces that combined to create the Tea Party will not stand down. They have the social commitment and organizational and financial wherewithal to keep going—certainly through 2012, and perhaps well beyond.

In this concluding chapter, we step back to consider the overall implications of the Tea Party. How might elite and grassroots Tea Party forces figure in the election of 2012? We cannot say for sure, but our analysis does suggest possibilities. Then we reflect on the paradoxes of the democratic citizenship exemplified by grassroots Tea Partiers, and conclude with an assessment of the overall impact of the Tea Party on American politics.

TEA PARTY FORCES HEADED INTO 2012

Throughout this book, we have gained insights by recognizing that the Tea Party is made up of a combination of forces: grassroots activists, national elites pushing ideas and directing funds to very conservative candidates, and right-wing media cheerleaders. Keeping this framework in mind helps us lay out the possible ways the various forces at work in the Tea Party may affect the electoral landscape and GOP candidates going into 2012. National advocacy forces want right-wing policy gains and aim to block GOP candidates who might not go along with their programs. The owners and editors of the right-wing media want GOP victories, and will soft-pedal the "Tea Party" brand if it seems to be hurting Republicans in the general electorate during 2012. And grassroots Tea Partiers have gained considerable clout inside the GOP. They are likely to keep that clout with GOP officeholders, but their influence in the general electorate will recede going into 2012. This mélange may lead the different parts of the Tea Party to operate at cross-purposes, and will certainly create a fluid and volatile situation for the Republican Party and the national electorate.

As we have learned, professionally run national organizations affiliated with the Tea Party include advocacy groups pushing long-standing right-wing policy nostrums along with political action committees that channel funds to Republican candidates who can be expected to toe the appropriate policy lines while in office. For the national organizations that have jumped on the Tea Party bandwagon, the GOP is a vehicle for realizing an agenda that includes reduced taxes on the wealthy and business; removal of regulations on business; and, if at all possible, radical restructurings of popular social programs to turn them into market subsidies rather than social entitlements. These policy goals are much more important to elite organizations in the Tea Party orbit than is the overall popular reputation of the Republican Party—although, of course, if Republican candidates lose in large numbers at the polls, it would be harder to push or protect favored free-market, low-tax policies.

After the November 2010 triumphs by the GOP, elite organizations riding the Tea Party wasted no time in urging newly elected DC representatives, governors, and state legislators to enact as many right-wing priorities as possible, and to do it as fast as possible. And indeed, no time was wasted. As we discussed in Chapter 5, the Republicans in the House of Representatives moved within months in virtual lockstep to adopt a highly ideological federal budget blueprint designed by Representative Paul Ryan. The Ryan plan was applauded in the auditoriums of the Heritage Foundation and the Cato Institute, but it quickly proved unpopular with the general public, above all because it promised to privatize Medicare, but for other reasons as well. In May 2011, the GOP lost a special election in an upstate New York House district that usually votes overwhelmingly Republican, and the victory of Democrat Kathy Hochul was widely attributed to her attack on the Ryan budget plan to eliminate traditional Medicare and ask the elderly to fund a greater proportion of their own health insurance on the open market. National Republican leaders and strategists maneuvered thereafter to neutralize what had clearly become a detriment for their candidates in 2012. Some political analysts decided that it might be possible for Democrats to retake control of the House of Representatives in 2012.

The Ryan budget, emblematic of GOP priorities in DC in general, was a clear instance of ideological overconfidence—misreading what happened in 2010. Voters put more GOP Representatives and Senators in office, but as was discernable at the time of the 2010 election, they did so mainly as a repudiation of Democrats who had failed to revive the economy. Voters were not endorsing radical budget cuts or restructurings of popular social programs. Where Medicare and Social Security are concerned, even Tea Partiers at the grass roots never proposed or demanded anything of the sort. Ideological elites, not voters sympathetic to the Tea Party, urged the GOP in Washington DC onto the thin ice of radical domestic policy-making.

In key states like Wisconsin, Ohio, Michigan, and Florida, new GOP governors and legislatures made equally abrupt policy moves right after 2010. Invariably, they cut taxes on business and dealt with overall budget shortfalls entirely through quick contractions of public spending on education and health care. GOPers in the states also moved quickly to ram through legislative blueprints disseminated by conservative think tanks—to curb the power of public employee unions, eliminate business regulations, and toughen up rules affecting how citizens register to vote or actually vote on election day.[2]

All of these moves in GOP-dominated states tended to be applauded by elderly Tea Partiers, who are happy to weaken unions and are sufficiently riled up about immigration to support legal rules to make registration and voting more difficult. Older white Tea Partiers are not fans of generous educational funding, either, because they fear paying higher taxes that benefit children of younger adults, who are much more racially and ethnically diverse than older cohorts. Grassroots Tea Partiers did not, for the most part, initiate the policy steps taken starting in early 2011 by GOP governors and legislators, but they approve them.

Many members of the general public, including many independents who supported GOP candidates in 2010, feel differently, however. So broadly unpopular were many of the GOP moves in the states that by the middle of 2011, the popularity ratings of governors such as Rick Scott in Florida and John Kasich in Ohio had taken a nosedive; recall elections were under way in Wisconsin and Michigan; and a centerpiece anti-union measure passed by the GOP in Ohio was scheduled for a referendum in the fall of 2011.[3] The very fact that these challenges occurred within months of GOP majorities taking over state capitols is another indication, like the Ryan budget in Washington DC, of the way in which ideological pressures can induce electorally dicey overreach among GOP officials.

Despite the danger of unpopular overreach, the attitude of right-wing policy advocates tends to favor forging full-speed ahead. They are not likely to let up the pressure on GOP officeholders during 2011 and 2012. Ideological elites on the right are confident to the point of arrogance, and they have a lot of resources to deploy. They expect that large infusions of campaign cash at the last minute can sway or bamboozle sufficient numbers of low-information voters to protect most of the GOP incumbents who vote their way on key policy matters and to secure victories for most of the GOP candidates they favor.

Elite Tea Party linked organizations also presume that measures disempowering their political opponents can help GOPers in 2012 and beyond. Requiring all voters to show photo IDs at the polls can discourage even legal immigrants and burden young people or poor people who do not have drivers' licenses.[4] Measures to undercut rival organizations are even better. Public sector unions will have less money to spend in 2012 if they cannot collect dues or deliver higher wages and improved benefits to members. From the point of view of the right-wing advocacy organizations operating through the Tea Party, immediate policy gains must be taken where they can, and any dips in GOP popularity corrected later, in the final months before the next election. So we can expect FreedomWorks, Americans for Prosperity, Tea Party Express, and their ilk to keep the pressure on GOP officials and candidates.

Media cheerleaders, especially at Fox News, may have a very different calculus, however. Back in 2009, the conservative media went all out to help the emerging grassroots activism of the Tea Party spread and take hold in many states and localities. Fox anchors and hosts, in particular, also helped to reinforce the narrative of the Tea Party as a grassroots force aimed at purifying and reforming the GOP (although, tellingly, Fox hosts urged Tea Partiers not to create a third party that would divide votes against Democrats). However, as the Republican Party and the nation move into the presidential election year of 2012, Fox News will take a pragmatic stance focused on helping whatever GOP presidential candidate emerges from the primaries maneuver to claim a national majority. If "Tea Party" activism still seems helpful to GOP electoral prospects in 2012, Fox will feature it. But if not—if independents remain wary of the Tea Party and the brand loses popularity—then Fox will switch gears. It will tout the supposed mainstream credentials and economic message of the GOP presidential candidate. Fox will feature whatever themes seem most likely to help Republicans win the presidency, gain control of the Senate, and hold the House. Quite likely, this will mean taking the spotlight off past policy moves of dubious popularity—like the Ryan budget of 2011—and also downplaying those grassroots activists so vividly featured in 2009 and 2010. The mainstream media may focus on the Tea Party as "controversial," but if the Tea Party continues to lose appeal to the general voting public, Fox and friends will try to change the focus. In an early sign of this likely change of network policy, Glenn Beck was sent packing by Fox management in early 2011.[5]

This brings us to the grassroots Tea Partiers themselves. What about their role leading into November 2012? In many Republican-leaning districts and states, the efforts of grassroots Tea Partiers to take control of GOP committees and keep a close eye on the votes of GOP elected officials will guarantee continued Tea Party clout inside the Republican Party itself. Many senators, representatives, state-level officials—and GOP candidates for those offices—will have to propitiate their local Tea Party leaders to maintain enthusiasm among core conservative voters. Yet as we discussed in Chapter 5, Republican politicians may have a hard time simultaneously satisfying Tea Party activists and the non–Tea Party voters they also need to win. GOP officials and candidates will struggle to appeal both ways, and they will not be able to turn fully away from Tea Partiers in most places. Even if the Fox spotlight shifts, and even if the national public registers wariness or negative evaluations of the "Tea Party" going into 2012, grassroots Tea Partiers in many places are organized, determined, and socially interconnected. Whatever Harry Reid may like to think, they will not go away.

Grassroots Tea Party involvement in the GOP presidential primaries may also be intense, but may not add up to a united effort for a winning candidate. In our interviews with Tea Partiers around the country, we asked about preferences for the 2012 GOP presidential nomination and got very scattered answers. Those who liked Sarah Palin considered her not viable as a general election candidate; and some did not like her. Many had nice things to say about Mike Huckabee before he decided not to run, and we presume that some of those Tea Partiers later took a liking to Michele Bachmann. We heard nothing positive about Newt Gingrich, and universal skepticism or negativity about Mitt Romney (because of his health plan, the precursor to ObamaCare, and because he is not considered trustworthy). This or that minor GOP candidate got a positive mention here or there—including Herman Cain. When Donald Trump was blustering about Obama's birth certificate, he got a chuckle and an "Atta boy" from some Tea Partiers, but no one seemed to take him seriously as a presidential contender.

The Tea Partiers we met in various states had no consensus or shared enthusiasm for any particular GOP presidential possibility in the early stages. One New Hampshire Republican linked to the Tea Party told us that he expects supporters to unite behind one candidate in late 2011 or early

2012. A broadly popular candidate like Rick Perry may inspire the Tea Partiers, who dislike Mitt Romney and would prefer that he not win the GOP nomination. The split between social conservatives and libertarians could become evident, as some Tea Partiers go for candidates favorable to Christian conservative priorities, and others deliver votes to Ron Paul. Two of the early GOP primaries, in Iowa and South Carolina, are likely to give strong voice to the socially conservative wing of the Tea Party. The New Hampshire primary could give greater leverage to libertarians, but that primary is an "open" contest, where independents and Democrats can vote as well as registered Republicans. Tea Partiers in New Hampshire may not have as much leverage as they hope in that critical early contest.

The key point is this: when the general election enters full swing in the spring of 2012, Tea Partiers as such will end up supporting whoever runs on the GOP line against the hated Barack Obama. The hard-core activists will all vote for Republicans down the line. Grassroots Tea Partiers will not, however, have very much sway in the broader electorate. Many Republicans not identified with the Tea Party, and many independents who could vote GOP, may be turned off by the grassroots Tea Party style and by far-right policy priorities. Even if mainstream Republicans and many independents join Tea Partiers to vote for the same GOP contenders in 2012 contests, the larger electorate will not be as open to the Tea Party message as it was in 2010.

Younger Americans, including people of more diverse ethnic, racial, and class backgrounds, will make up a higher proportion of the 2012 electorate than they did in 2010. The types of voters whose share of the vote will increase may or may not go for Democrats versus Republicans, but they are not very amenable to Tea Party messages or very likely to interact with Tea Party activists—except, perhaps, with an aunt, uncle, or grandparent at Thanksgiving dinner! In addition to shifting social categories and networks in the 2012 electorate, incumbent GOP officials who have taken strong right-wing policy stands will make the Tea Party–influenced agenda of the Republican Party much more visible to ordinary voters.

That agenda is not proving consistently popular. For younger, working-age adults, above all, the GOP budget ideas are a clear threat—not just to the social safety net, such as it is, but to education and health care funding on which many working people and their children depend. Younger Americans are also likely to be turned off by the anti-gay social policies pushed by

Christian conservative grassroots Tea Partiers, as well as by the racial and ethnic stereotypes underlying Tea Party ideology.[6] And many legal immigrants are repelled by the strong grassroots Tea Party emphasis on draconian border and police measures to harass and deport undocumented residents.

Ironically, the Ryan budget pushed by elite Tea Party forces has also raised concerns among middle-aged and elderly voters who might otherwise approve the GOP budgetary messages. Those messages, after all, stress holding down taxes and cutting public spending—above all, on programs that serve children and young adults. But a proposal to radically restructure Medicare, even if slated to take effect only in 2021, can easily frighten elderly voters. It certainly alarms adults 45 to 55 years old, the sons and daughters of today's elderly. After all, Medicare is not just an "old people's program," it is a cornerstone of family security because, in its absence, working-age adults would have to take funds from their family budgets to help cover health care costs for grandma and grandpa. Americans live in families, and most people will not sit still and watch grandmother or grandfather go without necessary health care.

In the electoral big picture, in sum, the Tea Party had the wind at its back between 2008 and 2010, but it is now headed into crosswinds if not counter-force gales. Americans will be dealing with more of a known Tea Party agenda in 2012, much of it unpopular stuff from right-wing think tanks; moreover, Americans will vote on it in greater, more diverse numbers than in 2010. Voters in 2012, including many younger people and minorities, won't merely decide if they like or dislike Democrats; they will be able to evaluate policies backed by Republicans at the behest of the ideological advocacy organizations identified with the Tea Party.

Social scientists are not good at predicting future events, so we stipulate that we do not know whether Barack Obama will be reelected in 2012, or how the balance of Republicans versus Democrats will sort out in the House, the Senate, and the states. At the national level, virtually any combination of outcomes is possible—from, on the one extreme, Obama winning reelection along with the Senate barely staying in Democratic hands and the House barely swinging back to the Democrats, to, on the other extreme, GOP victories sweeping the presidency and both houses of Congress. A mixed outcome is very possible.

It is irritating to be unable to prognosticate the institutional outcomes with any certainty because the policy consequences are likely to be quite different, depending on which scenario comes to fruition. A GOP sweep would lead to the hobbling if not repeal of the Affordable Care Act of 2010, and possibly put Medicare and Social Security on the privatization block. A Democratic sweep (even partial Democratic victories that include surprisingly large gains in the House) would sustain all of these social programs and probably lead to tax increases on the very rich. Another way to express the policy stakes of 2012 is to say that, even if the Tea Party loses coherence and popularity and weighs less heavily in an enlarged electorate, the enormous leverage it has gained over the national policy agenda after 2010 could survive and deepen anyway. Tea Party–backed conservative Republicans gained a lot of ground in 2010. And GOP victories in 2012, even with slight margins, would be sufficient to block tax increases on the wealthy and shift the fiscal burden toward cuts in major social entitlements inherited from the Great Society and the New Deal. The stakes in the 2012 election are very high.

THE PARADOXES OF TEA PARTY CITIZENSHIP

Prognostication aside, what is the normative bottom line for the Tea Party as a force in American democracy? Some readers may laugh at this question—assuming that the Tea Party is either laudable or damnably bad, depending on where one stands on its policy priorities. But the vitality of grassroots engagement in the Tea Party raises poignant questions even for observers who disagree strongly with what the Tea Party stands for.

This was brought home to both authors at a Harvard forum in March 2011. We had recently completed several rounds of interviews with grassroots Tea Partiers, and our findings came up during a discussion of Barack Obama's presidency and conservative reactions to it. Most people in the audience were liberals (or progressives critical of Democrats from the left). One questioner was a professor who has done important research on participatory democracy, and she knew that both of us care about active civic engagement and have studied its manifestations in America, past and present. The professor asked the most difficult question: "Even if you question their policy stands," she said, "what do you make of the active citizen engagement of Tea Partiers? Is their engagement a good thing for American democracy—or not?" The room fell unusually silent as we shared our reflections.

On the ground, in local rallies and regular meetings, the grassroots Tea Party is a model of active citizenship. Ordinary men and women, some previously active in politics and others with civic experience under their belts, take voluntary initiatives to make events happen and run meetings. Without pay, they pitch in to do everything from setting up chairs and handing out leaflets, to arranging for speakers, putting out newsletters, and preparing refreshments. At Tea Party meetings, people ask questions and make comments after a speaker has finished his or her presentation. And when groups discuss priorities and decide how to divvy up tasks, quite a few ordinary women and men step up to chair a task force or carry on a key duty. Tea Party meetings have the same "let's pitch in and get it done" air about them as clubs and lodges and church societies throughout America's past as "a nation of joiners."[7]

The willingness of grassroots Tea Partiers to plunge into new realms and learn about the nitty-gritty of politics is also remarkable. Midway through our interviews on the Middle Peninsula of Virginia, we were struck by a telling contrast. Between us, the two authors have attended many meetings of highly educated liberals in and around academic communities. In those meetings, detailed knowledge of public policies is common. People know exactly what is in Obama's health reform law, exactly how all kinds of taxes work, and can tell you who pays for and benefits from government expenditures. They can debate the intricacies of cap and trade versus carbon taxes. But even liberal PhDs are often extremely vague about how U.S. politics actually works. People will proclaim in meetings that President Obama should just give a speech on a particular priority—and act as if that would get it done, forgetting the complexities of Congressional rules and alliance-building. Opinionated, educated liberals often have no idea what happens in state legislatures, local government boards, or political party committees. Grassroots Tea Partiers, by contrast, know the rules and procedures for passing bills and advancing regulations in detail—for local, state, and national government. But at the same time, they hold wildly inaccurate views of what is in, or not in, public policies or legislative proposals. They know process, but flub content—the exact opposite of the academic liberals.

For Tea Partiers, a lot of study goes into mastering legislative and political processes. We saw evidence of that work getting done in almost every Tea Party locale we visited. A few members take it upon themselves to track all bills of a certain type in the state legislature, for example, to figure out who is voting on them and when. Using the official names and numbers of the bills, and explaining the steps for moving things through committees to floor votes, they let other Tea Party members in their area know exactly when to send a letter or email, and to whom, to push for preferred outcomes. The same thing happens with legislation in the national Congress, and with topics about to be taken up by local government committees and boards. Often, members of a Tea Party group also figure out the rules for nominations and decision-making for the Republican Party in their area—and mobilize people to attend the relevant meetings and make their voices heard, or cast their votes for key party offices. Leaders of local Tea Parties undertake this kind of research and orchestrate actions to take advantage of what is learned about pending legislation or key GOP decisions. But many regular members pitch in, too. They have learned to use the Internet to track government actions, and they exhibit a mastery of legislative process and arcane party rules that compares well to the knowledge of political scientists who specialize in these areas.

We found ourselves impressed by Tea Partiers' mastery of political processes. But we were also repeatedly shocked at the wildly inaccurate things people unblinkingly believe about what government does, how it is financed, and what is actually included (or not) in key pieces of legislation or regulation. In Virginia, for example, Tea Partiers confidently told us that the Affordable Care Act of 2010 ("ObamaCare" in their parlance) includes both death panels and the abolition of Medicare—although both claims are flat out untrue. One Virginian also told us she opposed Obama's health reform because it includes a "public option" that will drive private insurance companies out of business. This is completely untrue (though if it were true, we realized, most of our liberal friends would be very happy!). We were also assured that ObamaCare will be financed through a tax on all real estate transactions—another fantastic falsehood.

Other Tea Partiers were equally sure that half of Americans pay no taxes (this belief confuses the income tax with all taxes, because lower income Americans who do not owe income taxes pay heavy tolls in payroll taxes, sales taxes, and other kinds of charges). Still others made outlandish claims, ranging from the suggestion that the Obama administration plans to seize all 401k savings to pay off the deficit, to the prediction that federal authorities have plans to round up conservatives, seize their guns, and put them in concentration camps. Even if we leave aside the off-the-wall paranoid projections, the detailed policy claims made by Tea Partiers are, to put it politely, often not in touch with factual reality.

Grassroots Tea Party activism therefore marries participatory engagement and considerable learning about the workings of government with factually ungrounded beliefs about the content of policies. If people actively engage in the political process but on mistaken premises, is that good or bad for democracy? Our heads are left spinning. We admire the citizen participation and engagement we witnessed; we applaud the community organizers we saw at work. But it surely would be better to marry all that citizen energy to more accurate takes on what government does, or does not do.

Another paradox of Tea Party citizenship is the sharp bifurcation between generous, tolerant interaction within the group, and an almost total lack of empathy or sympathy for fellow Americans beyond the group. As we have commented, many local Tea Parties include both social conservatives, who feel strongly about traditional moral questions, and libertarians, who prefer to keep government and politics out of individual moral choices. That is quite a split, but in practice Tea Partiers of these different persuasions make a strong effort to understand one another and work together. For both politically pragmatic reasons and out of genuine social affection for other people in their group, they work to bridge and elide and accommodate the different outlooks within the Tea Party. We suspect that Tea Party participants usually find it difficult to stereotype and reject people they actually deal with face to face. That can also explain why Tea Partiers who dealt with us in person were invariably polite.

But Tea Partiers, as we have seen, freely wield demonizing stereotypes about fellow Americans in different age groups and life circumstances. When fellow Americans perceived as "freeloaders" come up, Tea Partiers' language becomes downright cruel. In one meeting we attended, public school teachers, who work hard for a living at modest salaries, were spoken of in hateful terms—simply because Tea Partiers resent public employee unions. We heard similar cruel stereotypes about Muslim-Americans, immigrants, and young people.

Stereotyping and hateful rejection become even more extreme where organized political opponents are at issue. Trade unionists are not seen as having the same rights to organize and exert collective political voice as Tea Partiers themselves. The former leader of the Service Employees International Union, Andy Stern, is a "Communist," one Tea Partier insisted to us (a laughably untrue statement, of course). Organized African-American and Latino rights groups are dismissed as threats to the nation. And so are Democrats—who are not discussed as legitimate competitors dueling with

Republicans. They are castigated as unpatriotic, portrayed as threats to national security, and scorned as detrimental to a healthy American society. "I hope you are not thin-skinned," a Tea Party member who hosted us said before we visited his local meeting, noting that we were likely to hear things we would not like about liberals and Democrats. Indeed we did, both at that meeting and at other Tea Party meetings as well, where the nasty stereotypes and demonizing dismissals flowed freely.

All in all, Tea Party citizen engagement in the democratic process—a positive thing—is married to a level of out-group intolerance and refusal to contemplate compromise and give and take that are surely worrisome for U.S. democracy. That the mostly older, white, middle-class conservatives who make up the grassroots Tea Party have found a new love of politics, a new willingness to get involved and work with others for desired outcomes—these are wonderful developments for anyone who cares about citizen involvement in U.S. politics. But the downsides are also inescapable because the new citizen energy is married to serious misconceptions about policy realities, and the solidarity among Tea Partiers is grounded in rejection of the needs and values and equally legitimate rights of other groups of Americans. Other people are not truly "fellow Americans" for many at the grass roots unless they are fellow "Patriots," that is, members of the Tea Party itself.

THE BOTTOM LINE

The more pathological aspects of Tea Party activism are arguably fueled by the content of right-wing media programming, above all the putative news delivered on Fox television. Well before the Tea Party burst on the scene, scholars looked into the content of Fox broadcasts, including so-called news coverage as well as interpretive programs. They established that Fox often propagates falsehoods, in many cases apparently as a deliberate editorial policy. The result is a viewership that knows less and believes many mistaken things about public affairs.

Fox News makes viewers both more conservative and less informed. The introduction of Fox News into the cable roster has been shown to have coincided with an uptick in voting for Republican presidential candidates.[8] The capacity to shift U.S. voting patterns suggests that Fox News has a very real persuasive power, although obviously people predisposed to be conservatives choose the network they watch. But Fox weighs more heavily—and in a way more worrisome for U.S. democracy—by spreading misinformation and evoking racial and ethnic stereotypes. Watch a day of Fox, and you will have the impression that illegal immigrants, criminals, and badly behaving people of color are overrunning America. You will also get the impression that federal officials and liberals are constantly plotting to take away the rights and ruin the family finances of regular Americans—all to aggrandize themselves and take care of "freeloading" supporters. You will hear dire warnings about the supposedly imminent collapse of the national economy and U.S. currency (and commercials will urge you to buy gold to ward off disaster in the looming economic collapse).

Fox News viewers are more likely than other news consumers to be misinformed on political issues. In 2010, Fox News watchers were fourteen points more likely to believe—mistakenly in most instances—that their own taxes had gone up, and thirty-one points more likely to believe that the health care reform law passed under Obama would increase the deficit (when in fact it is projected to significantly reduce the long-term federal deficit).[9] As mentioned above, we saw evidence of such policy misinformation in our interviews—in all cases speaking with Tea Partiers who reported regularly getting all or almost all of their news from Fox and other overtly conservative sources. In more than one instance, moreover, we tracked the falsehoods directly to Fox.[10] At a Tea Party meeting in Massachusetts, people discussed the possibility that the "SmartGrid" (an infrastructure improvement to the electricity grid, a plan approximately as controversial as road repair) was in fact a plan that would give the government control over the thermostats in people's homes. We wondered how such an outlandish conspiracy theory could have been accepted by the intelligent and well-educated people at this meeting—until we checked the Fox News transcripts. Glenn Beck had indeed raised this weird possibility on his show.[11]

Tea Partiers' factually inaccurate beliefs about many policy matters are particularly striking given their relatively high levels of education and overall savvy about the political process. It is hard to escape the conclusion that deliberate propagation of falsehoods by Fox and other powerful media outlets is responsible for mis-arming otherwise adept Tea Partiers, feeding them inaccurate facts and falsely hyped fears. If so, the elite media impresarios who have encouraged and helped to shape Tea Party activism are more responsible than the grassroots members themselves for marrying activism to falsehoods and stoking destructive social stereotypes that pit older white Americans—the Fox viewership—against younger, less privileged, often minority fellow citizens.

So far, we have disagreed with Harry Reid's declaration in January 2011 that the Tea Party will soon disappear. Whatever happens with the economy, we expect Tea Party forces to remain in the field for quite some time, even if the Tea Party label loses its charm. Many grassroots Tea Partiers will continue to attend meetings, and those who rarely attend will still respond to emails urging them to attend rallies or turn out at the polls to vote for conservative candidates. The right-wing media, too, will keep doing its thing—put out whatever Roger Ailes of Fox News and other key decision-makers think will favor the electoral fortunes of the GOP and advance conservative policy causes.

Even more certain to stay active are the national advocacy organizations, whose followings in email lists and on the Web have greatly swelled in the Tea Party period. Americans for Prosperity and FreedomWorks now have many more grassroots ties, and much greater reach into many states and localities, than they did before 2009. They will continue to stoke free-market preferences and engage grassroots citizens to push favored legislation—at the state level as well as nationally—and will do so with greater clout in and around the GOP than they had before the Tea Party emerged. The roving billionaires who fund these advocacy organizations are not going to let up either. They remain alarmed at Obama's presidency. In an era of steadily rising wealth and incomes at the very top, they have nearly unlimited wherewithal to influence public debates and elections—even as the Supreme Court has cleared away legal obstacles to the sway of fat cat money in politics.

Nevertheless, even if organization, resources, and strong networks keep its various parts active for some time to come, it is hard to see the Tea Party as such hanging together for many more years. The "Tea Party" label has become more ho-hum. Elites that find the label less than helpful for electoral or policy struggles will downplay it during the general presidential contest in 2012. The greater limitation for the Tea Party is the age of its participants. Grassroots Tea Partiers are mostly older people whose activism will of necessity wane in coming years. GOP supporters and Fox viewers, too, are disproportionately from the ranks of older white Americans. Both the Tea Party grass roots, and key institutions surrounding it, must find ways to appeal to younger cohorts of Americans, who are more racially diverse, or their decline is assured.

For the coming months and years, however, Tea Party activism and its elite supporters will sharpen social tensions in U.S. politics. As Brookings demographer William Frey and journalist Ronald Brownstein have pointed out, U.S. politics finds itself in a period of cultural mismatch between generational groups.[12] Older Americans are disproportionately white and often wary about paying taxes for programs to help younger cohorts, who are increasingly racially and ethnically diverse. The oldsters value Social Security and Medicare, to be sure, but feel they have already paid for them through lifetimes of work and tax contributions. When the federal budget is strained, older Tea Partiers want to make sure that cuts hit programs other than theirs.

The "grey" versus "brown" divide—a tension that superimposes divisions by age and experience, income, and ethnicity—is increasingly apparent for the United States as a whole. The mismatch is especially acute in certain states, including major Republican strongholds in the West and South, where recent immigrants coexist with older whites who were reared and began their working lives in an era of restricted immigration.[13] Budget battles can be more naked in the states, too, because potential tax increases to pay for public education and Medicaid would ask older, disproportionately white Americans to contribute more to sustain programs benefiting younger, more racially diverse residents. As we have seen, the Tea Party is very much a reaction by older white conservative Americans who resent and fear what they think might be the political accompaniments of a nation transformed by rising younger cohorts with different experiences, values, and social characteristics. Barack Obama's presidency, coming at a moment of national economic crisis that strained public budgets, only crystallized and heightened Tea Party fears on both the social and fiscal fronts.

If Obama is reelected in 2012, the generationally grounded fears will remain, and Republicans supported by Tea Partiers will continue to push against Democratic priorities. If Obama is defeated, the Republican president who replaces him will come under strong pressure to accept radical cuts in public programs that benefit younger Americans, as well as tax cuts for the wealthy that will necessitate restructurings of Medicare and Social Security for future cohorts of retirees. Elderly Tea Partiers themselves may be held whole by Republicans fearful of angering their most aroused followers, but the children and grandchildren of Tea Partiers will suffer from drastic GOP cutbacks along with all other younger Americans. The big winners will be the super-rich fat cats who have manipulated Tea Party activism with such glee.

"Tea Party" as a fashionable label is losing its luster, as the media and many conservative elites move on. But the outlooks, values, and heightened engagement of many older American citizens who gravitated toward this protest effort starting in 2009 will remain. Tea Party fears and outlooks are central to American politics in a period of culturally polarized generational change. For better and worse, Tea Party–style politics is likely to remain, for some time to come, a pivotal part of ongoing, fierce disputes about what U.S. government should do and not do. Tea Party activism is a generationally bounded variant of long-standing forms of conservative populism in America.

The Tea Party in all of its manifestations has pulled the Republican Party sharply toward the right, and shifted U.S. public debates at a critical juncture, blunting the reformist force of Barack Obama's historic presidency. The Tea Party's place in history, side by side with Obama, is assured. Even so, the longer-term results and after-effects of Tea Party mobilizations remain to be seen. Will elite and grassroots Tea Party efforts prove to have permanently shifted the center of gravity of U.S. politics? Will they have a long-term effect on the capacity of American government to respond to a changing society and ensure opportunity and security for citizens of all ages and backgrounds? These crucial questions remain as yet unanswered. Only time and future politics will tell.

Epilogue

How Tea Party Forces Are Dismembering the Republican Party

One rarely hears talk about of the "Tea Party" anymore, and polls suggest that the label now evokes more negative than positive responses from Americans. Even before President Obama was reelected in 2012, in fact, Republican leaders and conservatives were downplaying the Tea Party moniker. For the six months prior to the 2012 general elections, Fox News transcripts include fewer than 900 references to the "Tea Party." This was a huge drop-off from the more than 3,000 references during the same period in 2011—let alone the constant celebratory attention in 2009 and 2010. With conservative elites now downplaying the once-ubiquitous label, it is easy to imagine the Tea Party is over. But forces unleashed by the Tea Party have remade the Republican Party from above and below.

At the grass roots, anti-immigrant passions played a major role in spurring Tea Party activists to protest and form local groups from 2009 to 2011—and those passions live on in the hearts and minds of half or more of all rank-and-file Republicans.[1] At the top, many of the ultra-free-market professional advocates and funders who jumped on the Tea Party bandwagon so eagerly a few years now dictate much of the Republican Party's agenda. Far-right powerhouses like Heritage Action, along with Americans for Prosperity and other key operations in the comprehensive political network led by the multibillionaire Koch brothers, now control more resources than the Republican Party itself.[2] Virtually all national and state GOP officeholders and candidates espouse extreme positions pushed forward during the Tea Party era. No matter how solidly conservative their previous records, Republican contenders fear challenges from the right—fueled by billionaire ideologues or rebellious voters, or both.

In all but the most conservative districts and states, especially in high-turnout elections, the hard-right positions of the Republican candidates risk alienating moderate voters the GOP needs to win or hold elected offices. However, many elections are low-turnout affairs; and once in office Republicans can and do advance unpopular policies. Sometimes they prevail through sheer obstruction—blocking popular minimum-wage increases, for example. At other times, they use legislative majorities to push through unpopular measures as quickly and quietly as possible, hoping that voters will forget or opponents will fall short in the next election. In just this way, unpopular curbs to bargaining rights for public sector union workers have been pushed through in many states, as restrictions on voter registration and cutbacks in early voting periods designed to make it hard for Democratic constituencies to vote.

IMMIGRATION FEARS AT THE FOREFRONT

Fear of immigrants was a driving force of early grassroots Tea Party activism, and it continues to mobilize many conservative-base voters today. Republican candidates who demonize ethnic and religious minorities and call for once-unimaginable crackdowns on immigrants and minorities and cutbacks in help for the poor have been rewarded with tremendous outpourings of grassroots support on the right.

In the Tea Party era, xenophobic targets have varied in response to world events. In 2010, with the wars in Iraq and Afghanistan at low ebb, the anti-immigrant sentiments we heard from interviewees and in the conservative media were mostly directed at Latinos—though hatred and fear of Muslims was always freely expressed. Recently, however, the right-wing rhetorical focus has shifted. When the 2014 Ebola outbreak in Africa was in the news, leading conservative media figures stoked fears of an epidemic in the United States, called for a complete travel ban from the entire region.[3] A year later, in response to the Syrian crisis, Fox News claimed that lengthy federal processes for vetting refugee applications might nonetheless allow terrorists to enter the United States. Such claims soon jumped from conservative media to Republicans elected officials, including at least 28 GOP governors who pledged to block Syrian refugees from resettling in their states.

By the fall of 2015 and early 2016, extreme opposition to Islam and immigration dominated Republican primaries. Donald Trump built support among Republican primary voters by calling for mass deportation of the 11 million undocumented immigrants currently in the United States and proposing "a complete shutdown of Muslims entering the United States."[4] In September, neurosurgeon Ben Carson briefly rivaled Trump's popularity after he said a devout Muslim could not serve as president of the United States, and Ted Cruz became a leading contender after saying he would respond to the threat of terrorism by "carpet bombing" Iraq and Syria.

Such overt Islamophobia from leading Republicans in 2015 marks a true shift. As recently as the 2000 GOP National Convention, Republican National Committee chairman Jim Nicholson introduced a Muslim-American to offer a religious blessing drawn from the Koran.[5] And only days after the September 11th attacks, President George W. Bush told Muslims, "We respect your faith. It's practiced freely by many millions of Americans, and by millions more in countries that America counts as friends. Its teachings are good and peaceful, and those who commit evil in the name of Allah blaspheme the name of Allah. The terrorists are traitors to their own faith, trying, in effect, to hijack Islam itself. The enemy of America is not our many Muslim friends; it is not our many Arab friends."[6] In the contemporary context, it is almost unimaginable that a leading Republican candidate would make such a speech.

With fear of foreigners and immigrants now so central in appeals to the conservative base, immigration reform continues to be a stumbling block for the Republican Party. Business elites want reforms and many GOP leaders, consultants, and media supporters understand the increasing importance of Latino voters and would like to see a softening in opposition to immigration changes that could include a path to eventual citizenship for many current undocumented residents. Shortly after the GOP's big election defeats in 2012, for instance, Sean Hannity claimed to have "evolved" toward a more moderate stance on immigration.[7] In 2013, Republican presidential hopeful Senator Marco Rubio of Florida went so far as to sign on in 2013 to a bipartisan immigration bill that included a path to citizenship, clearly misjudging the potency of popular anti-immigrant sentiment in his own party. Faced with intense criticism, Rubio soon retreated and has been outdoing himself to take a hard line in the presidential primaries. Despite long-term electoral advantages, getting today's grassroots Republicans to go along with any kind of immigration reform remains very difficult.

THE HOLLOWING OF REPUBLICAN PARTY INSTITUTIONS

When grassroots Tea Party protests first spread in 2009 and 2010, many far-right elites tried to jump on the anti-Obama bandwagon, hoping to harness conservative voters to long-standing anti-government policy agendas. Republican elites and free-market advocacy groups mouthed Tea Party platitudes and flirted with popular nativism and racism because they wanted to win big in the 2010 mid-term elections amid a deep economic slowdown. If popular anger could be stoked to a fever pitch, perhaps conservative, white, older voters would turn out at even higher rates than usual. That is exactly what happened, helping to fuel huge GOP gains in the House of Representatives and across dozens of states in 2010. No sooner was the election over, though, than elites started to move the focus away from grassroots Tea Partiers.

Free-market advocacy groups and billionaire funders, especially those tied to the comprehensive political network orchestrated by Charles and David Koch brothers, proclaimed that the Tea Party wave in the GOP was all about furthering their long-standing agenda to cut taxes on the rich, slash welfare and social insurance, remove regulations on businesses, block environmental and climate-change policies, and curb union bargaining rights. In many states such as Wisconsin, Michigan, and North Carolina where right-wing Republicans gained full control, much of this agenda was rapidly passed and signed into law. Similarly, the Koch network leaders and other far-right advocates cheered on Republicans in the U.S. House as they repeatedly voted to repeal ObamaCare, cut taxes, and undercut environmental rules—and as they used fiscal deadlines in 2011 and 2013 to try to extort President Obama and congressional Democrats to accept huge reductions in government social spending.

Popular Tea Party activities had furthered—but did not cause—the policy shift of Republicans toward ultra-right free-market policy positions. Starting back in the early 2000s, ideological billionaires and millionaires assembled in twice-yearly donor conclaves led by the Koch brothers, who had already spent decades channeling funds into free-market think tanks and advocacy organizations.[8] Koch efforts to engage fellow wealthy conservatives in a long-term strategy to transform U.S. policy and politics ramped up under GOP President George W. Bush, who was criticized from the right for his willingness to spend tax money on programs like a new Medicare drug benefit; and these efforts reached new heights after Barack Obama and Democratic congressional majorities were elected in 2008. From 2002 to 2014, sharp shifts in the control of political resources unfolded, as the budgets of Republican Party committees declined and new far-right organizations gained huge infusions of donations and professional staffing. The hefty new players included Heritage Action, the Senate Conservatives Fund, and the Freedom Partners Chambers of Commerce plus Americans for Prosperity, central to the enlarged Koch political network.[9] In the 2010, 2012, and 2014 election cycles, right-wing spending expanded outside the Republican Party itself—and by now, as journalist Kenneth P. Vogel explains, "the Koch network rivals the GOP," deploying more money and paid staffers than Republican Party committees control.[10]

In this situation, the last thing GOP candidates or officeholders want is to face public challenges from far-right free-market elites. If they take stands the Kochs and their allies dislike on taxes, social spending, labor issues, or voting rights, GOPers know they can have Americans for Prosperity staging protests in their districts or right-wing fat cats funding primary challenges from their right. To fend off such challenges and get good ratings on scorecards publicized by the Club for Growth, Americans for Prosperity, and other enforcers, these politicians pledge fealty to extreme anti-government agendas. Even when Republican governors or congressional leaders try to persuade them to vote for must-pass budgets or business-touted measures such as highway taxes, most GOP legislators do all they can to avoid public criticisms and election challenges from the right.

The problem for Republicans, however, is that positions aligned with the Koch network and other ultra-free-market elites do not always appeal to other organized constituency groups or the voters. Dilemmas can be especially acute in dealing with conservative voters who rallied to the Tea Party banner not long ago. For those voters, the top priorities are often opposition to immigration, measures to outlaw abortion and gay marriage, and total refusal to compromise with Democrats to keep government functioning. Even very conservative Republican legislators can find themselves whipsawed between popular Tea Party–minded voters and free-market advocates who tried to harness popular anger but really have other policy priorities. Worse, Republicans often want or need support beyond the most conservative circles—from business interests and middle-of-the-road voters.

Middle-of-the-road voters often favor minimum wage increases, education spending, and laws to require paid sick days or family leave—measures that are anathema to the Koch network and other wealthy free-marketers, who stand ready to challenge Republican candidates and legislators who show signs of supporting any of them. As for business, groups like the Chamber of Commerce would like to see the GOP move forward with certain immigration reforms that nativist base voters will not abide. In addition, although business associations in the GOP orbit usually agree with free-market advocates (especially on measures to weaken unions and market regulations), sometimes these two elite forces break ranks. The U.S. Chamber of Commerce has pressed congressional Republicans to enact highway subsidies and agriculture bills, and to continue such programs as the Export-Import Bank; and in many Republican-run states hospital associations and chambers of commerce advocate accepting federal ObamaCare subsidies to expand Medicaid.[11] But all of these policies face strong opposition from the Koch network and other free-market advocacy groups, putting GOP legislators in a bind.

In sum, as extra-party elites on the far right weaken Republican leaders and hollow out party institutions, GOP politicians find themselves exposed to cross-cutting gale-force winds, and are not always well positioned to appeal to broader constituencies. The Tea Party that erupted in 2009 unleashed and intensified these contradictory forces now tearing apart the Republican Party and pulling it away from the American mainstream.

Nowhere is the hollowing of the GOP establishment more evident than in the rise of Donald Trump as the leading contender for the 2016 Republican presidential nomination. Trump may not even be a real Republican—he said in 2004 that "I probably identify more as Democrat"[12]—but party officials and other Republican presidential contenders struggled to gain any traction against him. Even the Koch network has not been able to deflect Trump's progress.

As a hijacker of the GOP presidential spotlight, Trump has several things going for him. Thrilling to the conservative base voters once called Tea Partiers, he touts nativism and immigration-bashing, and he is rhetorically willing to cross lines most other Republican contenders for state or national office have generally avoided traversing. Elites of all stripes may be horrified, but many grassroots conservatives are thrilled by Trump's willingness to express their fears and angers with no regard for "political correctness." Trump also hints at policy stands that are potentially appealing to grassroots conservatives, because he promises to combine immigration restriction with some higher taxes on the rich and steps to protect, not cut, Social Security and Medicare. As we showed in our research on ordinary Tea Partiers in 2011, most of them considered Social Security, Medicare, and military veterans benefits to be worthwhile protections for "real Americans," very different from "welfare." Trump does not sign on to the full Koch-style free-market agenda, and that is appealing to many voters. Equally important, billionaire Trump has funds of his own to use and does not to raise big money from other contributors, because he understands the new media landscape in which the Tea Party originally prospered. Using his fame as a reality TV star and his theatrically brash capacity to stoke outrage and controversy, Trump has been able to manipulate media outlets and make them his tools to gain public attention and build support in GOP primaries.

Whatever ultimately happens with the 2016 Republican presidential nomination, this billionaire loose cannon upended the nominating process and overshadowed competitors preferred by the GOP establishment, or the Koch network, or both. Trump has forced all contenders to compete over who will be toughest on immigrants, thereby undercutting Republican prospects to attract Latino votes in 2016 and beyond. Furthermore, the brash styles and blatant xenophobia Trump has helped to bring front and center in the GOP in 2016 presidential do not appeal to most Americans. In short, not only does the GOP find itself pushed to espouse often unpopular economic positions by free-market billionaires and advocacy groups, it also finds itself drawn by many angry populist voters and their preferred candidates to take extreme stands about immigrants and minorities likely to hurt Republican candidates in general election contests.

WHERE DOES THE REPUBLICAN PARTY GO FROM HERE?

Today the Republican Party finds itself rent by multiple civil wars—just eight years after the outbreak of "Tea Party" protests grabbed public attention, and just six years after big election victories by conservatives seemed to turn the tides of American politics and policy in the GOP's direction. In many states since 2010, far-right turns have indeed occurred—with voting rights cut back, union rights undone, taxes cut, social spending slashed, and environmental protections eviscerated. In Congress, especially following Republican take-overs of the House after 2010 and of the Senate after 2014, Republicans have tried to repeal ObamaCare, block immigration reform and environmental protections, and use budget deadlines and votes about raising the national debt ceiling as occasions to try to force Democrats and President Obama to accept huge cuts in federal government spending. In the Tea Party era, the ever-more radicalized GOP has scored accomplishments in Washington DC more by obstruction than through enacting right-wing laws, as it has been able to do in many states. Either way, however—whether obstructing in Washington DC or legislating in states they control—Republicans riding the Tea Party tiger have not been immune to the cross-pressures we have described in this epilogue. In Congress and many states, Republican candidates and officeholders are fighting among themselves and taking stands unlikely to wear well with most voters and many mainstream business interests. The 2016 GOP presidential primaries have simply shined a glaring national spotlight on intra-party struggles.

Many Democrats and media pundits seem to take a certain glee in watching Republicans move far from median voters and fight fierce internal battles. Will the Republican Party fall apart altogether? Will Democrats move into a commanding national majority? Today's Republican Party is certainly struggling—pulled in different directions and apparently locking itself into stands unlikely to win majority voter support in national or statewide contests, especially as the U.S. electorate becomes younger and more racially diverse. But no one should minimize the risks of one of America's two major political parties moving toward radical extremes—or presume that the GOP will never be able to gain new footing. It was only fifty years ago that the South was a solid Democratic bastion, and thirty-five years ago that Republicans were more supportive of abortion rights than Democrats. At some point, today's troubled Republican Party is bound to revamp its appeals and voting base.

But right now, GOP turmoil and extremism are risky for the entire country, because even nominating a patently unqualified White House nominee for 2016 might not put the presidency out of reach for Republicans. Drastic and unpopular policy shifts might quickly follow—including harsh measures toward immigrants, big cuts in education and health spending, new military buildups and foreign interventions, and eviscerations of U.S. workplace and environmental rules. The simple fact is that the United States has two major political parties, and many citizens who do not follow politics closely continue to think of them as interchangeable alternatives. If the economy slows, or if terrorist incidents happen, some voters will switch from one major party presidential candidate to the other, no matter who "the other" happens to be. Democrats tend to have demographic advantages in high-turnout national elections and in states with big diverse populations; but even in those elections Democrats' younger, lower-income, and minority supporters often do not vote at the same rate as angry white, older, conservative Republicans. So it does not take much to hand across the board victories to Republicans, even when they have moved to extreme positions and take policy stands most Americans do not approve.

Of course, truly unpopular actions are unlikely to stand forever. Even with Tea Party–minded Republican voters eager to vote, and right-wing billionaires able to fund elections and policy battles, larger swatches of American voters eventually have a say. If Republicans were somehow to win full control in Washington DC in 2017, they might face losses very quickly if they do all that ultra-free-market advocates or grassroots Tea Party nativists want them to do. Moreover, if the more likely scenario unfolds—with Republicans falling short of claiming the White House in 2016 and losing some ground in Congress and the states—then intra-GOP debates over the future of the party are sure to intensify.

When it comes sooner or later, the process of reorienting today's discombobulated GOP will be slow and fitful. True moderates hardly exist in the ranks of Republican officeholders any longer. And neither grassroots populists nor free-market billionaires are going to retire from the scene any time soon. Pushed from below and above by forces unleashed or accelerated in the Tea Party moment of 2009 to 2011, Republicans remain obdurately extreme in style and policy substance—and they are increasingly fighting among themselves, even as they compete to take stands most Americans do not support. Eventually, the Republican Party will either moderate or die, but not quickly. The after-effects of the Tea Party disruption will continue to weaken the GOP—and will also bedevil American government and politics for some time to come.

Notes

INTRODUCTION

1. Vanessa Williamson attended this meeting and took notes.
2. Theda Skocpol attended this meeting and took notes.
3. Vanessa Williamson attended this meeting and took notes.
4. More details and references appear in Chapter 3.
5. Johanna Neuman, "As Voters Go to the Polls to Pick His Successor, George W. Bush Hits New Low in Approval Rating," *Los Angeles Times*, November 4, 2008.
6. Allen Barr and Mike Allen, "Steele Trap? GOP Fears Grow," *Politico*, March 4, 2009.
7. See, for examples, the stories about a possible Democratic-led "*New New Deal*" in the November 24, 2010 issue of *Time*, which featured a memorable cover showing Barack Obama in an FDR pose, riding in an open convertible with a cigarette dangling from his grinning mouth.
8. Jeffrey M. Jones, "In First 100 Days, Obama Seen as Making a Bipartisan Effort," *Gallup*, April 24, 2009.
9. The first national media figure to bring significant attention to the Porkulus protests was Michelle Malkin. See her blog post from February 16, 2009: http://michellemalkin.com/2009/02/16/from-the-boston-tea-party-to-your-neighborhood-pork-protest/. In April, Malkin offered a snarky "cheat sheet" for reporters struggling to catch up with the Tea Party story: http://michellemalkin.com/2009/04/15/a-tax-day-tea-party-cheat-sheet-how-it-all-started/. (Both blog posts are available as of May 26, 2011.) In explaining the Tea Party's origins, Malkin featured the story of Keli Carender, who held an anti-Porkulus protest in Seattle in early February 2009. Malkin's framing of the Tea Party's origins was apparently quite successful; Carender later appeared prominently in *New York Times* reporter Kate Zernike's book. Kate Zernike, *Boiling Mad: Inside Tea Party America* (New

York: Times Books, Henry Holt, 2010), pp. 13–19. Like Malkin, Zernike credits Carender with organizing the original Tea Party protest. This is in tune with Zernike's overall emphasis on young libertarians as central to Tea Party activities. We find the origins story unconvincing, however, because there is no reason to believe that "Tea Party" activities would have spread like wildfire without persistent promotion from conservative media—and without a catchy name. "Anti-Porkulus" was not an electrifying rallying cry.

10. Video of the Santelli "rant" can be found at CNBC's website, available at http://video.cnbc.com/gallery/?video=1039849853 as of May 21, 2011.

11. The historical facts of the Boston Tea Party are not actually entirely in keeping with the common perception of the Tea Party as an anti-tax protest. For more information, see Joseph J. Thorndike, "A Tax Revolt or Revolting Taxes?" *Tax History Project*, December 14, 2005. Available at http://www.taxhistory.org/thp/readings.nsf/ArtWeb/1BC5839831CD15EE852570DD0061D496?OpenDocument as of May 26, 2011.

12. Mark Lloyd, "Why the Left Will Never Understand the Tea Party," *Tea Party Review* 1(1) (March 2011), p. 7. Note the grand-parental perspective from which Lloyd writes. He is speaking of the feelings of a movement mostly made up of older Americans worried that things will not be the same as they depart the scene.

13. Several Tea Party members we spoke to referred to this promise made by President Obama during his campaign for the presidency. See Angela Galloway, "Obama: We'll 'transform America,'" *Seattle Post-Intelligencer*, December 11, 2007.

14. Conservatives involved in the original February 27th Tea Parties hailed from the online networks Top Conservatives on Twitter and Smart Girl Politics; long-standing anti-tax campaigners including *American Spectator*, the Heartland Institute, and Americans for Tax Reform; as well as veterans of the mid-2008 "Don't Go" campaign that urged members of Congress to stay in session to lift the moratorium on offshore drilling. Instrumental to this early mobilization were loose networks organized around certain Twitter "hashtags"—the keywords Twitter users apply to tag the subject matter of their online comments—which allowed activists from a variety of different conservative networks to connect and combine forces.

15. Estimating the total crowd size of many protests held across the country is a difficult task. Data analyst and *New York Times* contributor Nate Silver came up with an estimate of "300,000+" on April 16th, 2009. You can see his calculations and data sources at http://www.fivethirtyeight.com/2009/04/tea-party-nonpartisan-attendance.html as of May 26, 2011.

16. Jean Casanave, "Losing Our Way," letter to the editor, *Gloucester-Mathews Gazette-Journal*, May 10, 2009.

17. See "Government Restraint Group Forms in Mathews," *Gloucester-Mathews Gazette-Journal*, June 19, 2009. The article has a picture of the founding members of the local Tea Party meeting around picnic tables, and ends with information on how others could get more information at the Peninsula Patriots website on Meetup.com. Another picture of larger numbers of Peninsula Patriots and others from the area preparing, signs in hand, to board two buses to travel to the national Tea Party protest march on September 12, 2009, in Washington DC, appears in the *Gloucester-Mathews Gazette-Journal*, Thursday, September 17, 2009, p. 22A.

18. The figure comes from ABC News, citing the Washington DC fire department. Russell Goldman, "Tea Party Protesters March on Washington," *ABC News*, September 12, 2009. Some conservative activists, including Matt Kibbe of FreedomWorks, dramatically inflated this number. For an analysis, see Nate Silver, "Size Matters; So Do Lies,"

available at http://www.fivethirtyeight.com/2009/09/size-matters-so-do-lies.html as of May 26, 2011.

19. More details and references on Tea Party Express are included in Chapter 3.

20. More details and references appear in Chapter 3. Journalist Kate Zernike does a good job of telling about the efforts of FreedomWorks to stoke the Tea Party. See her *Boiling Mad: Inside Tea Party America* (New York: Times Books, Henry Holt, 2010), chapter 2.

21. Lloyd, "Why the Left Will Never Understand the Tea Party," p. 7.

22. Taki Oldham, "The Billionaires' Tea Party: How Corporate America is Faking a Grassroots Revolution," DVD documentary distributed by the Media Education Foundation, Northhampton, Massachusetts, starting in March 2011.

23. This disconnection is documented and analyzed in Theda Skocpol, *Diminished Democracy: From Membership to Management in American Civic Life* (Norman, OK: University of Oklahoma Press, 2004).

24. Andrew Crutchfield and Will Eger worked for many hours to visit and catalogue the websites of every Tea Party group in the country.

25. The results are reported in Amy Gardner, "Gauging the Scope of the Tea Party Movement in America," *Washington Post*, October 24, 2010. We have had the chance to compare our findings to the dataset compiled by the *Post* team.

CHAPTER 1

1. As we explained in the Introduction, pseudonyms will be italicized the first time we use them in each chapter.

2. A more detailed discussion of survey research appears in Vanessa Williamson, Theda Skocpol, and John Coggin, "The Tea Party and the Remaking of Republican Conservatism," *Perspectives on Politics* 9 (1) (March 2011). We also look at polling in relation to media storylines in Chapter 4 of this book.

3. Nate Silver includes a figure with trends in favorable and unfavorable views in "Poll Shows More Americans Have Unfavorable Views of Tea Party," *FiveThirtyEight*, New York Times, March 30, 2011.

4. Alan I. Abramowitz, "Grand Old Tea Party: Partisan Polarization and the Rise of the Tea Party Movement," paper prepared for delivery at the Conference on the Tea Party Movement, University of California, Berkeley, October 2010, p. 12.

5. Larry J. Sabato, "Pendulum Swing," in *Pendulum Swing*, edited by Larry J. Sabato (Boston: Longman, 2011), p. 40.

6. For indications of basic active support, see evidence from the April 2010 *New York Times*/CBS poll summarized in Kate Zernike and Megan Thee-Brenan, "Poll Finds Tea Party Backers Wealthier and More Educated," *New York Times*, April 14, 2010; and evidence from a June 2010 NBC/*Wall Street Journal* poll discussed in Abramowitz, "Grand Old Tea Party," p. 12.

7. Our dataset, a tally of all local groups in all fifty states with any presence on the Internet, was last updated in the late summer of 2011.

8. The meetings we attended in the first half of 2011 fell in this range. In 2010, the *Washington Post* found that over half of Tea Parties had fewer than fifty participants at their last meeting, by their own count. Amy Gardner, "Gauging the scope of the tea party movement in America," *Washington Post*, October 24, 2010.

9. The very active Jefferson Area Tea Party in Charlottesville, Virginia, has about 100 members on its list, about half of whom tend to show up at any given meeting, according to our observations and reports from the group leader.

10. In Chapter 3, we will have more to say about the more particular life-circumstances and skills of men and women who founded local groups and provide ongoing leadership. In this chapter we stick to the characteristics broadly shared by Tea Party people.

11. CBS/*New York Times* poll, April 5–12, 2010.

12. The CBS/*New York Times* poll from April 5–12, 2010, found that three-quarters of Tea Party supporters are 45 or older. The Winston Group poll from April 1, 2010, found that 70% of Tea Party supporters are 45 or older.

13. NBC/*Wall Street Journal* poll, June 17–21, 2010.

14. "The Tea Party and Religion," report from the Pew Research Center, February 23, 2011.

15. CBS/*New York Times* poll, April 5–12, 2010.

16. John Green, political scientist at the University of Akron, was interviewed by phone by Theda Skocpol on April 8, 2011. He reported seeing both minorities and younger people at the Akron meeting, adding up to about a dozen out of 70 people in attendance. Green also attended a meeting near Columbus where all Tea Partiers were older—the youngest 55, he estimated.

17. Noted on the Greater Phoenix website in May 2011.

18. This point is ably elaborated and documented in Abramowitz, "Grand Old Tea Party."

19. Website accessed in March 2011.

20. For examples, see: Zachary Courser, "The Tea Party at the Election," *The Forum*, 8 (4), article 5; Sean J. Miller, "Survey: Four in 10 Tea Party Members are Democrats or Independents," *The Hill*, April 4, 2010; and Andrew Malcolm, "Myth-Busting Polls: Tea Party Members are Average Americans, 41 Percent are Democrats, Independents," *Los Angeles Times*, April 5, 2010.

21. In addition to polls cited here, see Stanley B. Greenberg, James Carville, Jim Gerstein, Peyton M. Craighill, and Kate Monninger, "Special Report on the Tea Party Movement," Democracy Corps, July 19, 2010. Available at http://www.democracycorps.com/strategy/2010/07/special-report-on-the-tea-party-movement/ as of May 21, 2011.

22. See, for example, the Quinnipiac Poll, March 16–21, 2010 and Stanley B. Greenberg, James Carville, Jim Gerstein, Peyton M. Craighill, and Kate Monninger, "Special Report on the Tea Party Movement."

23. Frank Newport, "Tea Party Supporters Overlap Republican Base," Gallup Survey Report, July 2, 2010. Available at http://www.gallup.com/poll/141098/tea-party-supporters-overlap-republican-base.aspx as of May 21, 2011.

24. NBC/*Wall Street Journal* poll, June 17–21, 2010.

25. "Tea Party's Hard Line on Spending Divides the GOP," *Pew Research Center Publications*, February 11, 2011. Ekins, "Character and Origins" also pulls together evidence from multiple surveys to document attitudinal differences between Tea Partiers and non–Tea Party Republicans. Similarly, 69% of "active Republicans" rated Obama negatively in 2008, for example, but 91% of Tea Partiers rated him negatively in mid-2010. Abramowitz, "Grand Old Tea Party," Tables 2 and 3.

26. "Most Want Budget Compromise but Split on Who's to Blame for a Shutdown," *Pew Research Center Publications*, April 4, 2011.

27. The collapse of the construction industry is a major reason that white unemployment, for the first time in recorded data, was more than half that of blacks. Data from: Anna Turner, "Jobs Crisis Fact Sheet," *Economic Policy Institute*, March 8, 2010.

28. Dannis Jacobe, "Nearly Half of Small-Business Owners May Never Retire," *Gallup*, October 1, 2010.

29. Peter Goodman, "Fuel Prices Shift Math for Life in Far Suburbs," *New York Times*, June 25, 2008. Conor Dougherty, "In the Exurbs, the American Dream is Up for Rent," *Wall Street Journal*, March 31, 2009.

30. Matt Nesvisky, "The Career Effects of Graduating in a Recession," *National Bureau of Economic Research*, November 2006.

31. "Most Want Budget Compromise but Split on Who's to Blame for a Shutdown," *Pew Research Center Publications*, April 4, 2011.

32. CBS/*New York Times* poll, April 5–12, 2010.

33. Emily McClintock Ekins, "The Character and Origins of the Tea Party Movement," unpublished working paper delivered at the Midwest Political Science Association, Chicago, Illinois, April 2011, p. 17.

34. In interviews in 2010 and 2011, Tea Partiers did not explain the Great Recession as a market failure. It is the result, in their view, of too much government interference, not too little. One example frequently cited by interviewees is the Community Reinvestment Act, which they believe created an unstable boom in homeownership among irresponsible people. We discuss Tea Party views of government in more detail in Chapter 2.

35. "Tea Party sign threatens gun violence if health care passes," Think Progress, March 20, 2010, available at http://www.thinkprogress.org/2010/03/20/code-red-gun/ as of March 14, 2010. An interesting analysis of the racial dynamic in the public response to violent rhetoric can be found in Tim Wise, "What if the 'Tea Party' were black?" *Alternet*, April 25, 2010, available at http://www.alternet.org/story/146616/what_if_the_tea_party_were_black as of May 26, 2010.

36. Andy Barr, "Tea Partiers told to 'drop by' Tom Perriello's home," *Politico*, March 22, 2010.

37. Ibid. and Andy Barr, "FBI investigates Virginia incident," *Politico*, March 24, 2010.

38. Ian Urbina, "Beyond Beltway, Health Care Debate Turns Hostile," *New York Times*, August 7, 2009.

39. Justine Sharrock, "Oath Keepers and the Age of Treason," *Mother Jones*, March/April 2010.

40. David Barstow, "Tea Party Lights Fuse for Rebellion on the Right," *New York Times*, February 10, 2010.

41. "Oath Keepers Battered by Members' Arrests," *Intelligence Report*, Southern Poverty Law Center, Fall 2010, p. 139.

42. The John Birch Society advertisement that includes this description of the Civil Rights movement appeared on page A10 of the Palm Beach *Post-Times* on October 31, 1965, and can be seen at http://news.google.com/newspapers?id=u4syAAAAIBAJ&sjid=ZbcFAAAAIBAJ&pg=4291,7598936 as of May 21, 2011. John Birch Society opposition to fluoridation has been widely reported, including on the December 23rd episode of the Rachel Maddow Show on MSNBC. In their response to the Maddow program, the John Birch Society claimed that they had opposed fluoridation as "a precedent for the socialized medicine" and "part of the Soviet communist state." See

http://www.jbs.org/jbs-news-feed/5785-rachel-maddow-recycles-falsehoods-against-the-john-birch-society, available as of May 21, 2011.

43. CBS News/*New York Times* poll, April 5–12, 2010.

44. "The Tea Party and Religion," The Pew Forum on Religion and Public Life, analysis published February 23, 2011.

45. Ekins, "Character and Origins," especially Figure 2, p. 30.

46. One of our Virginia interviewees told us about this, after hearing the story on a Tea Party Patriots national conference call.

47. CBS News/*New York Times* poll, April 5–12, 2010.

48. Brian Kates, "Tea Party Convention's Racial Brouhaha," *New York Daily News*, February 5, 2010. "About Dr. Scarborough," available at: http://www.visionamerica.us/about-us/about-dr-scarborough/ as of March 14, 2010.

49. CBS News/*New York Times* poll, April 5–12, 2010.

50. The question on political activity asked by the CBS/*New York Times* poll is an unusual one, but by any comparison, the Tea Party is an active group. In 1994, only 14% of American adults reported having worked for a party or candidate in the past three or four years. Gallup/CCFR Survey of American Public Opinion and U.S. Foreign Policy 1995, October 7–25, 1994: "Some people are quite active in politics, while others prefer not to take an active part. During the last three to four years have you done any of the things listed on this card? Just call off the number in front of any of the things you have done . . . voted in the Presidential election, voted in a local or state election, worked for a political party or candidate, gone to a political meeting to hear a candidate speak, asked someone to vote for your party or candidate, worn a campaign button or displayed a campaign poster, written or spoken to a public official about some personal need or problem, or written or spoken to a public official about some political issue or problem?" (Voted in Presidential election, 73 percent; Voted in local or state election, 68 percent; Worked for party or candidate, 14 percent; Gone to a political meeting, 22 percent; Asked someone to vote, 25 percent; Worn a campaign button or displayed poster, 25 percent; Written or spoken to a public official about personal need or problem, 23 percent; Written or spoken to a public official about political issue or problem, 25 percent; None of these, 20 percent.)

51. David Riley, "Holliston woman leads Boston Tea Party," *MetroWest Daily News*, February 22, 2010.

52. Sidney Verba, Kay Lehman Schlozman, and Henry Brady, *Voice and Equality: Civic Voluntarism in American Politics* (Cambridge, MA: Harvard University Press, 1995). Robert D. Putnam, "Bowling Alone: America's Declining Social Capital," *Journal of Democracy* 6(1) (1995), p. 65–78.

53. Saul Alinsky, *Rules for Radicals* (New York: Vintage, 1971).

54. Emily Ekins' breakdown of differences between social conservatives and libertarians in the Tea Party finds no gender difference. Both camps were tilted toward men in the surveys she analyzed. Emily Ekins, "The Character and Origins of the Tea Party Movement."

55. Theda Skocpol, *Protecting Soldiers and Mothers: The Political Origins of Social Policy in the United States* (Cambridge, MA: Belknap Press of Harvard University Press, 1995).

56. Rebecca E. Klatch, *Women of the New Right* (Philadelphia, PA: Temple University Press, 1988); and Kristin Luker, *Abortion and the Politics of Motherhood* (Berkeley and Los Angeles: University of California Press, 1988).

57. Skocpol, *Protecting Soldiers and Mothers*, which also contains many references to works on the prominent role of women in U.S. civic associations.

58. Theda Skocpol, *Diminished Democracy: From Membership to Management in American Civic Life* (Norman, OK: University of Oklahoma Press, 2004), chapters 1–3.

CHAPTER 2

1. Video of the Santelli rant is widely available online, including from CNBC's website: http://video.cnbc.com/gallery/?video=1039849853. Available as of May 5, 2011.

2. The statement appears at http://themaineteaparty.com/page/about-us. Available as of May 5, 2011.

3. Available at the Tea Party Patriots' Crawford Tea Party page, http://www.teapartypatriots.org/GroupNew/2888d2cb-20e5-418b-ae45-840c451d7efa/The_Crawford_Tea_Party, as of May 5, 2011.

4. Jill Lepore, *The Whites of Their Eyes: The Tea Party's Revolution and the Battle over American History* (Princeton, NJ: Princeton University Press, 2010). For a thoughtful review of this book, see Gordon S. Wood, "No Thanks for the Memories," *New York Review of Books*, January 13, 2011.

5. Notes taken by Theda Skocpol at the event on April 14, 2011 in the North Berwick Maine Community Center. No one followed up in the discussion, so we do not know if DeLemus really wanted to reinstate slavery or male-only suffrage. Other statements in the talk indicated he would probably be supportive of getting rid of the direct election of senators and the income tax.

6. Recounted by DeLemus in his talk in North Berwick Maine on April 14, 2011.

7. Sean Wilentz, "Confounding Fathers: The Tea Party's Cold War Roots," *The New Yorker*, October 18, 2010.

8. Available at the Greenville Tea Party website, http://www.greenvilleteaparty.com/freedom-of-religion.html/, as of April 5, 2011.

9. Available at the Greenville Tea Party website, http://www.greenvilleteaparty.com/freedom-of-religion.html/, as of April 5, 2011.

10. McNaughton's website includes a detailed description of each figure in the painting, from which these terms are drawn. Available at http://www.mcnaughtonart.com/artwork/view_zoom/?artpiece_id=353# as of May 6, 2011.

11. Andrew Romano, "America's Holy Writ," *Newsweek*, October 17, 2010.

12. Jeffrey H. Anderson, "Obama Misquotes Declaration of Independence, Again," *The Weekly Standard*, October 20, 2010.

13. Lawrence R. Jacobs and Theda Skocpol, *Health Care Reform and American Politics: What Everyone Needs to Know* (New York: Oxford University Press, 2010).

14. Lloyd Free and Hadley Cantril, *The Political Beliefs of Americans* (New Brunswick, NJ: Rutgers University Press, 1967); and Benjamin Page and Lawrence Jacobs, *Class War? What Americans Really Think about Economic Inequality* (Chicago: University of Chicago Press, 2009).

15. Peggy Noonan, "The Tea Party to the Rescue," *Wall Street Journal*, October 22, 2010. Other Noonan opinion pieces echo the same refrain.

16. From emails to Theda Skocpol.

17. For instance, David Brooks argued that "big business" was a target for Tea Party anger. David Brooks, "The Tea Party Teens," *New York Times*, January 4, 2010.

18. Several Tea Party members spoke of unions, particularly those representing public employees and auto industry workers, in terms that made them sound like Gilded Age plutocrats. A Boston Tea Party event was organized under the banner, "Collective Bargaining is EXTORTION." From a Boston Tea Party event listing, available at http://www.meetup.com/Boston-Tea-Party/events/16646263/ as of February 28, 2011.

19. CBS News/*New York Times* Poll, April 5–12, 2010.

20. Ibid.

21. Ibid.

22. In Arizona, Tea Partiers who told us they were unconcerned about social issues held their tongues when social conservatives voiced their views.

23. Rosalind S. Helderman, "Virginia fight over climate documents will continue," *Washington Post*, October 5, 2010. Available at http://www.washingtonpost.com/wp-dyn/content/article/2010/10/04/AR2010100406825.html as of May 12, 2011.

24. For a fascinating history of modern conservatism, see Allan Lichtman, *White Protestant Nation* (New York: Atlantic Monthly Press, 2008).

25. We almost never saw any member of a Tea Party audience question statements by visiting speakers, no matter how implausible.

26. CBS News/*New York Times* Poll, April 5–12, 2010.

27. Email to Theda Skocpol. Note that Rand likes the individual freedom he enjoys in the single-payer Medicare program, a program that is arguably the most socialized part of U.S. public social provision.

28. Mary Williams Walsh, "Social Security to See Payout Exceed Revenue This Year," *New York Times*, March 25, 2010, A1.

29. Daily Kos Weekly State of the Nation Poll (1001 registered U.S. voters; margin of error 3.1%), Public Policy Polling, January 23, 2011, pp. 7–8.

30. McClatchy/Marist poll, April 18, 2011. Available at http://maristpoll.marist.edu/wp-content/misc/usapolls/US110410/McClatchy/McClatchy-Marist%20Poll%20Complete%20April%2018th,%202011%20USA%20Poll%20Tables.pdf as of May 6, 2011.

31. DakotaPoll, "DakotaPoll Finds Large Majority of Tea Party Supporters Favor Sales Tax Increase for Education," February 14, 2011. Full results are also available at http://dakotapoll.com/category/february-2011-poll.

32. Asked about trade-offs in the South Dakota state budget between cuts in state support for public schools and nursing homes, on the one hand, and an increase in the sales tax during tourist season for the next three years, nearly three-quarters of the Tea Party supporters favored the tax increase.

33. Outside of Social Security and Medicare, Tea Partiers are generally not aware of all the forms of government assistance they have received—and they do not record these benefits in their mental ledgers of government's effect on their lives. Tea Partiers are mostly of the "baby boom" generation, and thus were recipients of very intensive federal spending on education and infrastructure in the post–World War Two era. Tea Party members we spoke to mentioned their own receipt of student loans, low-cost state college tuition, and public school education, among other government programs. But these comments were always made in passing, unconnected to their views of government as a whole. Less tangible expenditures, such as the energy subsidies, home mortgage deductions, and highway funding that make modern suburban life widely affordable, seemed almost entirely invisible to Tea Partiers. For all their concern about government intervention in the economy, many of the government's most significant redistributions in their favor simply are not on the Tea Party radar. Instead, they typically attribute their

own success to the functioning of the free market, and see their personal trajectory in the marketplace as resulting entirely from their own individual or family initiative. For more on government visibility, see Suzanne Mettler, 2010. "Reconstituting the Submerged State: The Challenges of Social Policy Reform in the Obama Era." *Perspectives on Politics* 8(03): 803–824.

34. DakotaPoll, "DakotaPoll Finds Large Majority of Tea Party Supporters Favor Sales Tax Increase for Education," February 14, 2011. Full results are also available at http://dakotapoll.com/category/february-2011-poll.

35. Because of the public nature of her role on the Tea Party Express tour, we do not use a pseudonym in this instance.

36. "Harper's Index," Harper's Magazine, March 2011, p. 13.

37. Liz Schott, "Policy Basics: An Introduction to TANF," Center on Budget and Policy Priorities, March 19, 2009. Available at http://www.cbpp.org/cms/?fa=view&; id=936 as of February 27, 2011.

38. Sandra's views on entitlements came up in a somewhat surprising context. Knowing that we were coming to interview her local Tea Party, Sandra had done some Internet research on her interviewers. She came across a presentation we had given on our research in Massachusetts, which made this same point about the differentiation between entitlements and welfare. Sandra was somewhat frustrated that we felt this was a point worth making. As she put it, "Well, obviously!"

39. Email to Theda Skocpol, February 24, 2010.

40. See Ronald Brownstein, "The Gray and the Brown: The Generational Mismatch," *National Journal*, July 24, 2010.

41. David Leonhardt, "In the Process, Pushing Back at Inequality," *New York Times*, March 24, 2010, A1 and A19. The equality-enhancing aspects of the Affordable Care Act of 2010 are more fully explored in Lawrence R. Jacobs and Theda Skocpol, *Health Care Reform and American Politics: What Everyone Needs to Know* (New York: Oxford University Press, 2010).

42. A photo of this sign, at a Tea Party rally in Madison, WI, can be seen at http://www.huffingtonpost.com/2009/04/16/10-most-offensive-tea-par_n_187554.html as of May 12, 2011.

43. Christopher Parker, et al., "2010 Multi-State Survey of Race and Politics," University of Washington Institute for the Study of Ethnicity, Race, and Sexuality. The website link appears in the following note.

44. Ibid. Parker's data suggests some very interesting subtleties to racial views in America more generally. Tea Partiers are more negative about everyone's hard work, intelligence, and trustworthiness. Sometimes, their views of blacks are much more negative than their views of whites. For instance, 14% more Tea Partiers described whites as hardworking than described blacks as hardworking. Skeptics of the Tea Party, by contrast, deem whites and blacks hardworking at almost exactly the same rate. But when it comes to trustworthiness, Tea Party *skeptics* have larger differences between their views of blacks and whites than Tea Party faithful. 72% of Tea Party skeptics rated whites trustworthy, while only 57% rated blacks trustworthy—a difference of 15%. Tea Partiers were less likely to see either blacks or whites as trustworthy, but the difference was only 9%. Though these data are only for white respondents, they do not control for other factors that may be significant, such as age. For these and other findings, see http://depts.washington.edu/uwiser/racepolitics.html, available as of May 5, 2011.

45. To some degree, this fear of outsiders was warranted, as the April 2010 Tea Party protest on the Boston Common was overrun with local college students and union members, many of whom were carrying ironic and purposefully misspelled signs, with slogans like "I forget what I'm angry about." or "Down with taxis."

46. From a description of upcoming guest speakers at http://www.daisymountainteapartypatriots.com/coming-to-dmtp.html as of February 27, 2011.

47. Muslims actually make up only 0.6% of the U.S. population. Data from the CIA World Factbook, available at https://www.cia.gov/library/publications/the-world-factbook/geos/us.html as of May 14, 2011.

48. Stanley's plan for immigration was remarkable in its moderation: "Secure the border, that's the first thing. Basically, what it amounts to, is a period of time of registration. Criminals are sent back across the border, and the rest are given green cards, they can work here, pay their taxes. At some point in time, if they want to become citizens, they pay a fine, get in the back of the line. There is a path to citizenship. But not amnesty." Stanley would presumably be disconcerted, if not horrified, to discover to what extent his views of immigration coincide with those proposed by President Obama. In a July 2010 speech, the President said: "Today, we have more boots on the ground near the Southwest border than at any time in our history. [. . .] We are committed to doing what's necessary to secure our borders. [. . .] We have to demand responsibility from people living here illegally. They must be required to admit that they broke the law. They should be required to register, pay their taxes, pay a fine, and learn English. They must get right with the law before they can get in line and earn their citizenship. [. . .] We can create a pathway for legal status that is fair, reflective of our values, and works." A transcript of this speech is available at http://blogs.wsj.com/washwire/2010/07/01/transcript-of-obamas-immigration-speech/ as of May 20, 2011.

49. John Lantigua, "Illegal Immigrants Paying Taxes?" *Palm Beach Post*, April 25, 2010. For a more complete understanding of the programs for which unauthorized immigrants are eligible, see "Overview of Immigrant Eligibility for Federal Programs," National Immigrant Law Center, available at http://www.nilc.org/immspbs/index.htm as of February 27, 2011.

50. James C. McKinley Jr., "Taking to the Streets and Court on Immigration," *New York Times*, July 23, 2010, A11.

51. Rehberg chairs the House appropriations subcommittee in charge of setting funding for the programs he denounced. He is quoted in Daniel Luzer, "The Lie About Pell Grants, the 'Welfare of the 21st Century,'" *Washington Monthly*, April 5, 2011. Rehberg has his facts wrong because most low-income Pell grant recipients who do not finish college drop out after a semester or two and are not a continuing cost to taxpayers.

52. Chris Isadore, "Job openings remain scarce for unemployed," CNN Money, October 7, 2010. See also "Unemployment rates by age, sex, and marital status," Labor Force Statistics from the Current Population Survey, Bureau of Labor Statistics, available at http://www.bls.gov/web/empsit/cpseea10.htm as of February 27, 2011.

53. Jacob S. Hacker and Paul Pierson, *Winner-Take-All Politics: How Washington Made the Rich Richer—and Turned Its Back on the Middle Class.* (New York: Simon and Schuster, 2010).

54. One person did cite the economic downturn. Asked to explain what rights of hers had been infringed, Arizonan *Cheryl Morse*, 49, said she "woke up" when her business failed. She had done all the right things, she insisted, and yet her business had gone under. As she saw it, her right to a fair economic shake had been taken away. For more

on the interaction of the economic downturn and conservative ideology, see in Chapter 1, "Economic Worries with a Political Edge."

55. Mary C. Waters and Tomás R. Jiménez, "Assessing Immigrant Assimilation: New Empirical and Theoretical Challenges," Annual Review of Sociology, Vol. 31 (2005), pp. 105–125.

56. The term "five-minute zones" was drawn from sustainable development literature intended to encourage walkable neighborhoods.

57. Paul Krugman's blog provides a good review of the bond market's overall health. See, for example, Paul Krugman, "Bond Vigilantes, Still Invisible," New York Times, December 8, 2010. Available at http://krugman.blogs.nytimes.com/2010/12/08/bond-vigilantes-still-invisible/ as of May 21, 2011.

58. Richard Hofstadter, The Paranoid Style in American Politics: And Other Essays (Cambridge, MA: Harvard University Press, 1996).

59. In emails to Theda Skocpol.

60. Mark Leibovitch, "Being Glenn Beck," New York Times, September 29, 2010.

61. From the website for the Southwest Metro Tea Party, available at http:///www.swmetroteaparty.com/educate-motivate.php as of May 5, 2011.

CHAPTER 3

1. With only a few exceptions—such as the work of Amy Gardner and other reporters at the Washington Post—journalistic accounts of grassroots Tea Partiers are based on buttonholing people who attend rallies for short interviews. Journalists also call up advocacy leaders based in Washington DC, and so their articles often quote these elites and attribute their ideological views to the Tea Party as a whole.

2. Quotes from our interview with Tom in February 2011 are used under his real name with his permission.

3. Jean Casanave, "Losing Our Way," letter to the editor, Gloucester-Mathews Gazette-Journal, May 10, 2009.

4. "Government Restraint Group Forms in Mathews," Gloucester-Mathews Gazette-Journal, June 19, 2009.

5. The account of Tea Party activities in Charlottesville comes from email exchanges and phone interviews Theda Skocpol conducted with Carole Thorpe in February and April 2011.

6. Cindy Pugh's and Mara Souvannasoth's real names are used because this portrait is entirely compiled form public records. The quote here from Mara is from their November 27, 2010 appearance on the radio show, "The Patriot," broadcast on AM 1280 in the Twin Cities. Both women recounted the story of how they met on that program, and also on "The Sue Jeffers Show," FM 100.3, on September 21, 2010.

7. Bob Cusack, "Bachmann Urges Confronting Lawmakers on Health Care Bill," The Hill, October 31, 2010.

8. Information on the Southwest Metro Tea Party's activities comes from its website available at http://mnteapartypatriots.ning.com/ as of May 11, 2011.

9. "How to Organize Your Own 'Tea Party' Protest," created February 21, 2009, 12:31 A.M., by Brendan Steinhauser and published at FreedomWorks.org.

10. Brandon is quoted in Chris Good, "The Tea Party Movement: Who's In Charge?" The Atlantic, April 2009.

11. Ibid.

12. The historical patterns and the post-1960 transition are documented in Theda Skocpol, *Diminished Democracy: From Membership to Management in American Civic Life* (Norman, OK: University of Oklahoma Press, 2003).

13. Marshall Ganz is a grassroots organizer who now teaches at the Kennedy School of Government at Harvard University.

14. See, for example, "Organizing for America catches heat," UPI, January 13, 2010.

15. Paul Bedard, "GOP Chairman Michael Steele Denies Tea Party Claim," *U.S. News and World Report*, April 10, 2009.

16. Amy Gardner, "Gauging the Scope of the Tea Party Movement in America," *Washington Post*, October 24, 2010.

17. Arizona, California, Florida, Georgia, Illinois, Indiana, Michigan, North Carolina, New York, Ohio, Pennsylvania, Tennessee, Texas, Virginia, Washington have more than thirty Tea Party groups.

18. For instance, Tea Parties that have a social networking component, using a service like MeetUp or Facebook or Ning, usually make visible the number of people who have joined online. We found online membership data for about one-third of the Tea Party groups; we believe larger groups are especially likely to have membership data visible because smaller groups tend to have less complex websites and are less likely to set up a social network component to their website.

19. Skocpol, *Diminished Democracy*, especially ch. 3 and pp. 130–131, Table 4.1.

20. In fact, several Tea Party organizers we spoke to were somewhat disdainful of 9/12 groups, claiming that those groups were less politically committed and less engaged.

21. Amy Gardner, "Tea-Party Activists Question if Rebel Political Movement has Changed for the Worse," *Washington Post*, December 31, 2010.

22. As we will see in the following chapter, conservative media were crucial to the spread of the Tea Party idea, and Fox News host Glenn Beck, in particular, helped encourage local meetings via his "9/12 Project."

23. Skocpol, Theda, Marshall Ganz, and Ziad Munson, "A Nation of Organizers." *American Political Science Review* 94(3): 527–546.

24. Our account is based on information from interviews with local Virginia Tea Party leaders who observed or participated in the formation of the state Federation.

25. On Federation lobbying, see Wesley P. Hester, "Tea-Party Backers Grill Va. Lawmakers," *Richmond Times-Dispatch*, January 6, 2011; and Anita Kumar and Rosalind S. Helderman, "Virginia Tea Party Aims to Put General Assembly Lessons into Practice," *Washington Post*, March 6, 2011.

26. Wesley P. Hester, "Tea Party All Grown Up and Planning for the Future," *Richmond Times-Dispatch*, October 10, 2010. The schedule of events is available at http://www.vateapartyconvention.com/schedule.php as of May 11, 2011.

27. Tyler Whitley, "Radtke Files for Senate," *Richmond Times-Dispatch*, December 29, 2010.

28. The Michigan Tea Party Alliance can be found at http://www.michiganteapartyalliance.com/ as of May 21, 2011.

29. See http://www.nctpp.net/tea-party-patriots-link-6-23.html for more information about this coordination effort. Available as of May 21, 2011.

30. Jacob S. Hacker and Paul Pierson, *Off Center: The Republican Revolution and the Erosion of American Democracy* (New Haven: Yale University Press, 2005); and Jacob S. Hacker and Paul Pierson, *Winner-Take-All-Politics: How Washington Made*

the Rich Richer—And Turned Its Back on the Middle Class (New York: Simon and Schuster, 2010).

31. Hacker and Pierson, *Winner-Take-All-Politics*, chapter 5.

32. Robert Frank, "Top 1% Increased Their Share of Wealth in Financial Crisis," *Wall Street Journal* blog, April 30, 2010. Available at http://blogs.wsj.com/wealth/2010/04/30/top-1-increased-their-share-of-wealth-in-financial-crisis/ as of May 28, 2011. To see the growth of wealth inequality over time, see http://voteview.com/Wealth_top_1_Percent.htm.

33. See, for example, Wendy Zellner, "The Gates Effect," *Fast Company*, January 1, 2006; Joanne Barkan, "Got Dough? How Billionaires Rule Our Schools," *Dissent*, Winter 2011; and Charles Piller and Doug Smith, "Unintended Victims of Gates Foundation Generosity," *Los Angeles Times*, December 16, 2007.

34. The power of the very wealthy has only been strengthened by the 2010 Supreme Court decision, Citizens United v. Federal Election Commission, which struck down major portions of America's campaign finance regulations. The Kochs have funded a number of the organizations that argued in favor of Citizens United, including the Cato Institute.

35. With $17.5 billion a piece, the two were tied for 24th on the 2010 Forbes list of the world's wealthiest people.

36. For a summary of the investigative reporting conducted about the Koch brothers by progressive bloggers in 2009 and 2010, see Jane Mayer, "Covert Operations: The Billionaire Brothers Who are Waging a War Against Obama," *The New Yorker*, August 30, 2010, p. 4.

37. Lee Fang, "In glitzy shadows, a health reform foe lurks," *Boston Globe*, December 6, 2009. See also Lee Fang, "MEMO: Health Insurance, Banking, Oil Industries Met with Koch, Chamber, Glenn Beck to Plot 2010 Election." Available at http://thinkprogress.org/2010/10/20/beck-koch-chamber-meeting/ as of May 11, 2011.

38. Kevin Grandia, "The Big Money Behind Americans for Prosperity," Desmog Blog, February 26, 2009. Available at http://www.desmogblog.com/big-money-behind-americans-prosperity as of May 11, 2011. See also Lee Fang, "From Promoting Acid Rain to Climate Denial: Over 20 Years of David Koch's Polluter Front Groups," *Think Progress*, April 1, 2011. Available at http://wonkroom.thinkprogress.org/2010/04/01/koch-pollution-astroturf-2deca/ as of May 11, 2011.

39. Sarah Owen, "David Koch Gives President Obama Zero Credit for Bin Laden's Death," *New York* magazine's Daily Intel blog, May 5, 2011. Available at http://nymag.com/daily/intel/2011/05/billionaire_conservative_david.html as of May 11, 2011.

40. Tom Hamburger, Kathleen Hennessey, and Neela Banerjee, "Koch Brothers Now at Heart of GOP Power," *Los Angeles Times*, February 6, 2011.

41. Kenneth P. Vogel and Ben Smith, "Kochs' Plan for 2012: Raise $88M," *Politico*, February 11, 2011, p. 1.

42. Dick Armey and Matt Kibbe, *Give Us Liberty: A Tea Party Manifesto* (New York: HarperCollins, William Morrow imprint, 2010).

43. "Koch Industries denies funding tea parties, but official filings say otherwise," *Crooks and Liars*, April 18, 2010. Available at http://crooksandliars.com/karoli/koch-industries-denies-funding-freedomworks as of March 22, 2011.

44. Background on AFP appears in Dan Eggen and Philip Rucker, "Loose Network of Activists Drives Reform Opposition," *Washington Post*, Sunday, August 16, 2009; and Eric Lipton, "Billionaire Brothers' Money Plays Role in Wisconsin Budget Dispute," *New York Times*, February 22, 2011, A16.

45. FreedomWorks has not received Koch funding since splitting from CSE, but it has replaced those funding sources with other corporate dollars from telecommunications companies, Phillip Morris, and MetLife. Kate Zernike and Jennifer Steinhauer, "A Power Again in Congress Years After He Left It," *New York Times*, November 15, 2010, A1 and A16. Dan Eggen and Philip Rucker, "Loose Network of Activists Drives Reform Opposition," *Washington Post*, August 16, 2009. FreedomWorks is led by Dick Armey, who after his term in the House became a lobbyist with strong ties to the oil, gas, pharmaceutical, and financial industries. "Oil and Gas Industries Fuel Unruly Townhall Meetings," *Political Correction*, August 6, 2009. Available at http://politicalcorrection.org/factcheck/200908060005 as of March 22, 2011. Amanda Terkel, "FreedomWorks, Run by Former Beverage Industry Lobbyist Dick Armey, Launches Attack Against Soda Tax," *Think Progress*, May 15, 2009. Available at http://thinkprogress.org/2009/05/15/armey-soda/ as of March 22, 2011. Pat Garofalo, "Dick Armey's Clients Required the Bailouts that Army's FreedomWorks is Now Protesting," *Think Progress*, April 15, 2009. Available at http://wonkroom.thinkprogress. org/2009/04/15/armey-financial-giants/ as of March 21, 2011.

46. Lipton, "Billionaire Brothers' Money," A16.

47. Amy Gardner, "Tea-party activists question if rebel political movement has changed for the worse," *Washington Post*, December 31, 2010.

48. Lipton, "Billionaire Brothers' Money."

49. "United States Congressman Paul Ryan to Receive Defender of the American Dream Award," AFP Wisconsin blog, available at https://americansforprosperity.org/ united-states-congressman-paul-ryan-receive-defender-american-dream-award as of May 11, 2011.

50. Paul N. Van de Water, "The Ryan Budget's Radical Priorities," Center on Budget and Policy Priorities report, July 7, 2010. Available at http://www.cbpp.org/cms/index. cfm?fa=view&;id=3114 as of May 11, 2011.

51. DeLemus is a founder and director of the Granite State Liberty PAC. Because New Hampshire plays a key role in presidential primaries, DeLemus is able to attract attention and sometimes contributions from GOP politicians entertaining a presidential run.

52. See, for instance, TeaParty.org, Tea Party Nation, Tea Party magazine, and Patriot Action Network.

53. "Tea Party's Big Money," *New York Times*, September 24, 2010, Editorial, A24.

54. Emi Kolawole, "A Spam Metamorphosis," The FactCheck Wire, October 28, 2008. Available at http://www.factcheck.org/2008/10/a-spam-metamorphosis/ as of May 22, 2011.

55. Data from Federal Election Commission filings.

56. Data on 2010 campaigns from Federal Election Commission filings. For TPE's 2012 targets, see Josh Kraushaar, "Tea Party's First Target: Richard Lugar," *National Journal*, February 8, 2011, and Steve Peoples, "Tea Party Express Names Snowe as Its Next Moderate Republican Target," *Roll Call*, February 10, 2011.

57. Zachary Roth, "Majority of Tea Party Group's Spending Went to GOP Firm that Created It," *TPM Muckraker*, December 28, 2009. The article's findings are confirmed by Federal Election Commission filings.

58. Laura Myers, "Thousands Gather for 'Tea Party Express' Event in Harry Reid's Hometown," *Las Vegas Review Journal*, March 27, 2010.

59. Jenny Beth Martin, a national coordinator for Tea Party Patriots, derided the Tea Party Express as "five people on a bus" in an interview with Vanessa in spring of 2010.

There have been significant legal tussles between TPE and TPP according to Stephanie Mencimer, "Tempest in the Tea Party," *Mother Jones*, December 30, 2009.

60. Before his involvement in Tea Party Patriots, Mark Meckler was a distributor for a dubious nutritional supplement company, Herbalife, that has been cautioned by the FDA for making false claims. Herbalife is widely promoted through "multilevel marketing," described by some as a pyramid scheme. Stephanie Mencimer, "Is the Tea Party Movement Like a Pyramid Scheme?" *Mother Jones*, October 19, 2010. Jenny Beth Martin's husband is also involved in Tea Party Patriots, serving as a treasurer for the group. Stephanie Mencimer, "Tea Party Patriots Investigated, Part 3," *Mother Jones*, February 16, 2011.

61. Ties between FreedomWorks and Tea Party Patriots have been documented by *Talking Points Memo* and Rolling Stone, though it is unclear to what extent FreedomWorks remained involved with Tea Party Patriots after 2009. Zachary Roth, "FreedomWorks Says Jump, Tea Partiers Ask How High," *TPM Muckraker*, August 11, 2009. Tim Dickenson, "The Lie Machine," *Rolling Stone*, October 1, 2009. The importance of FreedomWorks in the development of Tea Party Patriots was confirmed by Jenny Beth Martin in an interview on March 11, 2010. According to Martin, FreedomWorks was crucial to the group's original launch and was a primary funder for their national rallies. Martin also reports that operational funding for Tea Party Patriots was scant well into 2010, limiting the capacity of the group to take independent action. FreedomWorks has a history of creating homespun-looking websites like the original site of Tea Party Patriots that promote nominally grassroots causes. Michael M. Phillips, "Mortgage Bailout Infuriates Tenants (And Steve Forbes)," *Wall Street Journal*, May 16, 2008.

62. Zachary Roth, "FreedomWorks Says Jump, Tea Partiers Ask How High," *TPM Muckraker* website, August 9, 2009.

63. See, for instance, Wayne T. Brough, Ph.D. "Proposed Regulations Pose Threat to Internet," FreedomWorks, January 15, 2010. Available at http://www.freedomworks.org/publications/proposed-regulations-pose-threat-to-internet as of May 11, 2011.

64. This claim is from the Tea Party Patriots' "About Us" page, available at http://www.teapartypatriots.org/AboutUs.aspx as of May 11, 2011.

65. From an interview with Jenny Beth Martin on March 11, 2010. The number of participants on each call was confirmed by several local Tea Party organizers across the country who regularly participate in the calls.

66. As of May 2011, information about the summit was available at http://summit11.org/.

67. Stephanie Mencimer, "Tea Party Patriots Investigated," *Mother Jones*, February 14, 2011.

68. A quick glance at the Tea Party Patriots' home-spun website might give a visitor the impression of an entirely grassroots, volunteer-run organization. But the organization's actual structure is kept from public view. As of March 2011, the Tea Party Patriots website offered the visitor no information regarding their national leadership and no listing of the Board of Directors or staff. Without public disclosure, most available information about Tea Party Patriots comes from TPP itself. In an interview on April 26, 2011, Martin was unclear about precisely how many people were on TPP's payroll, estimating around a dozen. The number of coordinators on staff has varied over the past two years. When we spoke with Jenny Beth Martin in March of 2010, she reported that the organization employed nine national coordinators to help guide and coordinate local groups' actions. Emails from Tea Party Patriots to their supporters suggest that those numbers

have since been whittled down. In March of 2011, TPP emails were signed by a national coordinator team of only six people.

69. Bradford Plumer, "Can the Tea Party Be Controlled?" *The New Republic*, September 21, 2010. The anonymous donation to the TPP was announced at the National Press Club.

70. Stephanie Mencimer of *Mother Jones* has done extensive reporting documenting Tea Party Patriots' financial doings. Tea Party Patriots has used accounting tricks to avoid having to file their taxes or financial disclosure forms for almost two years, an especially troubling fact given the questionable business practices of Tea Party Patriots' leaders prior to their Tea Party activism. See Mencimer's three part series, "Tea Party Patriots Investigated," *Mother Jones*, February 14–16, 2011. See also: Stephanie Mencimer, "Is the Tea Party Movement Like a Pyramid Scheme?" *Mother Jones*, October 19, 2010.

71. Stephanie Mencimer, "Tea Party Patriots Investigated," *Mother Jones*, February 14, 2011.

72. "Americans for Prosperity Leader Speaks to Tea Party Tuesday," *KearneyHub.com*, November 27, 2010.

73. Information from the Americans for Prosperity of Nebraska website, which provides regular information on issues coming up at all levels of government and links to the national AFP website and to those of a full panoply of ultra-right, anti-government advocacy organizations.

74. Stephanie Mencimer, "Tempest in the Tea Party," *Mother Jones*, December 30, 2009.

75. Written as if from Ben Jealous, the president of the NAACP, the blog included lines like, "How will we coloreds ever get a widescreen TV in every room if non-colored get to keep what they earn?" The blog entry was removed from the original site, but a complete text of the letter is still available at http://gawker.com/#!5588556/the-embarrassing-racist-satire-of-tea-party-leader-mark-williams as of February 27, 2011. In another instance, Williams claimed that Muslims worship a "monkey god." Bill Hutchinson, "Tea Party leader Mark Williams says Muslims worship a 'monkey god,' blasts Ground Zero mosque," *New York Daily News*, May 19, 2010. Williams had previously claimed that, "it's impossible for there to be a racist element in the Tea Party." Charles Blow, "Dog Days of Obama," *New York Times*, July 17, 2010, A19.

76. The TPE road show, the only aspect of TPE that most Tea Partiers see, typically has a far more diverse line-up than the audiences in attendance. After attending an event similar to the rally that one of us (Vanessa) attended on the Boston Common, New York Times columnist Charles Blow described it as "a political minstrel show." Charles Blow, "A Mighty Pale Tea," *New York Times*, April 17, 2010, A17.

77. There are, of course, many other conservative organizations that offer training and guidance to conservative grassroots activists. We have focused on those most associated with the Tea Party in particular.

78. As we will see in Chapter 4, however, Fox News, and particularly Glenn Beck and his 9/12 Project, are far more frequently cited than any national advocacy organization.

79. When the Tea Party–backed candidate for the Colorado Governorship made similar claims tying bike lanes to a "very well-disguised" U.N. plot, he was quickly forced to recant, claiming his statements had been taken "out of context." The text of his August 9th, 2010, interview on MSNBC is available at http://wonkroom.thinkprogress.org/2010/08/09/maes-bike-plot/ as of May 6, 2011.

80. According to their MeetUp blog, the Peninsula Patriots called for volunteers for various working subcommittees in the months following the January 24, 2011 lecture. Most subcommittees got few volunteers, but there were multiple volunteers for the anti-sustainable development group, as well as for the group to fight the Muslim threat in the United States. Interestingly enough, fighting ObamaCare got no takers.

81. Even conservative columnist David Brooks admitted that the Ryan plan was so politically unpopular as to create an "opening" for Democrats. "Shields and Brooks on Public's View of Libya Efforts, Debate on Entitlements," PBS Newshour, April 22, 2011. The Ryan plan was reportedly also unpopular locally. See, for instance, John Nichols, "Paul Ryan gets an earful as tour bombs," *The Cap Times*, May 4, 2011.

82. Stephanie Mencimer, "Tea Party Patriots Investigated," *Mother Jones*, February 14, 2011.

CHAPTER 4

1. "Report: 'Fair and Balanced' Fox News Aggressively Promotes 'Tea Party' Protests," *Media Matters for America*, April 8, 2009.

2. Alex Isenstadt, "Town Halls Gone Wild," *Politico*, July 31, 2009. A *Politico* editor later bragged that his site had "been the first to establish the 'town halls gone wild' meme . . . ," according to Greg Marx, "An Oversteeped Tea Party?" *Columbia Journalism Review*, April 22, 2010.

3. Dan Eggen and Philip Rucker, "Loose Network of Activists Drives Reform Opposition," *Washington Post*, Sunday, August 16, 2009.

4. Paul Steinhauser, "Retreat for New Lawmakers to Emphasize Tea Party Goals," *CNN Political Ticker*, November 11, 2010. For more accurate coverage of the retreat, see Amy Gardner, "FreedomWorks gathers GOP lawmakers to refocus on tea party goals," *Washington Post*, November 12, 2010.

5. Kathleen Hall Jamieson and Joseph N. Cappella, *Echo Chamber: Rush Limbaugh and the Conservative Media Establishment* (New York: Oxford University Press, 2010).

6. Michael Schudson, *Discovering The News: A Social History Of American Newspapers* (New York: Basic Books, 1981).

7. That conservatives dominate the talk radio format is agreed upon by both liberals and conservatives. John Halpin, James Heidbreder, Mark Lloyd, Paul Woodhull, Ben Scott, Josh Silver, S. Derek Turner. "The Structural Imbalance of Political Talk Radio," *Center for American Progress*, June 20, 2007. Warner Todd Huston, "Top 100 Radio Host List, Dominated By Conservatives—Rush #1," *NewsBusters*, February 13, 2008.

8. See, for instance, Seth Ackerman, "The Most Biased Name in News," Fairness and Accuracy in Reporting, July/August 2001. Available at http://www.fair.org/index.php?page=1067 as of May 12, 2011. The introduction of Fox News into the cable roster has been shown to coincide with an uptick in voting for Republican presidential candidates. Stefano Dellavigna and Ethan Kaplan, "The Fox News Effect: Media Bias and Voting," *The Quarterly Journal of Economics*, August 2007.

9. "O'Reilly: 'Fox does tilt right'; said GOP 'very uneasy with Fox' even after Cheney, Ralph Reed touted Fox," *Media Matters for America*, July 21, 2004. Available at http://mediamatters.org/research/200407210007 as of May 12, 2011.

10. Danny Shea, "Fox News Dominates 3Q 2009 Cable News Ratings," Huffington Post, September 30, 2009. Available at http://www.huffingtonpost.com/2009/09/30/fox-news-dominates-3q-200_n_304260.html as of March 14, 2011.

11. "News Audiences Increasingly Politicized," Pew Center for the People and the Press, June 8, 2004.

12. Paul Fahri, "Limbaugh's Audience Size? It's Largely Up in the Air," Washington Post, March 7, 2009.

13. "Limbaugh holds onto his niche: conservative men," Pew Research Center for the People and the Press, February 3, 2009.

14. Ibid.

15. Michael Schneider, "TV viewers' average age hits 50," Variety, June 29, 2008; Michael Wolff, "Rush Limbaugh: The Man Who Ate the GOP," Vanity Fair, May 2009.

16. Danny Shea, "Fox News Audience Just 1.38% Black," Huffington Post, July 26, 2010, available at http://www.huffingtonpost.com/2010/07/26/fox-news-audience-just-13_n_659800.html as of March 14, 2011.

17. Peter Dreier and Christopher R. Martin, "How ACORN Was Framed: Political Controversy and Media Agenda Setting." Perspectives on Politics 8(03): 761–792 (2010).

18. Markus Prior, Post-Broadcast Democracy: How Media Choice Increases Inequality in Political Involvement and Polarizes Elections. 1st ed. (Cambridge: Cambridge University Press, 2007).

19. "Beyond Red vs. Blue: The Political Typology," Pew Research Center for the People and the Press, May 4, 2011. Available at http://people-press.org/2011/05/04/section-3-demographics-and-news-sources/ as of May 14, 2011.

20. Charles S.Taber and Milton Lodge, "Motivated Skepticism in the Evaluation of Political Beliefs." American Journal of Political Science 50(3): 755–769 (2006).

21. David Barstow, "Tea Party Lights Fuse for Rebellion on the Right," New York Times, February 16, 2010.

22. Paul Lazersfeld, Bernard Berelson, and Hazel Gaudet, The People's Choice: How the Voter Makes Up His Mind in a Presidential Campaign (New York: Columbia University Press, 1944).

23. Not just right-wing outlets, but also reporters at Huffington Post and Politico picked up the story via Drudge. So influential is the Drudge Report that these articles were actually covering the fact that Drudge was giving prominence to Santelli's performance on CNBC as much as the video itself. Jason Linkins, "Rick Santelli's Revolution: CNBC Reporter Freaks Out, Wants to Be Che Guevara," Huffington Post, February 19, 2009. Michael Calderone, "CNBC's Santelli fires up traders," Politico, February 19, 2009.

24. Michelle Malkin had earlier sent a tray of pulled pork to feed the dozens of attendees at one of the first anti-Stimulus protests in Seattle, weeks before the term Tea Party gained national currency. Michelle Malkin, "Gimme, gimme, gimme: More scenes from the anti-Obama entitlement backlash," Michelle Malkin blog, February 19, 2009. Available at http://michellemalkin.com/2009/02/19/gimme-gimme-gimme-more-scenes-from-the-anti-obama-backlash/ as of May 11, 2011.

25. Video of this speech was available at http://video.google.com/videoplay?docid=-2121564008630451568# as of May 12, 2011.

26. Video of this speech comes from Mike Gallagher's YouTube feed, and is captioned, "Mike appeared at a Tea Party in Greenville, SC sponsored by his radio affiliate News Radio WORD where more than 1000 people attended this very spirited event in

the upstate of South Carolina." Available at http://www.youtube.com/watch?v=jDrqlO MAFd4&;feature=related as of May 21, 2011.

27. "Backlash Against Those Suffering From Mortgages They Can't Afford," CNN Newsroom, March 5, 2009.

28. Greta Van Susteren, Fox on the Record with Greta Van Susteren, February 27, 2009. Glenn Beck, Beck, March 18, 2009.

29. Newt Gingrich, Fox on the Record with Greta Van Susteren, March 27, 2009.

30. Glenn Beck, Beck, April 7, 2009.

31. Sean Hannity, Fox Hannity, April 7, 2009.

32. Sean Hannity, Fox Hannity, April 8, 2009. Glenn Beck, Beck, April 8, 2009.

33. Glenn Beck and Arthur Laffer, Beck, April 13, 2009.

34. "Hosting the Party: Fox aired at least 20 segments, 73 promos on "tea party" protests—in just 8 days," Media Matters, April 15, 2009. Available at: http://mediamatters. org/research/200904150033?f=h_latest as of March 21, 2011.

35. Glenn Beck, Beck, April 6, 2009.

36. In the graphs below, peak CNN coverage of Tea Party activity is actually slightly higher than Fox News coverage; the may be due in part to the slightly more limited transcripts provided by Fox News compared to CNN. Three regular Fox News shows are not included in the transcripts available by either Lexis Nexis or Factiva: "Huckabee." "Fox and Friends Weekend," and "Red Eye with Greg Gutman."

37. Vanessa Williamson, Theda Skocpol, and John Coggin, "The Tea Party and the Remaking of Republican Conservatism," Perspectives on Politics 9 (1) (March 2011).

38. In the first two years of the Tea Party, both Sean Hannity and Bill O'Reilly actually referred to the Tea Party on more shows than Glenn Beck did. Moreover, fully half of the over 1800 transcripts referring to the Tea Party were not hosted by any of these top names.

39. The 9/12 Project was launched on-air on Beck's March 13th, 2009, show on Fox— about two weeks after the first tea parties were held.

40. The values and principles are listed at http://the912-project.com/about/the-9-principles-12-values/ as of May 14, 2011.

41. The figure comes from ABC News, citing the Washington DC fire department. Russell Goldman, "Tea Party Protesters March on Washington," ABC News, September 12, 2009. Some conservative activists, including Matt Kibbe of FreedomWorks, dramatically inflated this number. For an analysis, see Nate Silver, "Size Matters; So Do Lies," available at http://www.fivethirtyeight.com/2009/09/size-matters-so-do-lies.html as of May 26, 2011.

42. Ben Jones, for instance, described Beck as a "P.T. Barnum" and "a seller of soap," though he also commented positively on Beck's enthusiasm. Ben Armbruster, "Tea Party Leaders Criticize Beck's 8/28 Rally: 'All He's Doing Is Trying to Use Us to Promote Himself," Think Progress, August 24, 2010. Available at http://thinkprogress.org/2010/08/24/beck-tea-party/ as of March 21, 2011.

43. Quoted in Dana Milbank, Tears of a Clown (New York: Doubleday, 2010). p. 242.

44. A number of Tea Party Republicans in 2010 would only talk to interviewers on Fox, where they knew they would get a much friendlier reception than they would in other news outlets. Tea Party candidate Christine O'Donnell reportedly claimed to have Fox News anchor Sean Hannity in her "back pocket," available for a softball interview at a moment's notice. See "'Voice of the opposition': How Fox News won the 2010 election,"

Media Matters, November 2, 2010. Available at http://mediamatters.org/research/201011020054#6 as of May 14, 2011.

45. Asked why she went on Fox rather than more mainstream networks, Tea Party candidate Sharron Angle asked the Christian Broadcasting Network, "Well, in that audience will they let me say I need $25 dollars from a million people go to Sharron Angle. com send money?" "'Voice of the opposition': How Fox News won the 2010 election," *Media Matters*, November 2, 2010. Available at http://mediamatters.org/research/201011020054#6 as of May 14, 2011.

46. The misinformation promoted on Fox has been the subject of numerous books and documentaries; we discuss this point in more detail in the Conclusion.

47. CBS News/*New York Times* poll, April 5–12, 2010.

48. Vanessa Williamson, Theda Skocpol, and John Coggin, "The Tea Party and the Remaking of Republican Conservatism," *Perspectives on Politics* 9 (1) (March 2011).

49. These terms were repeatedly used on Fox News to describe the Tea Party; here we list only one example for each. Grassroots: Marianne Silber on *Special Report with Brett Baier*, April 14, 2009. Genuine: Mark Steyn, *Fox Hannity*, May 6, 2009. Organic: Carl Cameron, *On the Record with Greta*, February 4, 2010. Spontaneous: Karl Rove, *On the Record with Greta*, October 26, 2010. Independent: Sarah Palin, *Fox Hannity*, March 17, 2010. Mainstream: Charles Gasparino, *Fox Hannity*, March 26, 2010.

50. Ray Rahman, "Rupert Murdoch Talks Tea Party, China, and Fox Business . . . on Fox Business," *Mediaite*, November 16, 2010. Available at http://www.mediaite.com/uncategorized/rupert-murdoch-talks-tea-party-china-and-fox-business-on-fox-business/ as of May 11, 2011.

51. Glenn Beck, *Beck*, May 24, 2010.

52. Glenn Beck, *Beck*, January 19, 2010.

53. Greta Van Susteren, *On the Record with Greta*, April 16, 2009. John Fund, *Fox Hannity*, September 17, 2010.

54. See for example, the discussion on *Special Report with Brett Baier*, February 4, 2010.

55. Bill Kristol, Fox News Roundtable, February 21, 2010.

56. Rick Perlstein, *Nixonland: The Rise of a President and the Fracturing of America* (New York: Scribner, 2008).

57. Newt Gingrich, *On the Record with Greta*, April 17, 2009.

58. Jim Pinkerton, *Fox News Watch Saturdays*, April 18, 2009.

59. Bill O'Reilly, *The O'Reilly Factor*, February 8, 2010.

60. Glenn Beck, *Beck*, April 24, 2009.

61. Bill O'Reilly, *The O'Reilly Factor*, June 12, 2009.

62. Howard Kurtz, *The Situation Room*, April 13, 2009. Howard Kurtz, *Reliable Sources*, April 12, 2009.

63. David Carr, "Cable Wars Are Killing Objectivity," *New York Times*, April 20, 2009.

64. Howard Kurtz, *The Situation Room*, April 13, 2009.

65. CNN reporters tagged along and sent dispatches from two Tea Party Express bus tours. See Jonathan Martin and Ben Smith, "The Tea Party's Exaggerated Importance," *Politico*, April 22, 2010.

66. Alex Isenstadt, "Town Halls Gone Wild." *Politico*, July 31, 2009.

67. Mark Jurkowitz, "Town Hall Showdowns Fuel Health Care Coverage," Pew Research Center's Project for Excellence in Journalism, PEJ News Coverage Index:

August 3–9, 2009. Available at http://www.journalism.org/index_report/pej_news_coverage_index_august_39_2009 as of May 11, 2011.

68. A picture of the print ad is available at http://politicalticker.blogs.cnn.com/2009/09/18/networks-respond-to-false-fox-ad/, along with CNN's response, as of May 12, 2011.

69. Rick Sanchez, *CNN Newsroom*, September 18, 2009.

70. Wolf Blitzer, *The Situation Room*, September 18, 2009.

71. Jeffrey Toobin, *Campbell Brown*, October 23, 2009.

72. Peter Dreier and Christopher R. Martin, "How ACORN Was Framed: Political Controversy and Media Agenda Setting." *Perspectives on Politics* 8(03): 761–792 (2010). Kathleen Hall Jamieson and Joseph N. Cappella, *Echo Chamber: Rush Limbaugh and the Conservative Media Establishment* (New York: Oxford University Press, 2010.)

73. Brian Stelter, "Reporter Says Outburst Was Spontaneous," *New York Times*, March 3, 2009.

74. Rick Klein, "The Note, 4/15/09: Tea Time—Conservative grassroots flex organizing muscle on Tax Day," ABC News's The Note, April 15, 2009. Available at http://blogs.abcnews.com/thenote/2009/04/the-note-41509.html as of March 21, 2011.

75. Gail Collins, "Barack's Progress Report," *New York Times*, August 6, 2009. A29.

76. Bud Kennedy, "Burleson Tea Party is about taxes (and secession)," *Fort Worth Star-Telegram*, April 8, 2009. B2.

77. Previously, the Tea Party's only apparent electoral effect had been to hand a New York Congressional seat to a Democrat in October 2009. When a nominal "Tea Party" favorite, Doug Hoffman, pushed out a moderate Republican, Dede Scozzafava, she endorsed her Democratic opponent, Bill Owens, who went on to win the general election.

78. Evan McMorris-Santoro, "Marco Rubio's Tea Party Problem," *Talking Points Memo*, March 30, 2010. Available at http://tpmdc.talkingpointsmemo.com/2010/03/debate-exposes-marco-rubios-tea-party-problem.php as of March 14, 2011.

79. Sam Stein, "Scott Brown Held Tea Party Fundraiser Before Professing to Be Unfamiliar with Tea Party," *Huffington Post*, January 14, 2011. Available at http://www.huffingtonpost.com/2010/01/14/scott-brown-held-tea-part_n_423198.html as of March 14, 2011.

80. Ben McGrath, "The Movement: The Rise of Tea Party Activism," *The New Yorker*, February 1, 2010.

81. Ironically, the first beneficiary of the mainstream media's newfound interest was the February 2010 "Tea Party Convention"—a for-profit venture rejected by many of those most involved in the Tea Party.

82. Barstow, "Tea Party Lights Fuse for Rebellion on the Right," *New York Times*, February 16, 2010.

83. All data regarding the frequency of poll questions draws from the Roper Center's database of opinion data. Of course, the database is not a complete catalog of all poll questions ever asked—indeed, at least a few polls we have seen about the Tea Party are not included in the Roper Center's collection. The Roper database is, however, the world's largest archive of survey data and includes Tea Party polls from the major polling agencies.

84. Richard Wolf, "Afghan War Costs Now Outpace Iraq's," *USA Today*, May 31, 2010.

85. Jonathan Martin and Ben Smith, "The Tea Party's Exaggerated Importance," *Politico*, April 22, 2010.

86. President Obama received the votes of 70 million people, as FEC results attest. David Brooks, "The Geezers' Crusade," *New York Times*, February 2, 2010. FEC results available at http://www.fec.gov/pubrec/fe2008/2008presgeresults.pdf as of May 11, 2011.

87. Adele Stan, "The Tea Party Movement: A Force to Be Reckoned With," *Huffington Post*, May 7, 2010. Available at: http://www.huffingtonpost.com/adele-stan/the-tea-party-movement-a_b_567441.html as of March 14, 2011.

88. Mark Blumenthal, "Re: Tea Party Polling," Pollster.com, February 17, 2010. Available at http://www.pollster.com/blogs/re_tea_party_polling.php?nr=1 as of March 14, 2011.

89. E.J. Dionne Jr., "The Tea Party: Tempest in a very small teapot," *Washington Post*, September 23, 2010.

90. Lydia Saad, "Tea Partiers are Fairly Mainstream in Their Demographics." Gallup, April 5, 2010.

91. Glynnis MacNicol, "Look to Your Left, Look to Your Right . . . Everyone is a Tea Partier!" *Mediaite*, April 5, 2010.

92. Joe Garofoli and Carla Marinucci, "'Tea Parties' Protest Bailout; Anti-tax rallies," *San Francisco Chronicle*, April 16, 2009, A12. Glenn Reynolds, "Tax Day Becomes Protest Day," *Wall Street Journal*, April 15, 2009. Newt Gingrich, "A Rising Anti-Government Tide," *Washington Post*, May 22, 2009, A21.

93. In their first Tea Party ballot question, Fox News took an even more extreme approach. They removed the Republican Party altogether, asking respondents to choose between President Obama and a generic Tea Party candidate!

94. Scott Rasmussen and Doug Schoen, *Mad As Hell: How the Tea Party Movement Is Fundamentally Remaking Our Two-Party System* (Harper, 2010).

95. Dick Armey made these comments on Meet the Press on January 24th, 2010. David Brooks, "The Tea Party Teens," *New York Times*, January 5, 2010, A21.

96. See, for example, the *USA Today*/Gallup poll, March 26–28, 2010, or Winston Group poll, released April 1, 2009.

97. Bruce E. Keith , David B. Magleby, Candice J. Nelson, Elizabeth Orr, Mark C. Westlye, and Raymond E. Wolfinger, *The Myth of the Independent Voter.* (Berkeley: University of California Press, 1992).

98. John Barry, "Survey finds Tea Party supporters are mostly Perot-style libertarians (and often mad at Republicans)," *St. Petersburg Times*, April 4, 2010; Andrew Malcolm, "Myth-busting polls: Tea Party members are average Americans, 41 percent are Democrats, independents," *Los Angeles Times*, April 5,2010; Sean Miller, "Survey: Four in 10 Tea Party members are Democrats, Independents," *The Hill*, April 4, 2010.

99. Campbell Brown, touting her evening show on the afternoon Situation Room, February 3, 2010. See also Candy Crowley, *American Morning*, April 16, 2010.

100. Greg Sargent, "CNN justifies airing Bachmann speech: 'Tea Party has become major force in American politics," *Washington Post*'s "The Plum Line" blog, January 25, 2011. Available at http://voices.washingtonpost.com/plum-line/2011/01/cnn_justifies_airing_bachmann.html as of May 13, 2011.

101. Joel Meares, "There is No 'The Tea Party': East and West Coast *Time*'s Different Approaches to the Movement," *Columbia Journalism Review*, January 4, 2011.

102. We tracked the prominence of major "Tea Party spokespersons" Dick Armey, Jim DeMint, Newt Gingrich, Michele Bachmann, and Sarah Palin over the first two years of Tea Party activity. In the spring, summer, and fall of 2009, those spokespeople appeared in less than 10% of newspaper and wire stories on the Tea Party. By the winter of 2010, they appeared in almost a third of newspaper and wires stories on the Tea Party.

Representatives of Tea Party Express and Tea Party Patriots are far less prominent in the media, but their media appearances doubled during this time frame.

103. Comparison of published estimates for thirteen cities appear in Alex Seitz-Wald, "Analysis: Taxed Enough Already? Tea Party Rallies Significantly Smaller This Year Than Last," *Think Progress*, April 19, 2011.

104. Eric Boehlert, "Does a Tea Party Rally Attracting 'Dozens' Qualify as News?" *Media Matters for America*, April 1, 2011.

CHAPTER 5

1. There have been instances, most notably in upstate New York, where self-declared Tea Party candidates have run along with GOP candidates in general elections, splitting the vote in ways that help Democrats. But occasional instances of this sort are not equivalent to organizing a third party.

2. Theda Skocpol, and Vanessa Williamson, "Obama and the Transformation of US Public Policy: The Struggle to Reform Health Care." *Arizona State Law Journal* 42: 1203–1205.

3. Larry J. Sabato, "Pendulum Swing," in *Pendulum Swing*, edited by Larry J. Sabato (Boston: Longman, 2011); and Andrew E. Busch, "The 2010 Midterm Election: An Overview," *The Forum* 8(4).

4. Kate Zernike, "Tea Party Set to Win Enough Races for Wide Influence," *New York Times*, October 14, 2010. The *Times* defined 138 Congressional Tea Party candidates as "those who had entered politics through the movement or who are receiving significant support from local Tea Party groups and who share the ideology of the movement. Many have been endorsed by groups like FreedomWorks or the Tea Party Express, or by conservative kingmakers like Sarah Palin and Senator Jim DeMint of South Carolina, but those endorsements alone were not enough to qualify as a Tea Party candidate."

5. Maya Srikrishnan, Jared Pliner, Jennifer Schlesinger, Joshua Goldstein, and Huma Khan, "Which Tea Party Candidates Won?" November 3, 2010. Available at http://abcnews.go.com/Politics/2010_Elections/vote-2010-elections-tea-party-winners-losers/story?id=12023076 as of May 16, 2011.

6. "Biggest Election Winners—The Tea Party: Movement Flexes Its Muscles in Midterms," November 3, 2010. Available at http://www.nbcmontana.com/politics/25596591/detail.html as of May 16, 2011.

7. Carl Hulse, "Caught Between Compromise and Conviction," *New York Times*, March 17, 2011, A22.

8. Amy Gardner, "Gauging the Scope of the Tea Party Movement in America," *Washington Post*, October 24, 2010.

9. Stephen Ansolabehere and James M. Snyder, "Weak Tea," *Boston Review*, March/April 2011.

10. Ibid.

11. Several limitations of the Ansolabehere/Snyder exercise are clear. They measure "Tea Party candidates" by looking only at elite organizational endorsements, rather than grassroots engagement. They also fail to consider whether Tea Party winners were unusually conservative for their districts and states. Data we present below suggest that the latter may well be true—that the Tea Party helped to move the House GOP caucus sharply toward the far right.

12. Reid Wilson, "RNC Officials Feud Over Debt Reports," *Hotline On Call*, October 20, 2010. Kenneth R. Bazinet and David Saltonstall, "Republican National Committee spent nearly $2,000 at West Hollywood strip club Voyeur," *New York Daily News*, March 29, 2010.

13. Nate Silver, "Assessing the G.O.P. and the Tea Party," *New York Times*, September 20, 2010. Available at http://fivethirtyeight.blogs.nytimes.com/2010/09/20/assessing-the-g-o-p-and-the-tea-party/ as of May 12, 2011.

14. Mary Cheney, for instance, explained that the work being done by Karl Rove's Crossroads group "would normally be done with the RNC." Jim Rutenberg, "The Gloves Come Off Early for the Midterm Elections," *New York Times*, September 26, 2010. A1.

15. This paragraph draws on 2010 exit polls as summarized in Table 1.10 in Sabato, "Pendulum Swing," pp. 36–43. See also the discussions in Isaac T. Woods, "Bringing Down the House: Reliving the GOP's Historic House Gains," in *Pendulum Swing*, edited by Sabato (Boston: Longman, 2011); and Costas Panagopoulos, "The Dynamics of Voter Preferences in the 2010 Congressional Midterm Elections," *The Forum* 8 (4), article 9.

16. Though predictions are sufficiently varied that somebody is right or close to right each time!

17. Chuck Todd and Sheldon Gawiser, *How Barack Obama Won: A State-by-State Guide to the Historic 2008 Presidential Election* (New York: Vintage, 2009).

18. Sabato, "Pendulum Swing," pp. 29–30.

19. Sidney Verba, Kay Lehman Schlozman, and Henry Brady, *Voice and Equality: Civic Voluntarism in American Politics* (Cambridge, MA: Harvard University Press, 1995). Robert D. Putnam, "Bowling Alone: America's Declining Social Capital." *Journal of Democracy* 6(1): 65–78 (1995); Steven Rosenstone and John Hansen, *Mobilization, participation, and democracy in America* (New York: Macmillan, 1993).

20. Michael p. McDonald, "Voter Turnout in the 2010 Midterm Elections," *The Forum* 8(4), article 8, Table 1.

21. Todd and Gawiser, *How Barack Obama Won*.

22. Sabato, "Pendulum Swing," p. 37.

23. Adam Nagourney, "Politics and the Age Gap," *New York Times*, September 12, 2009. See also the Kaiser Health Tracking Poll (March 2011), available at http://www.kff.org/kaiserpolls/8166.cfm as of May 16, 2011.

24. Karl Rove, *Fox Hannity*, September 14, 2010.

25. A good overview of O'Donnell's career and the controversies she was involved in appear in Sandhya Somashekhar and Perry Bacon, Jr., "Delaware's O'Donnell is a 'Tea Party' Hero, but Controversy Casts a Shadow," *Washington Post*, September 18, 2010.

26. "Tea Party Backs O'Donnell in Delaware," *Wall Street Journal*, Washington Wire, August 30, 2010. It is worth noting that not all national Tea Party organizations got behind O'Donnell. Fearing she might be unelectable, FreedomWorks did not follow the lead of Tea Party Express. But this underlines that national advocacy groups are free-ranging. They operate separately from one another—as well as separately from formal GOP organs.

27. In the 2000 U.S. Census, Kent County had a population of 127,000 and Sussex recorded 157,000, making the two of them together significantly smaller than New Castle, with 500,000 people. This population imbalance among Delaware counties made it impossible for a GOP candidate who could not appeal to the voters of northern Delaware to defeat a Democrat with strong support there. But in the GOP primary, voters from central and southern Delaware weighed heavily, and these voters were older,

whiter, and much more conservative in their social, religious, and political views. For an overview of these facts about different regions of Delaware, we are indebted to the paper prepared for Theda's fall 2010 Harvard undergraduate seminar on "Inequality and American Democracy": Cedrick Yancey, "'Welcome to the Jungle': Examining Tea Party Involvement in Delaware's Senatorial Race and Its Implications for the Larger Republican Party."

28. An overview of the election appears in Samuel B. Hoff, "Of Witches' Brew and Tea Party Too!: 2010 Delaware Senate Race," in *Pendulum Swing*, edited by Larry J. Sabato (Boston: Longman, 2011). According to Hoff (p. 213), "Republican turnout exceeded Democratic turnout in the 2010 primary by an almost 3-to-1 ratio. The 32 percent turnout among registered Republicans doubled the turnout among voters in the party's primary that occurred in 2008 and quadrupled the turnout from 2006." The surge of voting from Christian conservatives is discussed in Jeff Montgomery, Beth Miller, and Ginger Gibson, "Delaware Politics: Rise in Evangelical Activism Tips Scales in Primary," *The News Journal*, September 19, 2010.

29. Karl Rove, *Fox Hannity*, September 14, 2010.

30. Jason Linkins, "Rove 'Endorses' O'Donnell, A Day After Calling Her 'Nutty,'" *Huffington Post*, March 14, 2011.

31. Facts about funding amounts and sources for the 2010 Delaware Senate race, as well as earlier O'Donnell races, come from Federal Election Commission data, made readily available by the Open Secrets project of the Center for Responsive Politics.

32. Hoff, "Of Witches' Brew," p. 215.

33. Ibid., p. 214.

34. Ibid., p. 215.

35. Ansolabehere and Snyder, "Weak Tea."

36. Michael Sokolove, "The Outsider's Insider," *New York Times*, November 8, 2009.

37. Our account draws on general media coverage, and on Rhodes Cook, "The Battle for the Senate: The Republicans Fall Short," in Sabato, *Pendulum Swing*, chapter 3.

38. Pat Toomey in Pennsylvania is sometimes called a Tea Party candidate who, first drove moderate Republican Arlen Specter out of the GOP, and then defeated the Democratic nominee in the general election. But Toomey is a former head of the Club for Growth and was an ultra-free-market-oriented Republican with his own sources of generous funding long before the Tea Party became a force.

39. Jon Craig, "Kasich: Passenger Rail is 'Dead,'" *Cincinnati.com*, November 2, 2010; Rebecca Stewart, "Scott Rejects Rail Funds for Florida," *CNN Politics, Political Ticker* blog, February 16, 2011; Joan Lowry and Kevin Frekin, "Wisconsin High-Speed Rail Money Goes Elsewhere . . . ," *HuffPost Chicago*, December 9, 2010; and Benny Sieu, "Assembly Passes Union Measure After Bitter Debate," *JournalInteractive*, March 10, 2011.

40. Abby Goodnough, "Maine Governor Gets Testy With N.A.A.C.P.," *New York Times*, January 14, 2011; and Steve Mistler, "LePage Orders Removal of Labor Mural, Sparking Outcry," *SunJournal*, May 16, 2011.

41. Adam Bonica, "Introducing the 112th Congress," *Ideological Cartography*, November 5, 2010. Available at http://www.ideologicalcartography.com/2010/11/05/introducing-the-112th-congress/ as of May 22, 2011. Bonica's measures use campaign finance data to pinpoint newly elected legislators on the left-right scale. His measurements correlate closely with well-established political science measures of the left-right voting patterns for sitting legislators. See Bonica, "How to Construct an Ideological Map of Candidates and Contributors Using Campaign Finance Records," *Ideological*

Cartography, February 15, 2010; and for a full presentation, Bonica, "Ideology and Interests in the Political Marketplace," unpublished paper, September 2010.

42. Republican Representatives are considered aligned with the Tea Party if they joined the Tea Party caucus by April 2011, or if the *New York Times* listed them prior to the November 2010 elections as receiving clear support from Tea Party groups. See Kate Zernike, "Tea Party Set to Win Enough Races for Wide Influence," *New York Times*, October 14, 2011, including linked list of Tea Party endorsed candidates.

43. Adam Bonica, "Introducing the 112th Congress," *Ideological Cartography* website, November 5, 2010.

44. Nolan McCarty, Keith T. Poole, and Howard Rosenthal, *Polarized Politics: The Dance of Ideology and Unequal Riches* (Cambridge, MA: MIT Press, 2008).

45. The following account draws especially upon Jacob S. Hacker and Paul Pierson, *Off Center: The Republican Revolution and the Erosion of American Democracy* (New Haven, CT: Yale University Press, 2005); and Barbara Sinclair, *Party Wars: Polarization and the Politics of National Policymaking* (Norman, OK: University of Oklahoma Press, 2006).

46. For an analysis of the sources of the current deficit and the debt, see Kathy Ruffing and James R. Horney, "Critics Still Wrong on What's Driving Deficits in Coming Years," *Center on Budget and Policy Priorities*, June 28, 2010.

47. Jacob S. Hacker and Paul Pierson, *Winner-Take-All-Politics: How Washington Made the Rich Richer—And Turned Its Back on the Middle Class* (New York: Simon and Schuster, 2010), chapter 1.

48. Ibid., pp. 207–210.

49. Neil King, Douglas A. Blackmon, and Jennifer Levitz, "Tea-Activists Prepare To Turn Aims Into Politics," *Wall Street Journal*, Thursday, November 4, 2010, A8.

50. Amy Gardner, "FreedomWorks Gathers GOP Lawmakers to Focus on Tea Party Goals," *Washington Post*, November 12, 2010.

51. Ibid.

52. Amy Gardner, "Tea Party Groups Holding Legislators to Promises," *Washington Post*, November 16, 2010.

53. Tom Hamburger, Kathleen Hennessey, and Neela Banerjee, "Koch Brothers Now at the Heart of GOP Power," *Los Angeles Times*, February 6, 2011.

54. Ibid. "Nine of the 12 new Republicans on the panel signed a pledge distributed by a Koch-funded advocacy group—Americans for Prosperity—to oppose the Obama administration's proposal to regulate greenhouse gases. Of the six GOP freshman lawmakers on the panel, five benefited from the group's separate advertising and grassroots activity during the 2010 campaign."

55. For example, see Matt Canham, "Revolving Door? Less Picks Top Lobbyist to Lead His Staff," *Salt Lake Tribune*, November 11, 2010; and Dan Eggen, "GOP Freshman Pompeo Turned to Koch for Money for Business, then Politics," *Washington Post*, Sunday, March 20, 2011.

56. Ryan described his own budget as a "cause" more than an actual budget. See Dana Milbank, "Paul Ryan's Dogmatic Budget," *Washington Post*, April 7, 2011. For a thorough analysis of the distributional effects, see Paul N. Van de Water, "The Ryan Budget's Radical Priorities," Center for Budget and Policy Priorities, July 7, 2010. For fact-checking and Ryan's reliance on ideologically cooked Heritage Foundation estimates, see Glenn Kessler, "Fact-Checking the Ryan Budget Plan," *Washington Post, The Fact Checker* blog, April 6, 2011. For Ryan's own presentation of his plan to a friendly

audience, see Paul Ryan, "The Path to Prosperity," American Enterprise Institute, Tuesday, April 5, 2011.

57. Harold Myerson, "Who's Hurt by Paul Ryan's Budget Proposal," *Washington Post*, April 7, 2011.

58. Raymond Hernandez, "Gingrich Calls G.O.P.'s Medicare Plan Too Radical," *New York Times*, Monday, May 16, 2011, A11.

59. Elspeth Reeve, "70% of Tea Partiers Don't Want to Cut Medicare Either," *National Journal*, April 19, 2011. Other surveys reported similar findings.

60. For example, a poll taken in late April 2011, found that "sixty-four percent of those polled said they favor raising taxes on people earning more than $250,000 a year in order to reduce the nation's deficits. Only 29 percent opposed higher taxes for those earners. . . ." Ian Swenson, "HILL POLL: Majority of Voters Reject Medicare Cuts to Reduce Budget Deficits," *The Hill*, May 2, 2011. See also Steven Thomas, "Poll: Best Way to Fight Deficits: Raise Taxes on the Rich," *McClatchy Washington Bureau*, April 18, 2011.

61. Charlie Cook, "Charlie Cook: Warning Signs Among the GOP," *National Journal*, April 4, 2011.

62. Juan Williams, "OPINION: Speaker Boehner in the Temple of Tea Party Doom," *The Hill*, April 11, 2011.

63. Examples include: Joshua Green, "Losing Steam," *Boston Globe*, May 12, 2011, A15; and Eliza Newlin Carney, "Tea Party Dogs GOP on Debt Ceiling," *National Journal*, May 8, 2011.

64. The "FreedomConnect" web tool is discussed in Gardner, "Tea Party Groups Holding Legislators to Promises." This tool also allows FreedomWorks operatives to see what local Tea Partiers are doing.

65. The quote comes from Jenny Beth Martin, coordinator of Tea Party Patriots, and appears in Jackie Kucinich, "Tea Party Group Releases Members' Personal Numbers," *Roll Call*, November 12, 2010.

66. Notes on this public lecture taken by Theda Skocpol at the April 14, 2011 meeting of the York County Constitutionalists in North Berwick, Maine, which is near Rochester, New Hampshire.

67. As we saw in previous chapters, this is one of many times when we heard Tea Partiers say that their tactics do, or should, imitate radical leftist tactics from the past.

68. Mark Murray, "Poll: Americans want compromise on debt, but nearly two-thirds of Tea Party supporters say leaders should hold their ground," MSNBC, July 19, 2011. Available at http://www.msnbc.msn.com/id/43813173/ns/politics/ as of July 20, 2011.

69. Sarah Schweitzer, "Hard Turn Right Worries GOP Moderates in New Hampshire," *Boston Globe*, February 1, 2011, A1 and A9.

70. Ibid., A1.

71. Harvard undergraduate Will Eger attended a Tea Party meeting in Manchester, New Hampshire, in May 2011 and saw a Pawlenty representative there. For a more general overview of state Tea Partiers in the 2012 presidential process, see Jonathan Weisman, "Tea Party Reshapes New Hampshire Calculus," *Wall Street Journal*, Saturday/Sunday April 16–17, 2011, A4.

72. Ibid., quote from activist Jane Aitken of the New Hampshire Tea Party Coalition.

73. "Tea Party Take-Over," *The Note*, ABC NEWS, January 24, 2011.

74. Kremer is quoted in Carney, "Tea Party Dogs GOP on Debt Ceiling."

75. Quoted in Carney, "Tea Party Dogs GOP on Debt Ceiling."

76. Danny Yadron, "Tea Party Targets Centrist Republican," *Wall Street Journal*, March 28, 2011; and Kirk Johnson, "3 Leading Mormon Politicians Feel Heat From Tea Party at Home in Utah," *New York Times*, March 15, 2011, A25.

77. The AFL-CIO and Chamber of Commerce issued a rare joint statement in support of infrastructure spending. Mike Hall, "AFL-CIO and Chamber Agree on Obama's Call for Infrastructure Rebuild," AFL-CIO Now blog, January 26, 2011. Available at http://blog.aflcio.org/2011/01/26/union-movement-business-back-obamas-call-for-infrastructure-rebuild-and-other-sotu-reactions/ as of May 16, 2011.

78. Jennifer Liberto, "Big Business: Quit Screwing Around on Debt Ceiling," CNN Money, May 12, 2011. Available at http://money.cnn.com/2011/05/12/news/economy/debt_ceiling_big_business/index.htm?section=money_mostpopular as of May 15, 2011.

79. "Debt Limit Harakiri," *Wall Street Journal* editorial, July 13, 2011.

80. Once people have chosen a political party, they tend to be pretty loyal to it. But to the extent that the types of people in the Tea Party come to define what it is to be a Republican, it could have a serious impact on how other people, especially young people, attach themselves to one party or another. "As people reflect on whether they are Democrats or Republicans (or neither), they call to mind some mental image, or stereotype, of what these sorts of people are like and square these images with their own self-conceptions. In effect, people ask themselves two questions: What kinds of social groups come to mind as I think about Democrats, Republicans, and Independents? Which assemblage of groups (if any) best describes me?" Donald P. Green, Bradley Palmquist, and Eric Schickler, *Partisan Hearts and Minds: Political Parties and the Social Identities of Voters* (New Haven, CT: Yale University Press, 2004). Elections can help shape people's view of what "kinds of people" are in each party. In California in the 1990s, the strong anti-immigrant ballot measures championed by Republican elected officials turned Hispanics and younger white people away from the Republican Party. Shaun Bowler, Stephen Nicholson, and Gary Segura, "Earthquakes and aftershocks: Race, direct democracy, and partisan change." *American Journal of Political Science* 50(1): 146–159 (2006).

81. Rachel Weiner, "Tea Party Unpopularity on the Rise," *Washington Post*, March 30, 2011.

82. Nate Silver, "Poll Shows More Americans Have Unfavorable Views of the Tea Party," *FiveThirtyEight* blog, *New York Times*, March 30, 2011.

83. These Fox News results were, unsurprisingly, seized upon by the progressive blogosphere. See Matt Corley, "More Americans have a 'favorable' opinion of the IRS than of the Tea Party," *Think Progress*, April 8, 2010. Available at http://thinkprogress.org/2010/04/08/tea-party-irs-poll/ as of May 11, 2011.

84. Steven Thomma, "Poll: Best Way to Fight Deficits: Raise Taxes on the Rich," *McClatchy Washington Bureau*, April 18, 2011.

85. Pew Research Center, "Tea Party's Hard Line on Spending Divides GOP," February 11, 2011.

CHAPTER 6

1. Quotes from the advance NBC transcript via Jason Easley, "Harry Reid Proclaims that the Tea Party is Dying," *PoliticusUSA* website, January 8, 2011. Available at http://www.politicususa.com/en/harry-reid-tea-party as of May 29, 2011.

2. The Cato Institute has been at the forefront of anti-union efforts. A policy forum held by Cato on July 28, 2010, was entitled "Union Influence on Public Policy," and asked, "Both private and public unions have undue political influence and use that power to seek privileges at the expense of consumers and taxpayers. Are unions good for America?" Video available at http://www.cato.org/event.php?eventid=7339 as of May 29, 2011. Cato scholars have also argued that public sector unions are responsible for making state government less efficient. Chris Edwards, "Unions and State Government Management," Cato at Liberty, April 6, 2010. Available at http://www.cato-at-liberty.org/unions-and-state-government-management/ as of May 29, 2011. Similarly, the Heritage Foundation has released "fact sheet" talking points such as "Government Unions 101: What Public-Sector Unions Won't Tell You." An accompanying video highlighted the argument that "Government unions actually campaign for higher taxes." Available at http://www.heritage.org/research/factsheets/2011/02/government-unions-101-what-public-sector-unions-wont-tell-you as of May 29, 2011. Heritage has also argued for many years in favor of voter restrictions. Hans von Spakovsky, "Stolen Identities, Stolen Votes: A Case Study in Voter Impersonation," Heritage Foundation, March 10, 2008. Available at http://www.heritage.org/Research/Reports/2008/03/Stolen-Identities-Stolen-Votes-A-Case-Study-in-Voter-Impersonation as of May 29, 2011. Heritage has also accused an Obama Administration official who registered to vote in Ohio of voter fraud. Conn Carroll, "Morning Bell: Stopping Voter Fraud," November 2, 2010. See also the October 18, 2004, event called "Stealing Elections: How Voter Fraud Threatens Our Democracy." Available at http://www.heritage.org/events/2004/10/stealing-elections-how-voter-fraud-threatens-our-democracy as of May 29, 2011.

3. Mike Thomas, "Rick Scott, the one-term wonder? Poll says yes," *Orlando Sentinel*, March 30, 2011. "Kasich's popularity plummeting," *Associated Press*, March 15, 2011. Available at http://www.sanduskyregister.com/news/2011/mar/15/00301bc-oh-ohiobudget3rdldoxml as of May 29, 2011. "Brutal numbers for Kasich, SB5," Public Policy Polling, March 15, 2011. Available at http://publicpolicypolling.blogspot.com/2011/03/brutal-numbers-for-kasich-sb-5.html as of May 29, 2011. Liz Halloran, "Recall Efforts in Wisconsin Face Tough Odds," NPR, March 8, 2011. "Rick Snyder Recall Election Effort Clears First Hurdle in Michigan," *Reuters*, April 29, 2011.

4. "The immense literature on the costs of voting has shown that costs ranging from the registration requirement to strict voter-ID laws do reduce voter turnout to some degree and that the impact seems to fall disproportionately on the least educated and the least wealthy." Marjorie Randon Hershey, "What we know about Voter-ID Laws, Registration, and Turnout," *PS: Political Science & Politics* 42 (2009), pp. 87–91. See also Matt Barreto, Stephen Nuno, and Gabriel Sanchez, "Voter ID Requirements and the Disenfranchisements of Latino, Black and Asian Voters." Paper presented at the annual meeting of the American Political Science Association, Hyatt Regency Chicago and the Sheraton Chicago Hotel and Towers, Chicago, IL, August 30, 2007.

5. Paul Farhi, "Glenn Beck to end daily TV program on Fox News Channel," *Washington Post*, April 6, 2011.

6. S. Bowler, S. P. Nicholson, and G. M Segura, "Earthquakes and aftershocks: Race, direct democracy, and partisan change." *American Journal of Political Science* 50(1) (2006): pp. 146–159.

7. Arthur M. Schlesinger, Sr., "Biography of a Nation of Joiners," *American Historical Review* 50 (1) (October, 1944): 1–25.

8. Stefano Dellavigna and Ethan Kaplan, "The Fox News Effect: Media Bias and Voting," *Quarterly Journal of Economics*, 122 (August 2007): pp. 1187–1234.

9. Simon Maloy, "UMD Report: Regular Viewers of Fox News More Likely to be Misinformed," *Media Matters*, December 17, 2010. Available at http://mediamatters.org/blog/201012170010 as of March 14, 2011.

10. We note only two examples we personally saw adopted by Tea Party members we spoke to. During the health reform debate, Fox News promoted the falsehood that the new health care law included "death panels" of doctors and bureaucrats with the power to euthanize elderly patients, and left unchallenged the claim that the law was to be funded with new taxes on all real estate transactions. See "The Evolution of the Death Panel Meme," *Talking Points Memo*, August 2009. Available at http://www.talkingpointsmemo.com/photofeatures/2009/08/the-evolution-of-the-death-panel-meme.php?img=1 as of March 14, 2011. This concern was raised by Bonnie Sims, one of our Virginia interviewees. Several Tea Party members in different states expressed concern that the health care bill would be funded with a new tax on real estate. The 3.8% real estate tax meme appeared on Fox News on November 2, 2010, in an interview with Dick Grasso. This idea seems to have come from a misinterpretation of some of the details of tax changes for very high earners. "A 3.8 Percent 'Sales Tax' on Your Home?" FactCheck.org, April 22, 2010. Available at http://www.factcheck.org/2010/04/a-38-percent-sales-tax-on-your-home/ as of March 21, 2011.

11. Brad Johnson, "Glenn Beck Attacks Smart Grid As Socialist Plot to Steal Our Thermostats," *Think Progress*, March 18, 2009. Available at http://wonkroom.think-progress.org/2009/03/18/beck-deadly-thermostats/ as of March 14, 2011.

12. Ronald Brownstein, "The Gray and the Brown: The Generational Mismatch," *National Journal*, July 24, 2010. Brownstein discusses and cites the work of Frey and other social scientists exploring the interaction of demography and political battles over generationally skewed public programs.

13. Ibid.

EPILOGUE

1. https://www.washingtonpost.com/news/monkey-cage/wp/2015/11/24/how-anti-immigrant-attitudes-are-fueling-support-for-donald-trump.

2. See Theda Skocpol and Alexander Hertel-Fernandez, "The Koch Effect: The Impact of a Cadre-Led Network on American Politics." Paper presented at the annual meeting of the Southern Political Science Association, San Juan, Puerto Rico, January 8, 2016. Available at http://www.scholarsstrategynetwork.org/sites/default/files/the_koch_effect_for_spsa_w_apps_skocpol_and_hertel-fernandez-corrected_1-27-16_3.pdf.

3. http://mediamatters.org/research/2014/10/06/conservative-media-advocate-travel-bans-from-eb/201031.

4. https://www.washingtonpost.com/news/wonk/wp/2015/11/24/its-not-just-don-ald-trump-half-of-republicans-shares-his-views-on-immigrants-and-refugees; http://www.slate.com/articles/news_and_politics/politics/2015/12/ted_cruz_s_latest_anti_muslim_rhetoric_is_beyond_shameful.html.

5. http://www.c-span.org/video/?c4565755/talat-othman-gives-prayer-2000-republi-can-national-convention.

6. http://berkleycenter.georgetown.edu/quotes/george-w-bush-addresses-muslims-in-the-aftermath-of-the-9-11-attacks.

7. Mackenzie Weinger, "Hannity: I've 'evolved' on immigration and support a 'pathway to citizenship,'" *Politico*, November 9, 2012. Available at: http://www.politico.com/blogs/media/2012/11/hannity-ive-evolved-on-immigration-and-support-a-pathway-149078.html#.UJxFjXBdw8Q.twitter.

8. Jane Mayer, *Dark Money: The Hidden History of the Billionaires Behind the Rise of the Radical Right*. New York: Doubleday, 2016.

9. See Figures 1 and 2 in Skocpol and Hertel-Fernandez, "The Koch Effect."

10. Kenneth P. Vogel, "How the Koch Network Rivals the GOP." *Politico*, December 30, 2015.

11. See Skocpol and Hertel-Fernandez, "Koch Effect"; and Alexander Hertel-Fernandez, Theda Skocpol, and Daniel Lynch, "Business Associations, Conservative Networks, and the Ongoing Civil War over Medicaid Expansion." *Journal of Health Politics, Policy and Law*, March 2016.

12. http://www.cnn.com/2015/07/21/politics/donald-trump-election-democrat.

Index

CPSIA information can be obtained
at www.ICGtesting.com
Printed in the USA
BVHW030722241021
619712BV00005B/14

9 780190 633660